Shakespeare

—— IN ——

Swahililand

Shakespeare

— IN —

Swahililand

IN SEARCH OF A GLOBAL POET

Edward Wilson-Lee

FARRAR, STRAUS AND GIROUX   NEW YORK

Farrar, Straus and Giroux
18 West 18th Street, New York 10011

Copyright © 2016 by Edward Wilson-Lee
All rights reserved
Printed in the United States of America
Originally published in 2016 by William Collins, Great Britain, as
Shakespeare in Swahililand: Adventures with the Ever-Living Poet
Published in the United States by Farrar, Straus and Giroux
First American edition, 2016

Library of Congress Cataloging-in-Publication Data
Names: Wilson-Lee, Edward, author.
Title: Shakespeare in Swahililand : in search of a global poet / Edward Wilson-Lee.
Description: First edition. | New York : Farrar, Straus and Giroux, 2016. | Includes
    bibliographical references and index.
Identifiers: LCCN 2016002076 | ISBN 9780374262075 (hardcover) / ISBN 9780374714444
    (e-book)
Subjects: LCSH: Shakespeare, William, 1564–1616—Appreciation—Africa, Central. |
    Shakespeare, William, 1564–1616—Appreciation—Africa, East. | Shakespeare, William,
    1564–1616—Stage history—Africa, Central. | Shakespeare, William, 1564–1616—Stage
    history—Africa, East. | Shakespeare, William, 1564–1616—Influence.
Classification: LCC PR3069.A37 W55 2016 | DDC 822.3/3—dc23
LC record available at https://lccn.loc.gov/2016002076

Our books may be purchased in bulk for promotional, educational, or business use.
Please contact your local bookseller or the Macmillan Corporate and Premium
Sales Department at 1-800-221-7945, extension 5442, or by e-mail at
MacmillanSpecialMarkets@macmillan.com.

www.fsgbooks.com
www.twitter.com/fsgbooks • www.facebook.com/fsgbooks

1   3   5   7   9   10   8   6   4   2

For my parents

Contents

PRELUDE

Beauty Out of Place

Once on a visit to Luxor in southern Egypt I was stopped by a man who called out to me from where he sat, crumpled in the shade of an August afternoon, with a famous line from Shakespeare's *Macbeth*: 'Tomorrow, and tomorrow, and tomorrow. . . .' It was the summer at the end of my first year of reading English at university, and though it was uncomfortable to stand in the throbbing heat swapping iambic pentameters, I was sure I was more than a match for this stranger with his long white *kanzu* shirt and papyrus mat. I responded with the next line, and he in turn; and, after that speech, we migrated on to others, though now I cannot remember which ones, and would almost certainly exaggerate my recitational prowess if I were to try to recall them. After a few minutes, we fell silent. I, at least, was probably out of breath (and lines) in the thick desert air, and panting like a lizard; I had no Arabic other than swearwords I learned at school, and if the man did have conversational English he showed no inclination to use it. We grinned at each other and I moved on, in search of another sweating glass of fresh iced lemon juice.

Odd as it seemed at the time, I am now very glad that I did not break the spell by drawing the encounter out. For although later I sometimes thought about what this moment might have been – an act of cultural comradeship or a defiant exhibition of superiority over the presumptuous tourist – it has more recently occurred to me that its poignancy was in part owed to its being out of place and unaccounted for. Shakespeare may have distantly heard of Luxor – though he would have known it as Thebes, from the ancient Greek romance *Aethiopica* which was popular in his day – but it is unlikely that he imagined lines written for performance in Shoreditch or Southwark would ever end up being spoken there, close by the feluccas sailing on the Nile and the acres of pharaonic ruins beyond. The poignancy was, I suppose, the experience of one's own culture as something exotic, like Tarzan finding a relic of the jungle in an English country house. The fact that I was so unprepared for this, however, seems to be in retrospect the most remarkable thing. After all, I had been brought up in Kenya, and had lived my life in a jumble of African places filled with things from elsewhere. These had, of course, included Shakespeare, though it seems to me now that I had always managed to keep his plays separate from the place in which I lived. It was as if his words, wherever spoken, were a foreign soil, like an embassy.

Many years later – now settled and teaching Shakespeare's works for a living – I happened upon the unexpected fact that one of the first books printed in Swahili was a Shakespearean one. Not a play, mind you, but a slim volume of stories from Charles and Mary Lamb's *Tales from Shakespeare*, published as *Hadithi za Kiingereza* ('English Tales') on the island of Zanzibar in the 1860s. Once again I felt that odd stirring of a beauty out of place. I began a small research project into this volume, its translator (the Missionary Bishop of Zanzibar Edward Steere), and the fascinating milieu in which he printed his books, with the help of former slave boys off the African coast. What I discovered during the momentous travels that followed, through Kenya, Tanzania, Uganda, Ethiopia and Sudan, was a hidden history that brought both Shakespeare and the land I thought familiar into richer focus than I had ever known them.

In part this was the story we already know of Africa – of the explorers who staggered through the interior of the continent, and the various eccentrics who developed a hothouse version of English culture as they tried to rebuild the Sceptered Isle on the African savannah – but made fresh by the disarming strangeness of the real experiences lived by well-known figures, figures whose stories are often reduced to cartoonishly simple fantasies of the 'Dark Continent' or of Happy Valley. But it was also a story of Africa less often told: a story of Indian settler communities coming to a land every bit as strange as that braved by white travellers; of African intellectuals and rebels in fledgling towns that grew up in the early twentieth century; of the private lives of the first African leaders of independent nations, and the Cold War intrigues that shaped the region at the end of the last century. Uncannily, what united all of these figures was their fascination with the British culture which was transplanted, like some exotic seedling, with the successive waves of settlers. More than anything else, this meant that they read, performed and idolized Shakespeare, who represented the pinnacle of that British culture. Though there were other challengers for Shakespeare's cultural pre-eminence – amusing episodes in which Tennyson, Burns and Chekhov raised their heads above the ramparts – none of them came close to unseating his place in East African life.

It was unimaginable that literary culture – let alone a single writer – should have assumed such importance in the politics and history of Europe or America at the time. Even the extraordinary story with which this book concerns itself might seem at first to be a series of coincidences, if the sequence of events didn't seem to take on an unstoppable momentum of its own. In uncovering the details of these lives and events two things became clear to me. I saw a new story of the land in which I grew up, an account which helped capture its history and its character not by focusing on matters of high government far removed from most people's lives, or describing the wilderness whilst ignoring the people and the towns, but instead by looking steadily at those moments when the many Africas I knew met: the bush and the tribal dwellings, yes, but also the towns and their neighbourhoods of Bantu peoples and Indians and Europeans. The stories I came across when following Shakespeare through East Africa were not neat accounts of the progress of history, but rather stirring resurrections of how that history must have felt to the people who lived through it. These stories also promised access to something else, something close to the Holy Grail of Shakespeare studies: an understanding of Shakespeare's universal appeal.

That Shakespeare *is* venerated throughout the world is not open for question – the Globe theatre in London, after all, staged each of Shakespeare's thirty-seven plays in a different language as part of the 2012 Cultural Olympiad, and most of the countries from which the performers came already had long and rich traditions of reading and performing the works.[1] But we have become less confident than we once were as to *why* this should be the case. In the nineteenth century the answer would have been easy: Shakespeare's *genius* gave him access to a transcendent, semi-divine reservoir of beauty, a beauty which naturally appealed to all men because it was above petty distinctions between one culture and another, and safe from becoming outmoded with the passage of time. Looking back, however, it is clear that there was more than a hint of aggression in how Shakespeare's universal appeal was asserted. It is, after all, as Kant points out, precisely in those matters of taste, so resistant to scientific demonstration, that we are most determined that others should agree with us; as W. H. Auden rather more wittily put it, 'A person who dislikes . . . the music of Bellini or prefers his steak well-done, may, for all I know, possess some admirable quality but I do not wish ever to see him again.'[2] In the twentieth century, a West chastened by reflecting on the atrocities of the Second World War and of colonialism – and former colonial subjects newly emboldened to speak – produced much less comfortable explanations for the global ascendancy of European culture and its totem Shakespeare: perhaps this 'love' of Shakespeare in exotic places was really just a pretence, a desire to curry favour with the British ruling class, who left their Shakespeare-worshipping public schools to administer an Empire which covered much of the globe? Perhaps even the colonial masters' love of Shakespeare was not something they came to naturally, but something drilled into them at public schools because it served the purpose of that ruling class to assert that the world's greatest mind was a white British man? Hard as it is to argue against this explanation (especially as a white man of British descent), it is less than wholly satisfying for all who have read Shakespeare with little feeling that they are being forced into it or trying to coerce others, and rather belittling for all those who *aren't* white and male and British, whose passion for Shakespeare was in danger of being written off as mere craven pandering to the overlord. My experience of teaching Shakespeare has been that he, almost alone among writers, defies such cynicism: whenever the time rolls around again to lead a fresh batch of students through the works, I wonder whether the reverence in which he is held might be some grand collective delusion, a truism rather than a truth. But, every time, the dawning freshness of a turn of phrase, a short exchange or an orchestrated speech makes dull the cleverness which wrote these impressions off as nostalgic. So what is it, then, that makes the writings of this obscure glover's son from a

Warwickshire village retain their power wherever they go, and even when they are taken out of the tongue in which he wrote them and the stage for which he designed them? Do Shakespeare's plays point the way beyond the jostling for power and prestige towards a shared humanity?

This book is the story of an attempt to answer these questions. In service of that attempt, it is also a travelogue and a cultural history of 'Swahililand', by which I mean those countries (Kenya, Tanzania and Uganda, as well as parts of Congo, Malawi and Sudan) into which the Swahili tongue was introduced by Arab traders and European missionaries and where it later became a pan–East African language of sorts.[3] The narrative sometimes has to leave Swahililand to fill in back stories or to follow stories out of Africa to their conclusions elsewhere, but it remains rooted in and dedicated to understanding eastern Africa.

It also became clear to me early on that any attempt to survey this landscape with an impersonal and objective eye would be not only dishonest but also doomed to failure. The questions I was asking were of so basic a nature, the story I was telling of trans-planted culture was so close to my own, that I could not pretend that my answers were unaffected by my own past. As I thought through these questions, about why certain phrases and stories are significant and beautiful to us, and how this relates to where the words came from and where they ended up, I caught the memories of my childhood creeping into my peripheral vision. It seemed disingenuous to exclude them, to pretend that my conclusions were reached through cold logic rather than by the insuppressible return of moments from the past, and so occasionally in what follows I allow these things to well to the surface, to give some sense of the tangle of emotions from which my judgements proceed: a sense of fierce belonging to the places of my youth, but one now made difficult by an awareness of the wider story of which

xiv

it was a part; a devotion and an atonement. It is, I suppose, no different from anyone else's love affair with the past.

The story reaches a climax, if not quite an end, in 1989, after which Shakespeare's prominence through most of East Africa abruptly evaporated, bringing this bizarre sequence of events to an even more mysterious close. I remember very clearly sitting that year on the floor of our kitchen in Nairobi, perplexed by my mother's joy as the BBC World Service gave daily bulletins on the collapse of the Soviet Union. I'm not sure I fully understand even now the exhilaration of this historical moment for many who lived through it; it is very difficult to inhabit the passions of the past, even though (as in this book) we cannot kick the habit of trying.

I am certain, though, that I did not understand it then. It seemed not to fit in with the house surrounded by woodland at the edge of Nairobi, with its makeshift cricket pitch between the washing lines, besieged by monkeys who would steal fruit from the kitchen table. That was a world of animals great and small, eating and being eaten and trying to stay clear of unruly children's traps. It did not seem to fit in with the life of the city either, where people queued endlessly on broken pavement to watch films like *Moonwalker* and *Coming to America*, which the main cinema played continuously and exclusively in that year and the next. But even if I had understood the Cold War and what its end meant to those who had lived through it, it would not have explained to me why, during the devastating withdrawal of billions of dollars of aid money meant to keep African countries from defecting to Soviet allegiance, the President of Kenya spent part of his summer defending the greatness of Shakespeare as a writer. It would not have made any sense of the fact that a new English-speaking country would appear on the upper reaches of the Nile in part through a young boy soldier's love for Shakespeare, and nor would it have solved the dozen other literary mysteries that I later came across during my travels through

Africa and through the archives. For that I would have to start long before the Cold War, and to understand something not just of the high politics and the many societies that make up Swahililand, but also of how beauty works in the world, how, in the words of Shakespeare's Joan of Arc,

> Glory is like a circle in the water,
> Which never ceaseth to enlarge itself
> Till by broad spreading, it disperse to naught.

1 Henry VI (I.ii.133–5)

For this, I began by looking at first contacts between the British and East Africa, and the strange story of how Shakespeare became an indispensable bit of safari kit in the nineteenth century.

THE LAKE REGIONS

Shakespeare and the Explorers

> . . . they take the flow o'th' Nile
> By certain scales i'th' pyramid. They know
> By th' height, the lowness, or the mean if dearth
> Or foison follow. The higher Nilus swells,
> The more it promises; as it ebbs, the seedsman
> Upon the slime and ooze scatters his grain,
> And shortly comes to harvest.
>
> *Antony and Cleopatra* (II.vii.17–23)

Although the world was beginning to open up during Shakespeare's lifetime, with Jesuit missions to the Far East and growing settlements in the Americas, he lived in an age in which the Mediterranean still merited its name as 'the middle sea', the place in the centre of the world. Around this great inland sea all places of importance were arranged – notably excluding the backwater island which Shakespeare never left – and through it man's greatest voyages had taken place. The classical geographer Pliny, still a respected authority in the Renaissance, declared that while men of the south were born burnt by the sun, and those of the north had frosty complexions, the blended climate of the middle lands made for fertile soils and minds. Only there, he contends, do the people have proper governments, while 'the outermost people . . . have never obeyed the central people, for they are detached and solitary, in keeping with the savagery of Nature that oppresses them'.[1] About half Shakespeare's plays are set in his native Islands; the rest, with the important exception of that strange beast *Hamlet*, arrange themselves around the Med. Its waters were so thick with history and myth that Odysseus's ten-year cruise from Asia Minor to the Greek Islands remained the archetypal sea voyage even long after Shakespeare's contemporaries had circumnavigated the globe through far more treacherous waters. And into this central body of water flowed the most famous and strangest of rivers, the Nile.

Every year, at the end of summer, the waters of the Nile rose above its banks and flooded the plains of northern Egypt, a potent symbol of the unexplained and irresistible force of nature. 'My grief', says Shakespeare's Titus Andronicus at the sight of his raped and mutilated daughter Lavinia, 'was at the height before thou cam'st / And now like Nilus it disdaineth bounds' (III.i.70–71). The destructive power of the Nile, however, was matched by its near-magical fertility. As the annual flood subsided, the river left behind water and silt rich enough for agriculture to flourish in the middle of a desert land. The power of the Nile mud to make things grow was held in such high regard that naturalists from ancient Greece to Renaissance Europe believed it capable of spontaneously generating animal life, though (as was fitting for a river whose source lay deep in an unknown continent) the 'fire / That quickens Nilus' slime' (*Antony and Cleopatra*, I.iii.67–9) could only produce monstrous serpents and crocodiles.

By the middle of the nineteenth century, much of the mythical aura had evaporated from the Nilotic delta. If the British biologist Thomas Huxley would soon suggest that all life *did* ultimately have its beginnings in the primordial slime, few believed any longer in life regularly emerging from the inanimate. Egypt had been invaded by Napoleon and had then fallen (as he had) under the growing British sphere of influence; its ancient artefacts were fast becoming familiar exotics in the museums of Europe. (By the end of the century, Sigmund Freud would plumb the middle-class European mind from a consulting room bursting with Egyptiana, including a mummy's mask that he liked to stroke.) The Egyptian floodplains had been given over to the industrial-scale production of cotton and fledgling tourism was starting to be seen in Cairo and on the river. Much of the continent from which the Nile flowed, however, was still completely unexplored, and the undiscovered source of the great river remained a tantalizing symbol of the stubborn resistance of parts of the world to the increasingly bullish European powers. Sir Roderick Murchison, the President of the Royal Geographical Society, blended the languages of intellectual and financial speculation when he declared (in his presidential address of 1852) that there was 'no exploration in Africa to which greater value would be attached' than establishing the source of the Nile, and that the men who achieved it would be 'justly considered among the greatest benefactors of this age of geographical science'.[2]

Though Vasco da Gama had pioneered the sea route to India around the Cape of Good Hope as early as the 1490s, European travel into the interior had not greatly progressed by 1800, and settlement was very thin and almost entirely restricted to the coast. Africa had, for a long time, been an extremely unattractive prospect to the white traveller: its landscape, its illnesses, and the extremes of its climate were death both to the unwitting European traveller and to the pack animals on which he was wholly reliant; and even if the central African environment had not proven quite so resistant, the interior of the continent offered few obvious prizes to adventurers, apparently having none of the great mercantile empires of the East Indies, nor the bottomless mines and rolling grasslands of the Americas. That Africa became suddenly and immensely attractive to Europeans and Americans in the mid-nineteenth century was the result of a number of factors which were closely related. The Industrial Revolution had both created new markets and reaped great wealth from them. Industrial philanthropy paid in large measure for the scientific and evangelical expeditions that made their way into Africa, and these expeditions saw the lack of 'civilization' in the continent as an opportunity rather than a deterrent. Africa would provide both souls for religious instruction and challenges to be overcome by the unstoppable leviathan of Western Knowledge. In the event, and not unpredictably, the altruism of these philanthropists was lucrative beyond imagining. Despite the fact that these ventures were thought of by contemporaries as foolishly benign, often being criticized for throwing good money after bad, they nevertheless produced raw materials which made new fortunes. Rubber, harvested from trees in the central African forest, was transformed by the discovery of vulcanization into an indispensable commodity; eastern Africa was found to be perfect for cultivating sisal (for rope fibre) and pyrethrum (for industrial pesticides). And if at the beginning of the century European governments were largely indifferent – even hostile – to the idea of colonies in Africa, by the end they were convinced of the vital strategic importance of not letting anyone else get there first. For Britain, the Nile would form the backbone of a British Africa which stretched from Egypt through Sudan to East Africa and Nyasaland, then down through Rhodesia to the Cape.[3]

East Africa, filled in with largely fanciful detail, on the 1564 Gastaldi map,
and Henry Morton Stanley pictured consulting one such existing
map on a cartographic expedition.

The expedition which finally succeeded in locating the source of the Nile left the coast of modern-day Tanzania in 1857 and was led by Captain Richard Francis Burton. Burton was not yet forty, but he was already the Victorian traveller *par excellence*; most notably, he had undertaken the pilgrimage to Mecca – the *Hajj* – with a shaven head and in disguise, and his account of the feat had made him celebrated for both his daring and his phenomenal linguistic skills.[4] In later life Burton would lead further expeditions throughout Africa and the Americas, while also finding time to translate the *Arabian Nights* and the *Kama Sutra* as well as writing learned treatises on Etruscan history, medieval literature and fencing. Even a bibliophile like Burton, however, could not afford to take much reading with him when heading into the African interior. The tsetse fly reliably killed off horses and pack-mules before they were a hundred miles inland, and the brigades of native porters also dwindled with terrifying speed as the journeys progressed. Some of them deserted early on while the coast was still in reach, undeterred by the loss of pay and the threat of execution by the expedition leader as he (often hysterical with fever and fear) struggled desperately to hold on to the remainder of his men. The rest of the native contingent was decimated by disease, starvation and punitive raids from the tribes whose land they were crossing. Available porterage was reserved, then, for ammunition, medicine and materials for trade with the locals, primarily American calico (called *merikani*) and copper wire, which was sold en route to tribes who wore it decoratively.

Burton did, however, find a little space for one or two volumes:

The few books – Shakespeare, Euclid – which composed my scanty library, we read together again and again . . .[5]

The volume of Shakespeare Burton took with him is lost, most likely destroyed in a warehouse fire which burned many of his possessions in 1861. (His edition of the *Sonnets*, which does survive in the Huntington Library in California, amusingly contains pencil corrections to Shakespeare's lines where Burton felt he could do better.[6]) But the extensive quotation from the works in the expeditionary account he published on his return suggests how intimately he knew them and how constantly he read them on that expedition. *The Lake Regions of Central Africa* was, like most of these narratives, written at great speed on the steamer voyage home in order to avoid being beaten to the punch by competing accounts from fellow expedition members, and Burton seems to have followed his (also lost) expedition diary closely in writing it, taking the Shakespeare-heavy description of the interior direct from the diary pages where he reflected on each day's events and reading.*

The competing account of the expedition, in this instance, was to come from the other European who accompanied him, John Hanning Speke, with whom Burton read Shakespeare intensively and repeatedly as the pair crossed the savannah scrubland. Their pages were undoubtedly marked, as mine were as I read my own *Complete Works* travelling through East Africa in their tracks, by sweat from the daytime and at night by winged insects drawn to the lamplight and trapped between the pages as they turned. There would have been periods, especially when their travel on foot was impeded by heavy rains which turned the dry land to bog, when reading would have been a welcome distraction from the frustrations of enforced indolence. It was important for expedition lead-

---

* The few other writers whom Burton occasionally uses to flesh out his description of Africa – Marlowe, Byron – give us a sense of the rather macho flavour of his Shakespeare.

ers to be close – they were, after all, heavily dependent on one another during long periods of malarial delirium – and their reading of Shakespeare seems to have been a central part of this: they read (as Burton says) 'together', and the way Burton quotes odd lines suggests this meant reading plays side by side and not simply passing the book back and forth to declaim famous speeches.

As the mention of Shakespeare alongside Euclid's geometrical treatise (the *Elements*) suggests, however, Burton had no room for books which were not useful as well as beautiful, and Shakespeare's lines are repeatedly called into service in *The Lake Regions* to provide English equivalents to local phrases and customs. In one instance, a Kinyamwezi saying ('He sits in hut hatching egg') is 'their proverbial phrase to express one more eloquent – "Home keeping youths have ever homely wits".'[7] The line is taken from *The Two Gentlemen of Verona*, a not entirely successful comedy about friendship and betrayal that is thought to be one of Shakespeare's earliest works. The frequency with which this play crops up in Burton's *Lake Regions* is rather surprising, given how minor a work it is usually thought to be. This might be explained in part by the fact that it was printed as the second play after *The Tempest* in Shakespeare's First Folio of 1623 and in almost every edition after that until the twentieth century; one is tempted to think that the *Two Gentlemen* was the beneficiary of many determined attempts to read the *Works* from cover to cover that foundered in the early pages.

Shakespeare's story of the noble Valentine betrayed by his treacherous friend Proteus seems, however, to have struck a deeper chord after the friendship turned sour, in large part because Speke had the unforgivable good fortune to discover the major source of the Nile – which he named Lake Victoria Nyanza – on a side expedition of his own. Burton may well in that moment have recalled Valentine's raw words at the betrayal of Proteus:

I must never trust thee more,
But count the world a stranger for thy sake!
The private wound is deepest. [. . .]

(V.iv.70–72)

In the first volley of a spat that was to continue for many years, Burton attempted in the *Lake Regions* to discredit Speke by rather ungenerously arguing that his discovery had been down to luck and not skill. In this he compares him not to *The Two Gentlemen of Verona*'s treacherous fair-weather friend Proteus, but (even more gallingly) to a maidservant in the play:

The fortunate discoverer's conviction was strong; his reasons were weak – were of the category alluded to by the damsel Lucetta, when justifying her penchant in favour of the 'lovely gentleman' Sir Proteus:

I have no other but a woman's reason.
I think him so because I think him so.[8]

The pettiness of Burton's sentiment might almost distract us from the exquisite strangeness of the whole situation: that a man ravaged by physical hardship and fever, surrounded by danger in an inhospitable land, racked by wounded pride and doubtless the feeling that he was both betraying his friend and being betrayed by him, should reach angrily for lines written for Elizabethan Londoners several hundred years earlier.

During the months I spent preparing for my first research trip to East Africa, I made my way through dozens of expeditionary accounts by Burton and those who came after him, looking for the books that they took with them on these jaunts out into the unknown. Reading about Burton's strong attachment to his Shakespeare, even when isolated in ways scarcely imaginable to modern minds, stirred my own memories of reading in remote places. I trace the beginning of my true devotion to literature to a volume of Auden's poetry given to me to read while in the Jiddat al-Harasis desert in Oman (though that properly belongs to another story). But the accounts of bush camps by Burton and others also cast new light on my own childhood, much of which was spent on safari in eastern Africa. I was born into a family of conservationists – my literary work is something of an anomaly, and a confusing one for them – so I spent most school holidays with my parents in areas chosen for their remoteness. These were, of course, entirely less dangerous affairs than the Victorian expeditions: convoys of Land Rovers, tented camps often with generators and two-way radios, and usually no more than a few hours from something recognizable as a road. What had not changed, however, since the time of those early adventurers, was the curious blend of luxury and primitiveness which characterized these travels. Even in the days of Land Rovers food supplies sometimes ran low, and among my clearest childhood memories is a scene of Samburu warriors in northern Kenya bringing to our camp the goat for which my father had bargained, its square and staring eyes as it bled out into a lip in its throat. Nothing was wasted, down to a coin-purse from the scrotum, and the goat meat was later fire-roasted by a cook as the adults had cocktails at sundown.

This blend of the primitive and the decadent seemed unremarkable to me at the time – simply part of *how things were done* – and it was only later that I became aware that many in Europe and America escape into nature with the conscious design of depriving themselves of life's comforts. An early twentieth-century traveller, the self-styled backwoodsman Theodore Roosevelt, complained repeatedly about the self-indulgence he encountered during his two-year hunting safari in Kenya, which he gave himself as a present on his retirement as US President in 1909:

> At Kapiti plains our tents, our accommodation generally, seemed almost too comfortable for men who knew camp life only on the Great Plains, in the Rockies, and in the North Woods. My tent had a fly, which was to protect it from the great heat; there was a little rear extension in which I bathed – a hot bath, never a cold bath, is almost a tropic necessity; . . . Then, I had two tent-boys to see after my belongings, and to wait at table as well as in the tent. . . . The provisions were those usually included in an African hunting or exploring trip, save that, in memory of my days in the West, I included in each provision box a few cans of Boston baked beans, California peaches, and tomatoes.[9]

The fine living which so disappointed Roosevelt would come to seem rather tame in comparison to the hedonism of later settlers, who added the fashionable sins of narcotics and promiscuity to these gastronomic indulgences; but it was certainly not entirely new either. While the porters held out, Burton's readings of Shakespeare would have been considerably enlivened by the bottle of port he insisted on drinking each day in the belief that it would stave off fever. Something of Burton's belief remained in my youth in the settler habit of drinking endless gins and tonic purportedly for the quinine in the Indian tonic water. But even as the medical justifications fell away, it remained customary for some of the trappings of safari life to be, if anything, *more* luxurious than they would be at home, even if the good wine had to be drunk from tin mugs.

These habits of indulgence also extended to art. For Burton it was Shakespeare; for Denys Finch-Hatton, the hunter whose relationship with Baroness Blixen was made famous in her memoir *Out of Africa*, it was the Greek poets and a gramophone that supposedly fascinated the houseboys on Blixen's farm:

> It was a curious thing that Kamante should stick, in his preference, with much devotion to the Adagio of Beethoven's Piano Concerto in C Major; the first time that he asked me for it he had some difficulty in describing it, so as to make clear to me which tune it was that he wanted.[10]

Roosevelt may have considered his expedition to be a pattern of self-denial – though many struggled to agree, given that he bagged thousands of trophies from 269 species, some from the cowcatcher of his own private train – but he had less stringent standards when it came to cultural cargo. For his two-year hunt he commissioned a fifty-five-volume 'pigskin library'; this was a veritable ark of Western culture to be carried into the wilderness, though Roosevelt (in his characteristic disregard for the proprieties of polite society) brashly mixed the undisputed classics of the Western canon with lighter fare from soon-forgotten authors. When the selection of books for the library, which are now kept at Harvard, occasioned a public debate with Harvard's then president, C. W. Eliot, on Roosevelt's return, Roosevelt quickly conceded that much of the selection was merely a matter of personal taste. The inclusion of three volumes of Shakespeare, however, caused no controversy; as Roosevelt suggested, there were only 'four books so pre-eminent – the Bible, Shakespeare, Homer, and Dante – that I suppose there would be a general consensus of opinion among the cultivated men of all nationalities in putting them foremost'.[11] For Roosevelt, as for the guests on the long-running BBC radio show *Desert Island Discs*, the need for Shakespeare was taken for granted when links with civilization were broken.

A souvenir print showing Roosevelt on his African adventure.

Despite the fact that the library weighed sixty pounds and that it required a porter all of its own, Roosevelt insisted (as Burton had) on the practical nature of the volumes:

> They were for use, not ornament. I almost always had some volume with me, either in my saddle-bag or in the cartridge-bag which one of my gun-bearers carried to hold odds and ends. Often my reading would be done while resting under a tree at noon, perhaps

beside the carcass of a beast I had killed, or else while waiting for camp to be pitched; and in either case it might be impossible to get water for washing. In consequence the books were stained with blood, sweat, gun oil, dust, and ashes; ordinary bindings either vanished or became loathsome, whereas pigskin merely grew to look as a well-used saddle-bag looks.[12]

There is a curious sense in Roosevelt's *African Game Trails* that these refined products of European literary culture somehow belong among the 'blood, sweat, gun oil, dust, and ashes', that reading them in the most inhospitable climes demonstrated both that the works' seeming delicacy was illusory, and that the reader's poetic soul was immune to the lures of barbarism.

As one quickly comes to realize in reading the accounts of explorers, naturalists, hunters and opportunists travelling the African wilderness, Roosevelt was following a tradition which had become firmly established between Burton's time and his; the only unusual thing about the President's actions was that he took so many books, whereas most travellers in the African interior publicly affirmed that they took Shakespeare as their only literary reading. Compiling an inventory of his own expeditionary supplies in 1886, Walter Montague Kerr protests at the meagreness of the baggage which accompanied him overland from South Africa to the Lakes, noting that his

> baggage . . . would have made a poor show beside the enormous stores carried by some expeditions to the interior of the dark continent . . . I also had some books – a small edition of Shakespeare, a Nautical Almanac, logarithmic tables, and Proctor's Star Atlas.[13]

Once again, a volume of Shakespeare is found nestled in among technical manuals, and after a while it does not seem out of place.

It becomes, in effect, a cultural tool as necessary for survival as any of the cartographer's manuals. Another traveller in the interior, Thomas Heazle Parke, writing from a sickbed just west of Albert Nyanza (in modern-day Congo), mentions that he is 'filling up [his] time reading Shakespeare and Allingbone's Quotations. The former, with the Bible, and Whittaker's large edition, are the best books for Africa when transport is limited.'[14] The printing of Shakespeare, like the Bible, in dense double columns on thin paper allowed for a great deal of powerful language to be squeezed into a small space. It is easy to forget, however, that Shakespeare's works were *made* portable because they were thought to be indispensable, and not the other way around. Roosevelt captured this perfectly when he said that his three volumes of Shakespeare were 'the literary equivalent of a soldier's ration – "the largest amount of sustenance in the smallest possible space".[15]

A riposte of sorts is delivered to this gung-ho world of expeditionary Shakespeares by one of the few female explorers to find a place in these overwhelmingly masculine ranks. Gertrude Emily Benham, who at the same time that Roosevelt was careening through East Africa on a private train was becoming the first woman to ascend Kilimanjaro (and who would later walk across the continent from east to west), similarly recorded the 'few books' that she took with her on this expedition and others: 'Besides the Bible and a pocket Shakespeare, I have *Lorna Doone* and Kipling's *Kim*.' *Unlike* her male counterparts, however, Benham professed never to have carried firearms on her expeditions, nor to have shot any game; she traded her own knitting for local produce as she went, and testified that she found all the locals she encountered pleasant and welcoming. Her Shakespeare, it bears mentioning, was not holstered in pig leather as Roosevelt's was; the cloth covers of her own making, she says, were enough to keep them safe during her travels on every continent.[16]

The nuances of these (male) travellers' attachment to Shakespeare start to become clearer in another passage where Parke, who served as medical officer on the celebrated Emin Pasha Relief Expedition of 1886–9, writes before setting out about how he came by the *Works* that he took with him:

> A former patient of mine presented me with a copy of Shakespeare, as a parting gift and remembrancer on my journey. I cordially appreciated the kind attention, and, now that I am about to penetrate *the undiscovered country, from whose bourn so few white travellers have safely returned*, I trust the perusal of the pages of the immortal dramatist will help me to while away many a weary hour.[17]

Though Parke is clearly trying to be witty, he cannot prevent his anxiety about the expedition from showing through, and the passage is riddled with worries about mortality. Africa here becomes the underworld, which in Hamlet's description is 'that undiscovered country from whose bourn / No traveller returns', and there is a sense in which the works, written by an 'immortal dramatist' and given as a talisman-like 'remembrancer', give Parke hopes of returning from the underworld, like the Golden Bough which allowed Aeneas to visit his wife in Hades and return to the land of the living. This fear is captured succinctly in Joseph Conrad's *Heart of Darkness*, where the madness of the colonist-run-amok Mr Kurtz is attributed (in part) to his lack of books:

> How can you imagine what particular region of the first ages a man's untrammelled feet may take him into by the way of solitude – utter solitude without a policeman – by the way of silence – utter silence, where no warning voice of kind neighbour can be heard whispering of public opinion? These little things make all

the great difference. When they are gone you must fall back upon your own innate strength, upon your own capacity for faithfulness. Of course, you may be too much of a fool to go wrong – too dull even to know that you are being assaulted by the powers of darkness.[18]

Kurtz's famous final words – 'The horror! The horror!' – gesture to exactly what Shakespeare was supposed to conjure away: the chaos, depravity and existential nihilism that lay just at the doorstep of Victorian confidence.

Parke may well have returned from his expedition with an even greater belief in Shakespearean magic than he had when he left, given that he survived relatively unscathed an expedition which shocked the world with revelations of barbarity unusual even for ventures of this type. The Emin Pasha Relief Expedition had departed in great fanfare to save a German national named Eduard Schnitzer, unremarkable before his life in Africa, who had set himself up as a petty king in the Sudan. Now named 'Emin Pasha', Schnitzer soon became embroiled in warfare with religious fanatics and ending up a hostage to his own subjects; he is the first upstart settler-king in this story, but he certainly will not be the last. The expedition quickly ran into trouble, however, and split into a vanguard scouting party (led by Henry Morton Stanley and Thomas Heazle Parke) and a rear column, in which the bulk of the Europeans remained with a small group of Zanzibari porters. Though they succeeded in building a makeshift fort, the rear column were constantly assailed by poison arrow attacks, and the maize they tried to grow was incessantly trampled over by elephants, reducing them to near-starvation only relieved by dire expedients including donkey tongues and grass. Their long wait inside their fort did, however, leave the rear column plenty of time for reading, and they had dutifully brought with them the *Works*, which by this point were almost issued as standard.* William G. Stairs, one of the Europeans in the rear column, dryly remarks in a diary entry on Monday, 29 October 1888, that 'if we stay here much longer we shall all be great authorities on Shakespeare & Tennyson'.[19] Though most of the Europeans did survive to tell the tale, the expedition became a scandal on its return to Europe, when it emerged that one of the officers in the rear column had beaten a man to death for the presumption of defending his wife from rape, and another had paid to watch a young girl being ritually eaten.

Although not all of the exploratory expeditions were quite so despicable, those who read Shakespeare in the course of them were often drawn towards the darker reaches of the works. The Shakespearean magic that lies buried in Parke's description comes out into the open in many of these stories, which multiplied as the tradition became established. Arthur H. Neumann, in his *Elephant Hunting in East Equatorial Africa*, recounts the following episode:

> Lesiat [his Ndorobo tracker] had for long been bothering me to give him a charm to increase his power in this pursuit [i.e., the hunting of elephants]. My assurances that I had no such occult powers merely made him the more importunate. He regarded my objections as a refusal to help him, and a proof of unfriendliness to him. When I was about to leave he became more pressing, promised to keep ivory for me against my return, as an acknowledgement, should I consent, and assumed a hurt air at what he regarded

---

* Amusingly enough, the German expedition, purportedly also mounted to rescue Emin Pasha (though in reality using this as a cover to extend German influence in Uganda through secret negotiations with the Kabaka), was also suffering infinite delays, time which the expedition leader spent reading the works of Shakespeare and Gibbon's *Decline and Fall*, borrowed from the English mission in Kampala. See Carl Peters, *New Light on Dark Africa: Being the Narrative of the German Emin Pasha Expedition* (trans. H. W. Dulken, Ward, Lock, 1891), p. 429.

as my unkind obstinacy. Squareface interceded for him, explaining to me that the Swahili always accede to such requests, the most approved charm being a verse of the Koran, written in Arabic on a slip of paper. Not wishing to appear unfeeling, and seeing that no harm could come of it at all events, it occurred to me that a line or two of Shakespeare would probably be quite as effective. Bearing in mind that the Ndorobo hunter owes his success – when he has any – mainly to the powerful poison with which his weapon is smeared, if he can only manage to introduce it, in the proper manner, into the animal's economy, it struck me that the following quotation would be appropriate; and I accordingly wrote it on a slip of paper, illustrating it with a little sketch of an elephant:

> I bought an unction of a mountebank
> So mortal that, but dip a knife in it,
> Where it draws blood no cataplasm so rare,
> Collected from all simples that have virtue
> Under the moon, can save the thing from death
> That is but scratched withal; I'll touch my point
> With this contagion, that, if I gall him slightly,
> It may be death.[20]

Neumann never mentions that he had a volume of Shakespeare with him, and though he gives the impression that he is able to pluck the perfect quotation from *Hamlet* out of thin air, it seems more likely that he had the works on hand for consultation than that he had these lines, which are rather unmemorable as far as *Hamlet* goes, by heart. Neumann is, like Parke, trying to be wittily xenophobic: the suggestion that 'a line or two of Shakespeare would probably be quite as effective' is intended to undermine the conjuring powers of the Koran, to show that Shakespeare's stage poetry has as much power as these supposedly holy words. But, just as in Parke's story, it is hard to escape the feeling that the belief in Shakespearean magic was not entirely ironic. It is a very dull reader who does not end this passage by wondering whether or not the charm worked, and it is tellingly frustrating that we never learn the outcome of Lesiat's next hunt.

The greatest Shakespeare expeditionary stories of all, however, come from Henry Morton Stanley, the man who had led the Emin Pasha Relief Expedition. In Stanley's defence it should be mentioned that all of the atrocities recorded on that expedition took place while he was away from the main party leading a scouting mission, though Stanley did not manage to keep his hands entirely clean during his long and extraordinary career. The man who would become 'Africa's Most Famous Explorer' was born out of wedlock as plain John Rowlands, and spent much of his youth in a Welsh workhouse; Rowlands invented 'Henry Morton Stanley' during his early manhood in the United States, where he lived in New Orleans and fought in the American Civil War (on both sides).[21] This new identity came complete with a fantastically rich and loving family, and Stanley never gave it up even long after the truth became common knowledge in the Victorian rumour mill. He rose to prominence as a result of his 1871–2 expedition, which found the celebrated missionary David Livingstone on the shores of Lake Tanganyika after contact with him had been lost for more than a year, though there are doubts now that his famously nonchalant greeting ('Dr Livingstone, I presume?') was actually spoken and not cooked up later to add charm to the story. Stanley found, however, that his celebrity was a mixed blessing. He was never forgiven by the members of the Royal Geographical Society for his vulgarity in undertaking the Livingstone rescue on a newspaper's dime and (more gallingly, one suspects) for having beaten the Royal Geographical Society at their own game. And though Stanley escaped much of the public opprobrium visited on other members of the Emin Pasha Relief Expedition, his reputation has been indelibly tarnished by his late-life association with Leopold II of Belgium's *Association Internationale Africaine*, an organization typical in its muddling of philanthropy with exploitation but extraordinary in the level of the atrocities it committed – atrocities to which attention was drawn back in Europe by Joseph Conrad's novel *Heart of Darkness* (1899). Having pioneered a route up the Congo from the west coast of Africa for the Emin Pasha Relief Expedition, Stanley would later put his expertise at Leopold's disposal and set in motion the execrable history of the Belgian Congo.

One of Stanley's main tasks was to negotiate with local chieftains treaties of mutual understanding that would allow Leopold's *Association* to plant trading stations on their lands (and, perhaps more importantly, to prevent the French from doing the same). These stations would set a precedent for the regions being within the Belgian 'sphere of influence', a type of *de facto* power which Belgium and other powers later asserted as *de jure* political control using spurious legal logic and adding many forged treaties to those actually signed in Africa. Stanley was not above using literary magic to get these treaties signed, as he did on one occasion in the late 1880s. A local chief, Ngaliema, furious that Stanley had made agreements which undercut his power, approached Stanley's camp with a view to scaring him off; but Stanley, forewarned of the attack, sat calmly in his tent porch with a gong, all the while placidly 'reading the complete works of Shakespeare'. The chief was unnerved by Stanley's calm demeanour, and demanded that Stanley strike the gong, undeterred by Stanley's warnings that this was a dangerous request. Stanley finally obliged; at the sound of the gong, a multitude of armed men leapt out from where they had been hiding, convincing Ngaliema of Stanley's sorcery.[22]

Stanley's little stage trick not only featured a volume of Shakespeare, but also has the feel of being borrowed from it, drawing both on the foliage-camouflaged army which brings Birnam Wood to Dunsinane to defeat Macbeth and on the 'strange and solemn music' through which the wizard Prospero controls both spirits and his adversaries in *The Tempest*. (Birnam Wood, as we shall see, later made its way into the folklore of the region.) If Stanley *was* taking his cue from Shakespeare, this would not have been the first time. An expedition which Stanley led in 1877 to see if the Lualaba River might have a claim to be the most southerly source of the Nile ended in a nightmarish descent of the Congo when the Lualaba drained into that river instead. From Loanda on the west coast of Africa Stanley sent a report to his employers at the *New York Herald* of an incident that had happened in the modern-day Democratic Republic of Congo:

Loanda, West Coast of Africa
Sept 5, 1877

. . . A terrible crime in the eyes of many natives below the confluence of the Kwango and the Congo was taking notes. Six or seven tribes confederated together one day to destroy us, because I was 'bad, very bad.' I had been seen making medicine on paper – writing. Such a thing had never been heard of by the oldest inhabitant. It, therefore, must be witchcraft, and witchcraft must be punished with death. The white chief must instantly deliver his notebook (his medicine) to be burned, or there would be war on the instant.

My notebook was too valuable; it had cost too many lives and sacrifices to be consumed at the caprice of savages. What was to be done? I had a small volume of Shakespeare, Chandos edition. It had been read and reread a dozen times, it had crossed Africa, it had been my solace many a tedious hour, but it must be sacrificed. It was delivered, exposed to the view of the savage warriors. 'Is it this you want?' 'Yes.' 'Is this the medicine that you are afraid of?' 'Yes, burn it, burn it. It is bad, very bad; burn it.'

'Oh, my Shakespeare,' I said, 'farewell!' and poor Shakespeare was burnt. What a change took place in the faces of those angry, sullen natives! For a time it was like another jubilee. The country was saved; their women and little ones would not be visited by calamity. 'Ah, the white chief was so good, the embodiment of goodness, the best of all men.'[23]

Stanley certainly succeeds in reproducing the conventions which were by then becoming established: here is the small but well-thumbed volume of Shakespeare, here is the 'caprice of savages' and their slightly ungrammatical language, here are the serious-joking words about the magic Shakespearean totem – it is 'medicine', it must be 'sacrificed'. Stanley repeated a condensed version of the story in his book of the expedition, *Through the Dark Continent*, in which he elaborates on his feelings at the moment of sacrifice:

We walked to the nearest fire. I breathed a regretful farewell to my genial companion, which during many weary hours of night had assisted to relieve my mind when oppressed by almost intolerable woes, and then gravely consigned the innocent Shakespeare to the flames, heaping the brush-fuel over it with ceremonious care.[24]

This account figures Shakespeare, the Man who is also Word, becoming Christ-like as he enters the inferno, guiltless but enough to sate the devils.

The sting in the tail of Stanley's story is that, like so much else in his life, it was a fabrication. As the modern editor of his *Herald*

Stanley in later life, here with the members of the Emin Pasha Relief Expedition. Stanley is seated in the centre with Emin Pasha to his left, and Dr Parke is seated second from left.

despatches notes, the account of this episode in his expedition diary has Stanley handing over no more to satisfy the furious natives than a sheet of paper upon which he had scribbled; this detail was subsequently revised for the newspaper account.[25] Stanley's instincts as a storyteller, as well as his finely honed sense of what he needed to do to fit in, told him that the mythic balance of the tale required the sacrificial victim to be Shakespeare. And the story itself is eerily reminiscent of the episode in Shakespeare's *Tempest* in which the savage Caliban plots to overthrow the magician Prospero with a band of drunken accomplices:

CALIBAN:
Why, as I told thee, 'tis a custom with him
I'th' afternoon to sleep. There thou mayst brain him,

Having first seized his books; or with a log
Batter his skull, or paunch him with a stake,
Or cut his weasand with thy knife. Remember
First to possess his books, for without them
He's but a sot as I am, nor hath not
One spirit to command – they all do hate him
As rootedly as I. Burn but his books.

The Tempest (III.ii.81–9)

It seems that Stanley and the other early travellers arrived in Africa expecting to find superstitious and violent natives who demanded that they burn their 'magic' books, for this image of the 'savage' had resided at the heart of English culture for centuries.

We are unlikely ever to be able to sort the truth of these accounts from the fantasies derived from the books that the explorers carried with them. Yet the truth of these stories is very much secondary to the purpose Stanley and others evidently expected them to serve. Instead of being straightforward accounts of what had happened in Africa, these stories form a kind of argument for how the 'Dark Continent' and its peoples should be understood. If Shakespeare is the universal genius of man, and his worth is evident to all humans, then those who do not appreciate him are, by extrapolation, *in some sense not human.* This insidious logic was nothing new; indeed, much the same tactic had been employed in Shakespeare's time to suggest that the inhabitants of the New World could not be human because they broke the deeply embedded European taboo of cannibalism.[26] Shakespeare's characters are themselves not immune to these chains of reasoning: it is constantly asked in *The Tempest* whether Caliban, whose name has not moved far from 'Cannibal', is fully human or not, and it is clear that the answer to this question will determine how he is treated by the

European colonizers. When Prospero and Miranda call him a 'slave', they are not simply describing Caliban's status as a captive but accusing him of a moral impoverishment which *justifies* the removal of his freedom and his rights. He was (Prospero claims) treated 'with human kindness', and Miranda 'took pains to make [him] speak'; and yet despite his aptitude for language, his ungrateful assumption that he was their equal (and could thus look on Miranda with desire) proved that their 'human kindness' – that quality of empathy which is both the mark of the human and only granted to other humans – was misplaced.

> But thy vile race,
> Though thou didst learn, had that in't which good natures
> Could not abide to be with; therefore wast thou
> Deservedly confined into this rock,
> Who hadst deserved more than a prison.

> *The Tempest* (I.ii.357–61)

Caliban, according to this argument, should look upon his enslavement as an act of mercy, after his criminal lust for the colonizer's daughter had earned him a worse fate. His savage hate of books – which Stanley echoed in his account of the *Dark Continent* – was an inescapable counterpart to this same unredeemable incivility.

This was, it must be said, a depressing place to start my quest to understand Shakespeare's universal appeal – with that very universalism being used as a tool to exclude from the bounds of the human. But though attempts to define what it is to be human have often been used in this way – to lever one group of people apart from the rest and deprive them of the right to be human – this does not characterize all thinking on the subject. It doesn't, in fact, even characterize all thinking on the subject in *The Tempest*. Indeed,

Caliban's *second* appearance in the play (II.ii) sets about parodying and upending the righteous judgements earlier levelled against him by Prospero and Miranda. The castaway Trinculo, coming upon a Caliban who is pretending to be dead, engages in an extended forensic analysis of the creature at his feet:

> What have we here? A man or a fish? Dead or alive? A fish: he smells like a fish; a very ancient and fish-like smell; a kind of not-of-the-newest poor-john. A strange fish. Were I in England now, as once I was, and had but this fish painted, not a holiday fool there but would give a piece of silver. There would this monster make a man; any strange beast there makes a man. When they will not give a doit to relieve a lame beggar, they will lay out ten to see a dead Indian. Legged like a man, and his fins like arms. Warm, o'my troth! I do now let loose my opinion, hold it no longer: this is no fish, but an islander that hath lately suffered by a thunderbolt.
>
> *The Tempest* (II.ii.24–34)

Trinculo's speech moves from lampooning the kind of judgement that decides on the essence of a thing by a few trivial external features (Caliban is a fish because he smells like a fish, he is dead because he is lying down) to turning the judgement back upon Shakespeare's audience. Trinculo's daydream – in which he takes Caliban to England to exhibit him to paying crowds – is, of course, a direct reflection of *The Tempest*'s audience, who themselves have paid to see this 'spectacle' of Caliban. It is clear that exotic peoples are made 'monsters' in England because there's money to be made from it – indeed, the word 'monster' *means* 'something to be shown to a spectator' – and this was as true in Stanley's day as in Shakespeare's. But it's also clear that it is the leering crowd that is in danger of losing its humanity in this bargain: in paying to see the 'strange beast' of a showman's exhibit 'When they will not give a doit [a small coin] to relieve a lame beggar', they reveal the loss of *charity*, of that 'human kindness' that makes them 'human kind'. Throughout the play, as the presumption that the European spectator is the arbiter of humanity ebbs away, we are given hints of qualities which Caliban *does* exhibit, qualities Renaissance thought toyed with as central to human nature – laughter, the love of wine, a sense of the political, and the ability to appreciate natural beauty and music – and which are increasingly attractive versions of humanity when set against the duplicity of the European settlers.[27]

So even if Shakespeare had been introduced to Africa by the explorers as a token of difference, as a demonstration that the Dark Continent could not absorb his genius, that didn't mean that everyone would be content to treat him in that way. Readers, in my experience, are unruly things, whose cooperation should not be counted on. I had generated a list of leads, of half-known stories and rumours, which gave reason to hope that Shakespeare's career in East Africa would be a lot richer and more varied than this, and that he would soon be prised from the hands of his cultural guardians and turned over to *real* encounters with Africa and its peoples. With this in mind, I packed my copy of the *Works* in the leather shooting bag I've always used as a satchel – a habit of which Roosevelt would doubtless have approved – and set off to follow in the tracks of Burton, Stanley and the tribe of readers that sprang up in their wake.

2

ZANZIBAR

Shakespeare and the Slaveboy Printworks

Sir, he hath never fed of the dainties that are bred in a book.
He hath not eat paper, as it were; he hath not drunk ink.
His intellect is not replenished; he is only an animal – only
  sensible in the duller parts.

Love's Labor's Lost (IV.ii.21–3)

Carrying Shakespeare into Africa felt momentous for Burton and
Stanley in part because they were escorting a treasure into the
unknown, where it did not seem to belong. Their feelings were not,
one suspects, altogether different from those of the missionaries
who dedicated themselves to bringing the Gospel into strange
lands, though of course the explorers showed little wish to share
Shakespeare's powerful language with the natives they met. Burton
carried Shakespeare with Euclid because both were felt to contain
unalterable, universal truths – in beauty as in geometry – and the
unshakeable nature of the works was demonstrated by carrying

them into unsettling places.* Yet though it is possible that the first white travellers met peoples who had not seen paper books before (if not likely, given that Arabic slaving caravans had long been visiting these areas), the sense that the works were wholly alien to Africa was largely an adventurer's fantasy during the time of the later safaris. By the time Roosevelt visited in 1909–10, a generation of young Africans were not only familiar with Shakespearean narrative, but had even been learning to read and write Swahili using the stories of Shylock and Lear.

It was to understand the setting in which this schoolbook – the *Hadithi za Kiingereza*, or 'Tales from the English' – was printed that I first returned to East Africa. Though Africa would long since have swallowed up any traces of Burton's and Stanley's encampments, the *Hadithi* was printed in a town which might retain traces of its genesis. Frustratingly, not a single copy survives of the book's first edition, printed by Edward Steere on the island of Zanzibar in 1867, and we are reliant on later editions for details of its contents.[1] Though a tragedy, this is no great surprise: such a slender volume, with pages sewed together by Steere's own hand, was designed for immediate use by the boys liberated from slaving vessels; copies of it would have quickly disintegrated in the dust and heat and sweat of excited, fearful, frustrated hands, and it was likely that no one thought it worth preserving a copy of such an ephemeral thing for the record.[2] Karen Blixen's Beethoven-loving houseboy, Kamante, was shrewd in casting doubt upon the merits of his mistress's typed manuscript pages:

---

* Even in Shakespeare's time, Euclid was carried into exotic places as a totem of the Christian West's access to universal truth – as when the Jesuit missionary Matteo Ricci presented Euclid's *Elements* to the Chinese Emperor, in hopes that the awestruck audience would accept the truths of Christian doctrine as equally indisputable.

'Look, Msabu,' he said, 'this [a leatherbound hardback *Odyssey*] is a good book. It hangs together from the one end to the other. Even if you hold it up and shake it strongly, it does not come to pieces. The man who has written it is very clever. But what you write,' he went on, both with scorn and with a sort of friendly compassion, 'is some here and some there. When the people forget to close the door it blows about, even down on the floor and you are angry. It will not be a good book.'[3]

Although the episode is intended to demonstrate Kamante's charmingly naïve assessment of a book by its cover, he is of course right: literary longevity has everything to do with a good solid binding. Though reasonably good records were kept of the missionary printing activities during the later years of Steere's stay in Zanzibar, the early print experiments like the *Hadithi* were not seen for what they would become: among the earliest physical relics of Swahili, a language spoken today by over a hundred million people in eastern Africa. It is one of the ironies of history that the true character of each age is lost in those things thought not worth preserving, and this was the fate of the first Swahili Shakespeare.

Steere's thin Zanzibari pamphlet consisted of four stories, taken from the pages of the popular children's book *Tales from Shakespeare* by Charles and Mary Lamb: *The Taming of the Shrew* (*Mwanamke Aliyefunzwa*), *The Merchant of Venice* (*Kuwia na Kuwiwa*), *The Tragedy of King Lear* (*Baba na Binti*), and *The Life of Timon of Athens* (*Kula Maji*). Steere's choice of these four stories seems baffling at first. They are not unified by genre, including as they do two comedies and two tragedies (though *Timon* is a slippery fish and doesn't sit easily in any category). Yet the idea that Steere might have chosen these four widely differing plays to give a sample of Shakespeare's range is also unconvincing: while the

Merchant and *Lear* are undisputed high points of Shakespeare's writing, it seems certain that no one choosing four Shakespeare plays to take to a desert island would settle for *The Taming of the Shrew* and *Timon of Athens*. The answer, it seems, must lie elsewhere, and my first guess is that these four plays suggested themselves to Steere as Shakespeare's clearest parables for everyday life: each of them is, in this highly simplified form, a morality tale about the proper relations between individuals, their families and the societies in which they live, and each offers a message that Steere might have expected to be acceptable to readers in an Islamic society. *Taming* warns of the dangers of unsubmissive women, and offers a path to bring them back to the desired obedience, while *Lear* shows the disastrous consequences of allowing children to wield power over their parents. *The Merchant of Venice* corrects the evils that arise in society from usury – a practice forbidden by Islamic law – and *Timon* demonstrates the fickleness of earthly possessions while portraying the sin of ingratitude. If this was Steere's motive in choosing these four tales, he would have been following a time-honoured missionary practice of focusing first on elements likely to be familiar to the culture to be evangelized, just as the early Apostles had portrayed Christ as a warrior when it helped to get more bellicose peoples on board. Whatever Steere's motives, they seemed to have struck a chord, as the collection was later taken up by the Society for the Promotion of Christian Knowledge and printed in regular editions (including at least eight between 1940 and 1972), forming part of their schoolbook distribution in eastern Africa, which would exceed 100,000 books a year in the middle of the twentieth century.[4]

The language of the *Hadithi* is simple in the extreme, easily legible even to me with the impoverished Swahili that I have retained from my childhood. Each tale begins with a storybook formula: 'Palikuwa na mtu, akikaa Venezia, mji wa Uitalia, jina

Hadithi za Kiingereza.

lake Shailoki, kabila yake Myahudi; kazi yake kukopesha fedha na mali' – 'In the beginning there was a man, living in Venice, a town in Italy, named Shylock, of the Jewish people; his business was to lend money and property.'[5] The use of this opening formula is striking, because Steere used the same words a few years after his Swahili Shakespeare to translate the haunting first words of the Gospel of John – 'Mwanzo palikuwa na Neno, Neno akawa kwa Muungu, Neno akawa Muungu' ('In the beginning was the Word, and the Word was with God, and the Word was God').[6] To the young boys and girls who were his first readership, the boundaries between Steere's evangelizing mission and his role as a cultural ambassador must have seemed very hazy indeed, introduced as they were by the same man with identical formulas.

There were no simple, physical signs by which to distinguish storybook Shakespeare from the Word of God: each of these early Swahili books is a flimsy, pocket-sized pamphlet, and while the title of *Hadithi* ('stories') might seem to signal that these are lighter fare, things may not have been so simple to children who had heard of the *hadith* that are the foundations of Islamic law. Hoping to find out more about Steere and the world into which he brought this oddity, I started my travels where the *Hadithi* did – in Zanzibar.

Shakespeare set two of his finest plays, *The Comedy of Errors* and *The Tempest*, on magical islands where all expectations are confounded, and he could have done worse than take his inspiration from Zanzibar, which was in his lifetime receiving its first visits from merchants of the newly founded East India Company.* The main city, called Stone Town to differentiate the whitewashed coral stone palaces on the seafront from the earthwork dwellings that once lay inland, is a labyrinth of narrow alleys winding between high smooth walls, topped by arabesque parapets. These walls are punctuated only by brass-studded heavy wooden doors and windows opening onto fretwork balconies, which for all their artistry give the stranger few distinguishing marks by which to find his bearings. Shakespeare's own disorienting island of Ephesus provokes his traveller Antipholus to describe the feeling of getting lost in just such a warren of streets in some of the finest lines from this underrated gem of early Shakespeare:

---

* Shakespeare would also have had access to information about Zanzibar from John Pory's translation and edition of the *Geographical Historie* of Leo Africanus, first published in 1600, where the inhabitants are described as 'much addicted to sorcery and witchcraft'. The *Geographical Historie* is largely confined to northern and north-western Africa, and Pory's supplement on sub-Saharan Africa was drawn from the reports of other travellers.

I to the world am like a drop of water
That in the ocean seeks another drop,
Who, falling there to find his fellow forth,
Unseen, inquisitive, confounds himself.

The Comedy of Errors (I.ii.35–8)

Getting lost today in Stone Town can be a befuddling affair: one is as likely to happen upon a palace as a slum tenement, a mosque blaring anti-Western rhetoric from the loudspeaker as a European church in the neo-gothic style. To add to the effect, this puzzle of streets smells strongly – as indeed the whole island does – of cloves, which with other spices (cinnamon and nutmeg) are the main local crop.

I came once to Zanzibar as a child, and my sense of it as a place of wonder was doubtless set by those early memories. We arrived for our visit on a hydrofoil, a ship-sized hovercraft which a local entrepreneur had recently acquired on credit to ferry passengers from the mainland to Stone Town. The hydrofoil disappeared soon after with its insolvent owner, to the confusion of the local police, who had little means of following an ocean-going hovercraft. It turned up years later, I believe, off in the Gulf, as an air-conditioned pirate ship for the modern day. Of Zanzibar itself I remember taxicabs carpeted inside with Persian rugs, and the catamaran fishing dhows spilling their resplendent cargo on the shore.

The Zanzibar archipelago is made up of two main islands – Unguja and Pemba – lying off the coast of modern-day Tanzania, and the location of these islands made them a prized seat for a succession of colonizing powers. Not only are the islands marvellously lush, but they are also far enough offshore to be safe from all but advanced maritime nations, as well as being directly in the path of the seasonal tradewinds that circulate between Africa, the Middle East and India. Indeed, so attractive were the islands that the Busaidi dynasty, who had controlled Zanzibar since 1698, moved their seat from Oman to the southern island of Unguja early in the nineteenth century. Arabic merchants built an empire there through the trade in spices, ivory and (above all) slaves, and expended their wealth on the palaces which line the seafront of Stone Town. The immensely powerful Busaidi dynasty soon caught the interest of the Western powers, and by the middle of the nineteenth century American and European consuls were resident in Stone Town. When Edward Steere arrived in 1864, then, Stone Town was anything but the barbaric wilderness that he feared when he left England. Indeed, it was considerably more cosmopolitan than his former parish in the remote Lincolnshire town of Skegness. He remarked on arrival that 'the whole aspect of the place from the sea is more Italian than African', and was surprised to see riding in the harbour the Sultan's latest acquisition, the battleship *Shenandoah*, which had recently been retired from Confederate service in the American Civil War.[7]

The organization that sent Steere to Africa, the Universities' Mission to Central Africa (UMCA), had been founded by four universities (Oxford, Cambridge, Durham and Trinity College Dublin) in response to an appeal made by David Livingstone in a speech to the Oxford Union in 1857. Livingstone, who had spent nearly two decades evangelizing in Africa by that time, was considered a saint in his own lifetime, a veneration that does not seem to have been reduced by the fact that he reputedly managed to convert only a single person to Christianity during all his mission work (and that convert lapsed soon afterwards).[8] It was not only, however, Livingstone's Christian zeal which captured the enthusiasm of the earnest Victorian university men; rather, it was his principled stand against the Indian Ocean slave trade, against which he

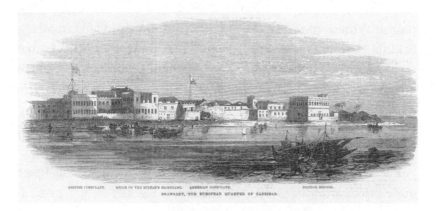

The European quarter of Zanzibar.

railed in speaking tours while on periodic return to Britain, making him a philanthropic celebrity. The UMCA had quickly gathered steam, and had sent their first Missionary Bishop out in 1861, though the incumbent died shortly after arriving on the mainland, living only long enough to send home reports of pestilence, famine and war. Steere travelled out in the entourage of the second appointee, Bishop Tozer, and before retreating to the safety of Stone Town the pair had made a concerted attempt to set up in the interior, where Livingstone felt the main work of conversion and education was to be done. Among the many bleak descriptions of this voyage up the Zambezi in Steere's letters, now kept in Rhodes House (Oxford), is a delightful description of Steere holding one of the new patent steel-ribbed oilcloth umbrellas over the Bishop's head.[9]

It must have been just such first encounters with Europeans that made the factory-produced umbrella a universal symbol of status through much of Africa. For people relentlessly assaulted from above by sun or driving rain, this was an infinitely more impressive invention than others of which European civilization was so proud. I cannot help thinking, after reading Steere's description, of a senescent *askari* (guard) who worked at our house outside of

Nairobi. Vuli would arrive promptly at sundown and fall fast asleep in a chair outside the house, and on the few occasions he did wake (usually roused by his own snoring) he summoned the entire household, having convinced himself that one of the Labradors was a leopard. On his days off Vuli would walk to market, wearing a shower cap and armed with an umbrella and a squash racquet, the inalienable markers of his civility.

For all the amusement afforded by the image of Steere and Tozer under their umbrellas on the Zambezi, Steere's letters paint a sobering picture of torturous illness within the mission party and vicious warfare on the riverbanks (though, following the tradition instituted by the explorers, they responded to these hardships with evening readings of Shakespeare).[10] Having tried but failed to establish a foothold at various locations closer and closer to the coast, he and Tozer eventually left for Zanzibar at the end of August 1864, having decided that their ends would be best served by setting up a seminary on Zanzibar to train local priests for redeployment in the interior. Though Steere's nineteenth-century biographer defends the move as a 'tactical retreat', it was seen as a shameful capitulation by many, including Livingstone himself, who dismissed the Zanzibar mission as nothing more than a chaplaincy to the consulate.[11]

Even if Steere setting up in Stone Town was in many ways an admission of defeat, he nevertheless applied himself fiercely to the tasks at hand, the most urgent of which was to get the Sultan (and the local British Navy vessels) to take seriously the anti-slavery 'Moresby' treaty the two had signed decades earlier. The disregard for the ban on trading human cargo was underlined by the fact that upon their arrival the Sultan gave the UMCA party, along with a palace in which to set up operations, five slave boys as a welcoming gift. These and all the UMCA's first subjects for evangelization – including those whom Steere taught to work his printing press when it arrived – were *literally* a captive audience, boys from mainland tribes who had been lured away from their families in southern Tanganyika by *tende halwa* ('sweet givers').[12] A small number of these, including most of those at the UMCA mission, were then confiscated from the slavers by the Royal Navy. Steere later recorded his first impression of his encounter with the boys presented by the Sultan:

> Now if you can imagine yourself standing opposite to five little black boys, with no clothing save the narrowest strip of calico [*merikani*] round their middles, with their hands clasped round their necks, looking up into your face with an expression of utter apprehension that something more dreadful than ever they had experienced would surely come upon them, now that they had fallen into the hands of the dreaded white men, you will feel our work somewhat as we felt it. And then, how are you to speak, or they to answer? You have not one word in common. Yet these are the missionaries of the future.[13]

Steere's confidence that these damaged boys would find a vocation in the church might seem delusional, and yet the future was to see some of his hopes come to fruition. Among these boys was John Swedi, who became the first East African to take holy orders, and Francis Mabruki, who spent a year at Rickinghall in Suffolk, where he inspired the destitute farmhand Samuel Speare to follow him back to Zanzibar as a missionary. Another of the young recruits, Owen Makanyassa, was put to work in the printing office, where he was soon in charge and running a brisk business for local clients as well as setting the pamphlets composed by Steere.[14] Ironically, the boy christened 'William Shakespeare' was considered among those 'who shew no sign of teaching power', and was put out to apprentice as a mason.[15]

It is hard to decide quite what to think of the evangelizing activities of Steere and his kind. The intentions with which Steere embarked upon his life in Africa were undoubtedly noble ones, just as his life before Zanzibar had been a catalogue of selfless aspiration. Though he had followed his father and studied law at University College London, he was distracted (as I was when an undergraduate there) by the variety of the metropolis and spent most of his time in the Reading Room of the British Museum studying ancient tongues, as well as learning to print (and learning botany, conchology and brass rubbing). (Admittedly, my own distractions were not always as salubrious.) He was called to the bar in 1850, but soon left in hopes of helping the needy. He sold all of his books and other possessions to support his work in various Brotherhoods dedicated to helping the London poor, though he left this life in disgust at the internal politics and what he viewed as the lack of zeal in many of the participants.

Joining the church seemed the next logical step, and Steere volunteered for one of the least desirable postings in the British Isles, where his Skegness parishioners remembered him as a 'downright shirt sleeve man, and a real Bible parson'.[16] When even this proved insufficiently testing, he signed on to accompany Bishop-elect Tozer into what could only have seemed to him the last place on earth. So if Steere's actions in offering safety and a livelihood to utterly helpless orphans in exchange for their adherence to his own Christian beliefs strikes me as hard to sympathize with, it is nevertheless clear to me that Steere was benevolent and believed unquestioningly that what he was giving these boys was salvation. He was, I suppose, not asking of them anything more than what he was asking of himself, and this sets him apart from the explorers. As his translation of the *Tales from Shakespeare* suggests, Steere's belief in the equality of our souls meant he also believed in the possibility of shared thought, language, culture, of a common humanity which reversed the fragmentation of human society after the Tower of Babel.

This is not to say that Steere could not be rather self-righteous, perhaps even too much for the woman he married in 1858, Mary Bridget. It seems clear that there was a separation between Steere and the woman who persuaded him to accept the African posting, for all that the biography written soon after Steere's death gives an (amusingly melodramatic) explanation for why they never lived together again:

> Mrs. Steere had bravely consented to his former sacrifice [his solitary move to Skegness], and now she bade him God speed on his second venture [to Africa], and quite intended following herself, accompanied by a sister. We may add that the idea was not definitely abandoned until some years afterwards, when delicacy of health, ending, alas! in disease of the brain, rendered it impossible.[17]

Although Steere and his wife never lived together again, their letters and papers do show rather touchingly that she spent much of her remaining life visiting English churches to sketch the masonry and woodwork that Steere would copy for the vast neo-gothic cathedral he erected in Stone Town, on the site of the Zanzibar slave market he had helped to put out of commission.

My progress in reconstructing the Stone Town of Steere's day is immeasurably slowed during my first days in Zanzibar by the fact that Ramadan is being observed. For this I have calculated: things would be open erratically (if at all), and any officials whom I do manage to locate will be hungry and uncooperative from observing their daytime fast. This is fine – I have a pile of nineteenth-

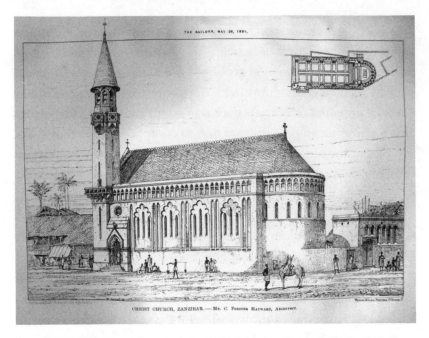

Christ Church, Zanzibar, the cathedral that Steere built during
his time as Missionary Bishop to Central Africa.

century accounts of Zanzibar to work my way through, and a list
of infidel contacts whose availability should be less affected by the
religious calendar. What I had not realized, however, is that
Zanzibar is practically alone in the Islamic world in not observing
a set date for the end of Ramadan: instead, Eid al-Fitr will only be
declared when the new moon is actually *seen* by the famished and
expectant faithful. Each cloudy evening, then, will mean another
day's wait, and a day less of my limited time in the archives. I
spend my days, then, walking the alleys that have remained
unchanged since Steere's time, trying to pinpoint the location of
the UMCA mission and of Steere's printing venture. Here is what
was once the American Consul's house, where Henry Morton
Stanley spent nights on the roof in his tent to prepare himself for
the hardships of his expedition to find Livingstone. This palace

became the club for colonials in the twentieth century, where Evelyn Waugh spent a week trying to weather the unbearable heat by sitting under a fan with *eau de quinine* on his head; it is now a public hotel selling smart cocktails at souvenir prices to visiting cruise passengers. Here is Steere's cathedral, and nearby the chains that serve as reminders of the slave auctions once held on the site. Here would have stood the building where a princess, Seyyida Salme, was kept under house arrest during Steere's time after assisting her brother in a failed coup. Seyyida Salme, who will play a part in Steere's life in Stone Town, is a figure whose daily life is recorded in unparalleled detail in the intimate memoirs she left of life in the harem.

The brother whose rising she supported, Barghash, did eventually become Sultan, and his palace, the Beit al-Ajaib (or 'House of Wonders'), is now a sparsely filled museum, with exhibits in the corners of its vast reception rooms. As an Arab palace, the Beit al-Ajaib is of an open design to allow the sea breeze to draw the hot air out of the upper floors, and many of the lighter exhibits seem on the point of fluttering away. The rickety vitrines, dwarfed by the echoing and palatial rooms, contain the few surviving pieces of Limoges porcelain and Venetian glass with which Barghash tricked out his palace, pieces which in their exotic fragility seem faintly like butterflies pinned to their velvet boards. Among these moulting remnants of Barghash's splendour and their curling typewritten labels, I come across an intriguing early photograph of a group of men, both black and white, working in a large room filled with what are unmistakably typesetting cases: inclined desks, like architects' drawing-tables, with dozens of cubby holes for the pieces of moveable type that will be put together to make a printed page. The photograph is labelled 'Universities Mission to Central Africa, Mambo Msiige', and by the look of their dress the photograph was taken at the end of the nineteenth century. There is no one to ask for further information other than the small crowd of women lazing on the verandah at the front of the palace, of whom all and none seem to be employed by the museum. I shall have to see The Director; The Director is unlikely to be in until after Ramadan; my existing ticket will certainly not allow me to enter the museum again to see if he has returned.

After several unsuccessful return visits I manage to secure an interview with The Director. No further mention is made of new tickets, and indeed after my first reappearance I have the run of the museum, as the women have evidently become bored by the whole matter and make no protest at my comings and goings. I find my way to The Director's office, which turns out to be another cavernous reception room in which he occupies a small desk at the far end, by one of the two walls of windows, which remain firmly shuttered in an attempt to keep the stacks of paper on his desk. The Director is a small, round man in a navy blue suit, squared off by shoulder pads of a remarkable breadth. He invites me to take a seat, an offer which occasions some confusion on my part as the only two chairs in the near-empty office are next to one another behind his desk. I take a seat behind the desk, though it becomes clear that this is not the commencement of the interview, as The Director is engaged in Solving a Problem. On his desk is a computer; on another table, a good thirty feet away across the palace room, is a printer. These two are evidently plugged into the two power sockets in the room. The Director returns to the printer, which he seems to have been examining for some time, and walks the printer cable to its full extent, leaving him a good twenty-five feet short of the computer. He places it calmly on the ground and walks to the computer, where he stops and looks back at the printer, before once again pacing the ground in between. I am unsure whether it would be wise to offer some observations at this point, so I remain quiet.

The Director spends some time over at the printer, contemplating (it seems) whether he had best move the printer table towards the desk, or give the matter up entirely. Employing a tactic once suggested to me as a response to official delays, I remove my volume of Shakespeare from my satchel and begin to read. Emitting a sigh of resignation, The Director comes and sits down at my side.

Leaning towards me on his elbow with chin in hand, but still looking out into the body of the room rather than in my direction, he asks me the nature of my inquiry. Assuming what seems to be the only logical posture at this point, I also speak out into the room, telling him who I am and asking whether he might be able to provide any information on the photograph in the gallery below. There are the inevitable questions about letters of introduction, of which I am thoughtlessly unprovided. (Later in my trip I take to writing these on my own behalf from inventively named referees; my university identity card, which would have been infinitely more difficult to forge, is of no interest to such authorities as I meet.) After several repetitions of my question have produced no impression whatsoever on the mind of The Director, it appears that the only thing to do is to descend together into the gallery to inspect said photograph. This involves a great process of informing secretaries and locking offices – one or other of which one might reasonably have expected to suffice. The Director has evidently never set eyes on the photograph before, and indeed seems rather taken by the display as a whole. It is, he agrees, very interesting, but he can tell me nothing further about it.

Luckily I have another appointment, this time with a local watercolourist of Goan descent, John Baptist da Silva, who seems unnervingly to have been present at all significant events in the last seventy years of Zanzibar's history. (It is, I suppose, a small island.) We sit on an open gallery overlooking the courtyard of his house; as with many townhouses in the old quarter, this one has inherited the Arab disdain for outward magnificence, and the heavy door which gives entrance to the elegant quarters opens off an alley which might easily be mistaken for an untended gap between buildings. His granddaughter brings us mugs of achingly sweet tea flavoured with husks of cardamom, and we look over portfolios of his exquisite paintings, which expertly capture the blend of rubbish and Moorish glamour that characterizes Stone Town. We discuss the irritability of the island during Ramadan, and I comment on the increased number of women wearing the full *niqab* covering since I was last here. Unfurling his glinting eyes from among their wrinkles, John Baptist smiles and tells me that they are, however, experts at flirting with their eyes, and often provocatively dressed underneath. My 'flat' in Stone Town confirms this sense of female freedom when off the streets. The 'flat' is, in fact, merely a room perched above a first-floor court-yard, reached by something more ladder than stairs; the entrance from the street is through the back of one of the many lean-to stores selling *kikoi* wraps, up stairs to a landing that has been converted into a hair salon by means of odd mirrors and chairs, and then into the courtyard which serves the dozen or so other residents of the tenement for all of life's necessities. The ladies in the hair salon seem to have an arrangement by which each of them is dresser and each customer, without too much bothersome distinction between. One voluminous lady quickly senses my unsureness about local gender relations, and asks increasingly daring questions about my romantic interests, to gales of laughter from the other ladies.

When I tell John Baptist why I've come to Zanzibar, he is charmingly unfazed by the idea that I might try to understand Shakespeare (or anything else, for that matter) by coming to

Zanzibar. He immediately recalls his own childhood experience of being made to learn *Julius Caesar* by rote for the Sisters of his Catholic convent school. His early memory is reminiscent of the semi-autobiographical passages in the novel *By the Sea* by the excellent Zanzibari novelist Abdulrazak Gurnah, which features a 'teacher of English . . . who was a pious Muslim and an ardent Anglophile without contradiction or anxiety', and whose efforts culminate in a bravura performance of Brutus's speech in praise of Caesar, given by a young Zanzibari boy in an alley like that outside John Baptist's house.[18] It is rather poignant to think that Steere's island would one day be populated by boys fluent in iambic pentameter.

John Baptist can confirm that the UMCA mission house was at Mambo Msiige, and that it later became (among other things) an embassy and part of the government telegraph office. Though it is still standing, he doubts that I am likely to find anything there; it is currently an empty shell, marooned in a legal battle over whether its proprietors should be allowed to convert another Zanzibari heirloom into a luxury hotel. He tells me not to expect too much in the archives or museum records: at independence in 1963 the new officials carted the records out of offices all over town in wheelbarrows and set fire to them on the front lawns, intent that the New Zanzibar should not be burdened by the clutter of the past. Much of Stone Town was appropriated under the subsequent socialist programmes of President (and Shakespeare translator) Julius Nyerere, given over to tenants who had no funds to maintain the merchant palaces in which they squatted.

I am shown the dozens of photograph albums John Baptist was given by a member of a Goan photographic dynasty, days before he was murdered in the looting that followed independence. John Baptist has since acquired more photographs and postcards of

Zanzibar from visits to specialist fairs near Paddington railway station, which seems to be the only reason for which he leaves the island. The albums contain page after page of bug-eyed Victorian official portraits, as well as pictures of the town during the latter part of Steere's life and a surprising number of louche pictures of all-male theatricals and costume parties on board navy vessels anchored off the island. Among the pictures is an old picture post-card depicting the UMCA mission house on Mambo Msiige, where Shakespeare first became Swahili in the thin pamphlet of stories. John makes a gift to me of the postcard, and, slugging the cardamom sugar at the bottom of my mug, I leave him to his after-noon nap.

A few days later, as I am carefully porting a paper plate full of barbecued seafood back to my rooms from the open-air market, the cry of *Eid Mubarak!* announces that Ramadan is at an end. A man from the crowd streaming down to the Forodhani gardens on the waterfront stops to tell me with no apparent irony that it is 'not permitted' to eat the street food in my flat, and (while dubious of the legal logic this entails) I take this as an invitation to join the revels down in town. The sense of relief is general. Even the dread-locked Somali zealot I had watched a few days previously lambast-ing a tourist for wearing shorts during Ramadan seems to be letting his hair down.

When the archives finally open, and I have waited long enough for several ranks of officials to scrutinize my very august letter of introduction, I start on the boxes of UMCA papers. The going is slow, in part because I am only allowed one box at a time – the box being the natural unit with which the scholar can be trusted – and there are long intervals while a new one is fetched. The papers when they do arrive are terrifyingly brittle, and have to be handled like dried flowers. More than once it seems clear that I will be the last to read a letter or a diary page, and only reluctantly do I return the crumbling papers to their boxes and send them away into the hot-dry limbo in which they wait hopelessly to be read. Still, my time is short and I want to find out something about Steere's printing works and his day-to-day life. So I pass over the touching details of the young slave boys' daily routines, and the arrival of the first liberated slave girls, and the growth of outposts of the UMCA mission elsewhere on the Zanzibar islands and (slowly) on the mainland.

Here and there I come across a rich detail, such as the mission logbook entry which tells me that on 24 January 1867 – the very year in which Steere would set his printing press to the task of producing the *Hadithi za Kiingereza* – the mission staff (and perhaps some of the boys?) attended a 'Theatrical Performance on board *HMS Highflyer*'; they also on that occasion received from the ship two further boys taken from slaving vessels.[19] Even if this is no more than a tantalizing lead, I already know something about the contexts of this ship visit, which makes me thrill at the discovery. After all, the last time the *Highflyer* had been at Stone Town it had weighed anchor in the middle of the night, slipping away in secret to take with it Princess Seyyida Salme, the sister of the pretender Barghash, who had during her house arrest fallen in love with a German banker, Heinrich Reute. The ship's party must have spent part of the evening, before settling down to watch their play, congratulating Captain Thomas Malcolm Sabine Pasley on his successful part in this storybook romance, by getting the princess safely to Aden, from where she could pass on to Hamburg, to live out the rest of her life as Emily Reute, a prosperous *burgeress* and celebrated author of harem exposés. The logs and letters are silent about what the play was – though it strikes me that Shakespeare's own *Winter's Tale* of rescued princesses would have served the mythic balance – but it is still fascinating that these people, far removed from England and every day facing danger and confronted by disease and deprivation, retained a loyalty to the cultural rituals of their homeland.*

Days of sifting – sometimes literally – through the disintegrating documents in the archives shows me that I will learn little more of the *Hadithi za Kiingereza* (at least here). This is, of course, a disappointment, but it is one that those interested in the past become accustomed to. There is a tightness in the gut which comes from the sense that something wondrous is slipping ever further from us, like the vertigo in one's bones when handling something delicate. Though this tightness never disappears completely, it is sometimes relieved when a fragment brings us closer to the disappearing past, like a ghostly hand clasped for a moment. The feeling is succinctly captured in Shakespeare's famous Sonnet 30:

When to the sessions of sweet silent thought
I summon up remembrance of things past,
I sigh the lack of many a thing I sought
And with old woes new wail my dear time's waste.
Then can I drown an eye, unused to flow,
For precious friends hid in death's dateless night,
And weep afresh love's long-since canceled woe,
And moan th'expense of many a vanished sight.

---

* Indeed, some indication of the success of Steere's project to plant bardolatry on the East African coast is given by the action of Seyyida Salme's brother, Sultan Barghash, during his state visit to London in 1875. Not only did Barghash insist on pausing to pay respect to the bust of Shakespeare in Westminster Abbey, but Shakespeare also helped to avert a diplomatic crisis: after the Sultan objected, during a ceremonial dinner given by the Worshipful Company of Fishmongers, to the use of the epithet 'Worshipful' for anyone other than God, he was apparently placated by the information that the company was sufficiently venerable to have merited a mention in the works of Shakespeare (*The Times*, 26 June 1875, p. 12). Although some commentators at the time suggested that Barghash was being coached by his British escorts into locally appropriate behaviours, they seem not to have considered that Barghash may have been evangelized for Shakespeare before setting foot in Britain.

Though convention required that Shakespeare turn in the end to a rather anodyne comment on the power of love ('But if the while I think on thee, dear friend / All losses are restored, and sorrows end'), the force of the sonnet lies in Shakespeare's unmatched evocation of loss. The phrases are riddling – how does one 'sigh a lack' or 'moan an expense'? – but they summon precisely the defeat of language in the face of 'time's waste', 'death's dateless night', a defeat that can be brought on by the loss of 'precious friends', yes, but also by the loss of 'things' or even those 'sights' which are by nature ephemeral. The 'sessions of sweet silent thought' that characterize scholarship are often driven by much the same yearning.

Later, however, I do come across one enticing story which deserves to be told here even if it happened many decades afterwards. Though Steere and his printers were long dead, the episode takes place on the island of Zanzibar and is reported by a member of the Universities' Mission to Central Africa – it is, in fact, a throwaway anecdote in one of their newsletters from 1934.[20] In it he reports a large gathering of Africans, Arabs, Indians and Europeans at the village of Mbweni, where a troupe of local men were putting on an impromptu performance. The text on which the drama is based, it transpires, is none other than *Kuwia na Kuwiwa*, the rendering of *The Merchant of Venice* from the *Hadithi za Kiingereza*.[21] The production, it is reported, was very basic: a petrol lamp, a table, a chair and five actors – Antonio, Bassanio, Shylock, a Judge and the 'ugliest man in the village' as Portia. The setting was only indicated by signs (*Nyumba ya Portia*, 'Portia's House', etc.); and the tale of the Jewish moneylender had been turned, as it would often be afterwards in East Africa, against the wealthy Indians who were closer to their own lives. The punchline of the anecdote – and what particularly intrigues me about it – is that *the cast of the play have no idea of its connection to Shakespeare, or even that it was once a dramatic text.* For the correspondent in the newsletter this is evidently amusing – like Arthur Neumann putting Shakespeare into the hands of his unwitting elephant hunter; but I think we might take it rather differently. This, after all, is Shakespeare in the hands of those who have no reason to think of it as 'Shakespeare'; 'all ignorant of Shakespeare's efforts', we are told, they 'decided it had great possibilities of dramatization'. While the appeal of Shakespeare's play to a group of provincial Zanzibaris who had no reason to revere the text as canonical is not unassailable proof of Shakespeare's universal appeal, it certainly has the flavour of a beginning.

Before leaving Zanzibar to follow the spread of Shakespeare on the mainland, I go to visit the Universities' Mission house at Mambo Msiige, approaching it by walking along the beach among joggers and fishermen. I also pass groups of Maasai *elmorani* (warriors), long and thin and draped in their traditional plaid, like tartan Giacomettis; these nomadic herders from the inland plateau, disconcertingly out of place, have been imported by luxury hotels to give the place an authentically African air which the Arab coastal Africans apparently lack. The building is, as John Baptist had said, more or less abandoned – almost, that is, save for the dozen or so security guards, who in grand African tradition are armed to the teeth in blithe disregard for the fact they are sentries to a hollow shell. My original romantic notion of breaking into the empty building is replaced by an equally romantic notion that I will bribe my way in. It is very rare for Shakespeare scholars to have the opportunity to cover up criminal proceedings in the course of their research, so this was clearly an opportunity not to be missed. In the event, the guard I approach seems delighted that anyone had been tempted to breach the cordon, and offers to guide my tour personally.

We traipse around for a considerable time up narrow staircases comically unsuited to luxury, and through stripped-bare low-ceilinged spaces furnished only with curling posterboards with mockups of the high-ceilinged ballrooms the hotel will contain. Eventually, we find the nondescript room captured in the museum photo, where the Universities' Mission had set up its printing operation. This was where my first Swahili Shakespeare had been typeset by fingers that had come from inland villages down to the coast in cages, out to sea in bondage, back to shore on ironclad Royal Navy ships. I have worked with old-fashioned hand-presses myself, and even to someone who knows what to expect they are a frightening confusion of pistons and levers and traps; I imagine the boys must have felt, like Conrad's native boiler feeder in *The Heart of Darkness*, as if they were in 'thrall to some strange witchcraft'. They did, however, seem to accommodate themselves to their new surroundings with reasonable speed, aided in part by the clearing up of certain misunderstandings. As Steere says,

> It was not long before even the natives perceived that our boys had an air and a bearing such as their old companions never had. It was their Christianity beginning even so soon to show itself, as sound religion must, even in their speech and bearing. We taught our children that white men might be trusted. They have told us since that their impression was, that first night they slept in the house, that they were meant to be eaten.[22]

Steere is unfailingly confident that it was his religious teachings which made the boys feel superior to those around them, though being inducted into the mysteries of print may in and of itself have had a powerful effect on them. It is difficult for us, who spend our lives trying to keep above a sea of printed matter that threatens to drown us, to remember the strangeness and power of a process that produces uncannily identical objects, objects which constrain those holding them to speak the same words.[23] Indeed, it is often far from clear in his writings that Steere felt he had come to the Dark Continent to bring the Christian message, rather than the tools of language which were only supposed to be servants in the Lord's work. In a series of letters in 1872, prompted by Bishop Tozer's resignation and the likelihood that he would succeed as Bishop, he wrote repeatedly to the UMCA asking to be left to his translation and printing: he was, he said, more 'useful to the Mission as an interpreter of European thoughts to negroes and of negro thoughts to Europeans'.[24] For Steere, it seems, establishing a shared culture had overtaken the task of religious conversion. A belief that we owe our existence to a single god might suggest that there are other things that link us – a shared morality a culture which is similar at its heart for all the superficial differences. But this logic could also be reversed: evidence that there are shared, universal aspects to our culture might serve as proof that we derive from a single point of origin, an Edenic and united past.

We should not forget, however, the power that even this cultural authority was to confer on Steere and his kind. Looking out from the UMCA house on Mambo Msiige at the same seascape Steere would have seen, I am reminded of two Shakespeare quotations which evidently meant much to him. They are quoted prominently in his commonplace book, where Steere (like many readers before the twentieth century) gathered his most treasured bits of text. The first of these is from *The Tempest*, that perennial lens through which Englishmen saw Africa:

My Library
Was Dukedom large enough . . .[25]

This sentiment is voiced by Prospero (*The Tempest*, I.ii.109–10), magician and exiled Duke of Milan, whose death we saw being plotted by Caliban in the last chapter. As suggested by the need to burn his books before murdering him, Prospero's library, like Samson's hair, is the immediate source of his strength, and destroying it will leave him vulnerable. But Prospero's library has a more complicated relationship with power in the play than simply providing him with magic tricks. It is, in the first place, the reason that he has lost his Dukedom: Prospero's bookish belief that his 'library / Was Dukedom large enough' distracted him from the dangers of his court and the conspiracy which unseated him. As so often in Shakespeare, however, a lack of interest in political power is the best evidence that someone deserves it. Two of Shakespeare's great actor-politicians, Julius Caesar and Richard III, demonstrate their awareness of this when they make a great show of refusing a tyrant's crown when it is first offered to them, only to condescend at the appropriate moment to accepting the burden. In a similar way, Prospero's books are both a symbol of his lack of interest in power and the ultimate proof that he deserves it – as shown when he is reinstated to his Dukedom at the end of the play.

The suspicion that these lines are the key to Steere's personality is confirmed by the fact that the second treasured quotation encapsulates the same paradox of power and books, even if it comes from a different play. The lines are from the opening of the second Act of *As You Like It*, where the ousted Duke Senior is praising his woodland exile over the cares of court. The lines (mis)quoted by Steere are given here in italics:

Now, my co-mates and brothers in exile,
Hath not old custom made this life more sweet
Than that of painted pomp? Are not these woods
More free from peril than the envious court? [. . .]

Sweet are the uses of adversity,
Which like the toad, ugly and venomous,
Wears yet a precious jewel in his head.
And this our life exempt from public haunt
Finds tongues in trees, books in the running stream,
Sermons in stones, and good in everything.

As You Like It (II.i.1–4, 12–17)

Duke Senior argues that simply being away from the corridors of power has such a salutary effect that the very woodland becomes like a library in the reflections it affords. Again, like Prospero, it is the very fact that Duke Senior is content to give up his ducal rule for a bookish wilderness which advertises his fitness for authority, and he is duly returned to his Dukedom at the end of the play. So when Steere wrote these lines in his commonplace book, was he stirred by their humility, their idyll of a life contented with books, or with the righteous claim to power entailed by that humility?

Steere's awareness of the role that printing and language-teaching would play in the struggle to dominate Africa meant that the relationship between power and books may not have been a subconscious one. As he wrote about one tribe shortly after an expedition into the interior, 'It seems to me morally certain that the Yaos will be Christians or Mahommedans before very long, and I think the question will turn a good deal upon which is the first to write and read their language.'[26] So the boys who learned to print in this room looking out to sea from Stone Town were, unbeknownst to them, building an arsenal which would conquer the inland communities from which they had been kidnapped. I thank the security guard, who is wavering between boredom with and suspicion of my glassy-eyed pensiveness in an empty room, and leave.

3

INTERLUDE: THE SWAHILI COAST

Player-Kings of Eastern Africa

STEFANO (to Caliban):
Monster, I will kill this man. His daughter and I will be king and queen – save our graces – and Trinculo and thyself shall be viceroys. Dost thou like the plot, Trinculo?

The Tempest (III.ii.101–3)

If *The Tempest* ensured that the Victorian explorers arrived in Africa with readymade ideas about the book-burning savages they expected to meet, it also provided predictions of how the colonizing powers would behave towards them. The prescience of its narrative – the occupation of land through various legal and technological tricks, initial belief in the aptness of the native for education, followed by horror when the same natives begin to demand to be treated as their education merits (as Caliban does in casting a desiring eye upon Miranda) – was not lost on East African observers, who after gaining independence repeatedly reflected on the way in which Shakespeare's works both predicted and served as patterns for colonial actions.[1] The breakthrough novel (*A Grain of Wheat*, 1967) of Kenya's most celebrated writer, Ngugi wa Thiong'o, includes the story of a local official in the Kenyan colonial administration whose grand plan to Anglicize the local Africans is laid out in a tract entitled PROSPERO IN AFRICA. That Prospero's colonization project ended in the enslavement and torture of Caliban is, of course, entirely lost on Ngugi's deluded visionary.

Interestingly, however, Shakespeare's *Tempest* provides not one but *two* prophecies of colonization, and if Prospero's overlordship takes the form of tragedy, the second version is unmistakably in the key of farce. This subplot features the clowns Stefano and Trinculo, who are shipwrecked in the storm that opens the play and who imagine themselves the sole survivors to have been washed up on the island. In a series of burlesque episodes that run parallel to the main action of the play, Stefano (fuelled by the vat of wine on which he drifted ashore) conceives a plan to murder Prospero and rule over the island with the aid of Caliban, who (in his inebriation) believes Stefano to be a god. In the first great colonial narrative in English, at that time largely a matter of speculative fiction, Shakespeare had not only predicted with uncanny accuracy the course of Britain's future colonial empire, but also the many comically botched and bungled amateur attempts at colonization which preceded it.

A few days after Eid I pick my way down to the dock, back past the Beit al-Ajaib and the shorefront restaurant celebrating Queen's frontman and local boy, Freddie Mercury, in search of a passage to the mainland. Ferry travel here, as in so many parts of the Third World, creates a class system with stark boundaries: a relatively comfortable passage for me and other travellers who can afford it, and dangerously overcrowded hulks for those who can't. The number of sunken vessels is astonishing, though for one reason and another they hardly register a blip on the Western media radar. The week after I make the short hop over warm waters to the mainland a cheap-passage ferry, with an official capacity of 645, capsizes with 3586 people on board; 2976 of them – roughly the number of excess passengers – are drowned.[2]

Though it is not the hovercraft on which I came to the island as a child, my ferry is sufficiently commodious for me to continue to read during the crossing, and to think about the first performances of Shakespeare in East Africa. Striking as John Baptist's photographs of shipboard actors are, they cannot claim to record the first English stage plays acted on (or off) the coast of Swahililand. In fact, one of the most incredible stories in all of Shakespeareana recounts how Shakespeare's work was acted off the East African coast during the poet's own lifetime. The performances in question are said to have taken place on the *Dragon*, which led the *Hector* and the *Constant* on the third voyage of the East India Company between 1607 and 1610, years during which Shakespeare's Sonnets were published and when he was himself writing about sea travel in *Pericles* and *The Winter's Tale*. While the *Constant* made a swift passage around the Cape of Good Hope to its destination of the Molucca Islands (the fountainhead of the early modern spice trade, now in modern Indonesia), the *Dragon* and the *Hector* were beset by a litany of disasters and spent much of the next year and a half coasting slowly around Africa. In extracts supposedly taken from the diary of Captain William Keeling of the *Dragon*, first published as a postscript to an article on *Hamlet* in *The European Magazine* of 1825–6, we hear that the ship's crew were distracted from more dangerous temptations by being allowed to stage two of Shakespeare's plays on board:

Sept. 5, 1607. I sent the Portuguese interpreter, according to his desire, aboard the Hector, where he broke fast, and after came aboord me, where we had the TRAGEDY OF HAMLET; and in the afternoone we went altogether ashore, to see if we could shoot an elephant.

Sept. 29, 1607. Captain Hawkins [of the *Hector*] dined with me, when my company acted KINGE RICHARDE THE SECOND.

March 31, 1608. I invited Captain Hawkins to a fyshe dinner, and had HAMLET acted aboord me, which I permit, to keepe my people from idleness and unlawful games, or sleep.[3]

The first two performances, in September 1607, would have taken place while the *Dragon* was riding at anchor off Sierra Leone (and trying to lay in fresh fruit to counteract a bout of scurvy), and may in fact represent the very first recorded performance of *Hamlet*.* Even more remarkably, this would mean that the earliest recorded production of *Hamlet* was a command performance for a Portuguese-speaking native of the West African coast. By the time of the third performance, in March 1608, the *Dragon* had made it around the Cape, and was meandering between the various islands north-west of Madagascar. According to Keeling's diary, then, Shakespeare was being acted off the Swahili coast even as Shakespeare was still alive and writing plays for the King's Men in London.

Fuller extracts from Keeling's account of this period on the East African coast, published in the great compendium of Renaissance English travel accounts *Purchas his pilgrimes* in 1625, make for

---

* Although no earlier records of productions survive, it is clear that *Hamlet* was performed before this, with two quarto editions (1603 and 1605) attesting to the popularity it had already gained on the stage. Indeed, one of these, the first so-called 'bad quarto' of 1603, has long been believed by many to be a 'pirated' text compiled for the printer from memory by the actor who played the minor character Marcellus.

fascinating reading. The swing from the now-familiar (such as monsoon patterns and elephants) to the utterly fantastical can be somewhat disorienting for the modern reader, though it must be remembered that they were faced with constantly sorting between the astounding things they witnessed and fictional reports (many of which probably had more in common with their European traditions and experiences). A selection of Keeling's observations from around the time that his men were supposedly performing *Hamlet* to help the digestion of Captain Hawkins's Zanzibari 'fyshe dinner' gives a flavour of his writing:

[20 March 1608] *George Euans*, one of the *Hectors* Company, was shrewdly bitten with an *Alegarta*. [. . .]*

The people are circumcised, as some affirmed to have seene. Here we found the beautifull beast. [. . .]

THE *Moores* of this place affirme, that in some yeeres, pieces of *Amber-greece* [sperm-whale gland] are found, Poiz twentie kintals, of such bulke, that many men may shelter themselves under the sides thereof, without beeing seene. This is upon the coasts of *Mombasa, Magadoxo, Pata Braua*, &c. being indeed all one long Coast.[4]

While Burton and Stanley used Shakespeare as a talisman of Englishness during their expeditions, to set themselves apart from their exotic surroundings and perhaps keep themselves from 'going native', Shakespeare had nothing of this iconic status as transcend-

---

* Shakespeare had been the first to use this word in a printed English text when in the 1597 quarto Romeo buys his suicide dram from an apothecary 'Whose needie shop is stufft / With beggarly accounts of empty boxes: / And in the same an *Aligarta* hangs, / Olde ends of packthred, and cakes of roses' (V.i.45–8). In the 1599 quarto the word has moved closer to its modern spelling and appears as 'allegater'.

ent genius and national poet in 1607–8. The performances on the *Dragon* would, then, be an even more intriguing episode of happenstance, whereby Shakespeare found his way to Africa as merely one of a jumble of shipboard occupations, nestled within a bewildering array of scarcely imaginable new experiences for the Englishmen coasting along East Africa.

As suggested by the tentative manner in which this superb story has been told, however, a range of question marks lingers over its basis in truth.[5] To begin with, the journal of Keeling's from which the clearly pseudonymous 'Ambrose Gunthio' transcribed these passages in 1825–6 no longer survives, and the (admittedly chaotic) records of the East India Company suggest that it may already have been lost by the inventory of 1822. A number of experts have seen in this delightful episode the hand of the Shakespeare scholar and notorious forger John Payne Collier. Collier, who lived at the centre of Romantic intellectual and literary circles, and could name Wordsworth, Coleridge, and Charles and Mary Lamb among his friends, was later exposed as having fabricated a wide range of documents (purporting to be Tudor and Stuart originals) in support of his editorial scholarship and biographical writings. Other modern scholars have reinforced suspicions about the Keeling entries by questioning the likelihood that a group of shiphands would have been capable of performing not one but two long and complex Shakespeare plays on a crowded deck, or that they would even have *wanted* to during stifling days off the African coast.*

---

* There is, however, a range of interesting evidence to suggest that early modern travellers were driven to literary consolations when stranded in exotic climes: among notable examples are Camões's composition of part of *The Lusiads* while shipwrecked on the Mekong delta in 1559 (another poem, now lost, was written when he was stuck on the island of Mozambique), and the story of François Leguat, a Huguenot exile who planned to set up a French Protestant colony in Mauritius, but ended up marooned with his fellow colonists on the uninhabited island of Rodrigues. During his time on the island he wrote a long poem recounting his experiences (including allusions to being raped by the other sailors), and hid the poem in the hollow of a tree.

While all of these doubts are reasonable, it is hard to understand why the supposed forger would allow his trick to remain unremarked upon by Shakespeare scholars for nearly half a century, when the story gained a wider currency. To this the sceptics can only respond that the delight of the forger is in having performed his chicanery in public, and not necessarily in it obtaining widespread approbation. If these stories *were* a forgery, however, the form they took began to make perfect sense in light of the exotic Shakespeare stories I was collecting during my travels: whether this episode only came to light in the nineteenth century, or was actually cooked up to suit nineteenth-century tastes, it fits comfortably into the compulsive desire of the English at that time to see Shakespeare rear his head in the Dark Continent, to sing (as the text of Bishop Tozer's first Zanzibar sermon would have it) 'the Lord's song in a strange land' (Psalm 137).[6]

As I read through the memoirs of the early travellers and settlers, a pattern becomes increasingly clear. This was, in effect, a strange feedback loop in which fortune hunters, drawn to East Africa by literary fantasies cobbled together from accounts by Stanley and others like him, returned with yet more travellers' tales which confirmed to the hungry audiences at home that the reality matched their fevered expectations. Evelyn Waugh joked, on his return from a tour of the region, about that time when travellers

have been home from abroad for a week or two, and time after time, in response to our friends' polite inquiries, we have retold our experiences, letting phrase engender phrase, until we have made quite a good story of it all; when the unusual people we have encountered have, in retrospect, become fabulous and fantastic, and all the checks and uncertainties of travel have become very serious dangers; when the minor annoyances assume heroic proportions and become, at the luncheon table, barely endurable privations ... [.][7]

What Waugh fails to mention, however, is how these tales can set the course of history for the regions about which they are told. These stories were to crop up again and again in the early history of East Africa, blurring the boundaries between historical record and fictional narrative, and though at first their profusion of characters seemed like a distraction from the Shakespearean story I was following, it slowly became clear that this was the missing link between colonialism and the literary texts that I was studying.

The great fountainhead of the African adventure story was H. Rider Haggard, whose phenomenally popular boys' adventure novels drew on his three years' experience in the Transvaal in southern Africa (1878–81), but took much of their material from explorers' accounts such as those by Burton and Stanley, and from letters written by his brother, Jack, who was British Vice-Consul at the ancient Arabic city of Lamu on the Kenyan coast from 1881 to 1885.[8] The novel that made Rider Haggard famous (and very wealthy) was *King Solomon's Mines* (1885), an extraordinary yarn about a voyage into central Africa to discover the legendary source of the biblical king's wealth, which the heroes find in a Lost Kingdom resembling ancient Phoenicia beyond snowcapped mountains. Their access to Solomon's mines, however, is forestalled by a battle in the kingdom between two rival claimants to the throne, one of whom is supported by the ghastly witch Gagool.

Rider Haggard's novel was astonishingly popular. In part this was down to his publishers' use of the first guerrilla advertising campaign to promote it, clandestinely covering the London streets on the night before publication with posters that read: 'KING SOLOMON'S MINES – THE MOST AMAZING BOOK EVER

WRITTEN' – a claim that the still-innocent consumers of 1885 could not resist testing.[9] But *King Solomon's Mines* also gave the British public a purer version of what they had already been reading in the explorer's accounts, a wish-fulfilment fantasy in which Men of Courage could find Untold Wealth in the heart of the Dark Continent. The stories also conveniently served the purposes of a British government desperate for recruits to staff its rapidly expanding colonial service, a need greatly increased after the 1885 Berlin Conference defined the 'spheres of influence' allotted to each of the European powers and set in motion the 'Scramble for Africa'. Haggard's hero, Allan Quatermain, sums it up in an entirely unembarrassed passage:

> But then that is what Englishmen are, adventurers to the backbone; and all our magnificent muster-roll of colonies, each of which will in time become a great nation, testify to the extraordinary value of the spirit of adventure which at first sight looks like a mild form of lunacy.[10]

While this theme of 'Imperial Duty' was nothing new – the great Victorian art critic John Ruskin had used it as a call to arms in his inaugural lecture as Slade Professor of Fine Art at Oxford in 1870 – it was now the stuff of bestsellers, captivating an entire nation with a heady cocktail of national pride, moral righteousness and the enticements of wealth and power.[11]

Rider Haggard quickly followed up his bestseller with a sequel (*Allan Quatermain*) and a newly cast adventure story (*She*), both published in 1887. Each of these stories copies the formula of *King Solomon's Mines* very closely, and both again rely heavily on African explorers' tales and the letters of his East African brother, Jack Haggard. This is especially the case in *Allan Quatermain*, in which the same band of characters – the eponymous hero, accompanied by his old team of Captain John Good (reportedly based on Jack Haggard) and Sir Henry Curtis (an idealized, almost proto-Aryan English nobleman) – depart from Lamu up the River Tana in search of a mythical kingdom of white men somewhere in the interior of modern Kenya. Along the way they ward off an attack by Maasai warriors, and their canoe is sucked into an underground cavern, where they are forced to survive by eating giant black crabs. The underwater cavern – like the jagged peaks of 'Sheba's Breasts' in *King Solomon's Mines* and the vast catacomb tunnels leading to the kingdom of She-who-must-be-obeyed in *She* – marks the transition from heightened reality to pure fantasy. On the far side of this cavern they reach the land of the Zu-Vendi, whose capital, Milosis, is strangely reminiscent of England:

> In another minute we perceived a great golden dome, not unlike that of St Paul's piercing the morning mists . . .
>
> . . . the climate is, comparatively speaking, a cold one, being very similar to that of southern England . . . Sometimes, again, we went hawking, a pastime in great favour among the Zu-Vendi, who generally fly their birds at a species of partridge which is remarkable for the swiftness and strength of its flight.[12]

After taking the side of Nyleptha against her sister-queen, Sorais, in a civil war, Sir Henry Curtis marries her and remains behind in the Lost Kingdom as King of the Zu-Vendi.

Rider Haggard had, in effect, hit upon the archetype of African adventure stories, a model from which to reproduce endless tales in which every Englishman worth his salt had a kingdom waiting for him in the heart of Africa, ripe for the taking.[13] Even better, these kingdoms did not have the inconvenience of exotic natives – their inhabitants were usually varieties of European lost tribes – nor

'For there . . . were Sheba's breasts': an illustration from the
1888 edition of *King Solomon's Mines.*

had they suffered the ravages of industrialization.* They were, in fact, little versions of Old England, hidden just through the looking-glass landscape of the African wild. The reading public were evidently happy to allow for the possibility of such kingdoms, even while they had struggled to believe the announcement in 1849 that snow had been sighted on Mounts Kenya and Kilimanjaro, a claim that flew in the face of long-held notions about the tropics and was laughed to scorn in the learned societies of Europe.[14]† In a sense, these fantasy stories found a middle way between the explorers' and the missionaries' approach to the Dark Continent: the traveller could expect to wield power (like Stanley) over the people that he found in Africa, but he needn't worry about 'going native' because these hidden kingdoms had a shared culture – they were, in fact, just little Englands.

Rider Haggard, posing as the 'editor' of a true story told by the hero Allan Quatermain, makes it clear early on that Quatermain is cut from the same cloth as other Shakespeare-toting adventurers, though with a sly twist. He glosses a Shakespeare quotation mis-attributed to the Old Testament with the following note:

---

* Rider Haggard's fantasy of a lost Mediterranean culture in central Africa was later formalized in the 'Hamitic Hypothesis' championed by the English anthropologist C. G. Seligman, who argued for cultural links between ancient Egyptian and 'primitive' central African tribal societies. These largely unsubstantiated ideas had a long reach, not only through the use of Seligman's writing in colonial service training, but also through the influence of his pupil Bronisław Malinowski, who set the tone for a generation's work on African ethnography (including Jomo Kenyatta's work on his own Gikuyu tribe). Julius Nyerere's brother himself believed that their Zanaki tribe was descended from a race of ancient Egyptians; see Thomas Molony, *Nyerere: The Early Years* (James Currey, 2014), pp. 24–5.

† Incidentally, the German missionary Johannes Krapf, who made this sighting, spent many years dreaming of founding his own theocratic kingdom, 'Ormania', in eastern Africa.

Readers must beware of accepting Mr Quatermain's references as accurate, as it has been found, some are prone to do. Although his reading evidently was limited, the impression produced by it on his mind was mixed. Thus to him the Old Testament and Shakespeare were interchangeable authorities. – *Editor*.[15]

In light of *Steere's* evident belief that 'the Old Testament and Shakespeare were interchangeable authorities' – that translating Shakespeare and converting souls were two sides of the same coin – this lighthearted comment about Quatermain's approach to book-learning seems less like a joke.

For all Quatermain's 'limited' reading, *King Solomon's Mines* is littered with Shakespeare quotations; but Rider Haggard's debt to the explorers' tales of Shakespeare in the bush do not end there. In a climactic scene, the heroes are saved from the machinations of Gagool the witch when they astonish the inhabitants of the lost kingdom by pretending to bring on an eclipse while reading from the only book that they have with them.[16]* This celebrated scene is, in fact, a blend of two real-life travellers' tales which Haggard was echoing. One of these is the prediction of an eclipse by Christopher Columbus on 1 March 1504, which won him the obedience of the awestruck native Indians of Jamaica; the other, of course, is Stanley's story about taming the tribesmen he encountered with his magic volume of Shakespeare. Rider Haggard, who added to his public reputation as a gruff man's man by confessing himself 'no great reader', increases the humour of the scene by replacing the conventional explorer's volume of Shakespeare with a penny-dreadful collection of ghost stories, *The Ingoldsby Legends*. Once

---

* In the first editions of *King Solomon's Mines*, Rider Haggard had his travellers astonish the natives by predicting an eclipse of the sun by a full moon; this was changed in all post-1887 editions for an eclipse of the moon, it having been pointed out to Rider Haggard that his first eclipse was an impossibility.

again, there is a creeping sense that Shakespeare was thought of as having too much *real* power by the Victorians to serve effectively as a comically mistaken magic book.*

These fantasies seem to have taken on an unstoppable life of their own, and the boundary between Rider Haggard's fantasy and reality soon became hopelessly confused. Some readers, caught up in the excitement, were determined to head for Africa to locate King Solomon's mines themselves. Every traveller who had met Haggard in Africa – and many who hadn't – claimed to be one of the models for his characters. Further muddling matters, the explorer Joseph Thomson both accused Rider Haggard of plagiarizing from his expeditionary account *Through Maasai Land* and also took to writing Haggard-esque fantasy novels himself. Archaeologists working on the ruined city of Great Zimbabwe, which had been visited by various expeditions since 1871, declared in 1891 that it was the seat of Solomon's companion the Queen of Sheba, and that the civilization that built it must (like Rider Haggard's Kakuana tribe) have been Phoenician; a number of landmarks surrounding the site were named after characters from *King Solomon's Mines*. Rider Haggard claims not to have known of the Great Zimbabwe excavations when writing his novel, though the ruins were widely discussed when he lived just south of them in Natal, and the similarities make his claim hard to believe.[17] It is just possible, though, that the influence ran the other way – that the team who claimed Great Zimbabwe for the Queen of Sheba (J. Theodor Bent and his patron, Cecil Rhodes) were trying to hitch their wagon to Haggard's in an attempt to borrow some of his celebrity.

---

* In a further twist to this curious tale, the supposed inspiration for Quatermain, the Great White Hunter Frederick Courtney Selous, was himself inspired to seek adventure in Africa by the romantic childhood atmosphere created by his uncle, the Shakespeare illustrator H. C. Selous.

Rhodes, like Haggard, was a younger son in a large gentry family and (also like Haggard) had been thought too dull to follow his brothers to Eton or Winchester. Both men were sent to Africa in hopes that they could make something of themselves there – or at least fail to do so in a place where they were not in the public eye, and would be less of a drain on the family resources. Haggard and Rhodes each succeeded in triumphing over low expectations, becoming the most celebrated men of the age (unlike their brothers). But whereas Haggard's kingdoms were the figments of a fertile imagination, Rhodes succeeded in building a vast dominion which existed in the world outside the boys' adventure story. Through a mixture of canny entrepreneurial manoeuvring and willingness to use prison camp setups to control his workers at the Kimberly diamond mines, Rhodes succeeded in turning his De Beers enterprise into the largest company in British history. From this position of strength, he was able to found the British South Africa Company, a joint stock venture which soon held vast mining concessions in central Africa, concessions covering much of modern-day Zimbabwe, Zambia and Malawi, and serving as the basis for the eventual formation of his fiefdom of Rhodesia.

When the fabulous gold concessions Rhodes and his partners had promised their shareholders were slow to materialize, it must have been a useful distraction to be able to claim that the Great Zimbabwe ruins were the celebrated lands of Sheba (and must, therefore, contain their storied wealth). The Sheba story undoubtedly held an attraction for Rhodes, who – like Haggard and many of their compatriots – lived a life which curiously blended hard-nosed entrepreneurship with occult dabblings.* Many of the uses

---

* Another adventurer who attempted to find King Solomon's mines in Africa – this time in Mozambique – was Carl Peters, the leader of the German Emin Pasha expedition. Peters's writings were to inspire the Freeland Association (discussed below) to decide on East Africa as the site for their socialist Utopia.

to which Rhodes directed his vast fortune have become famous, such as Rhodes House in Oxford, where the papers of Steere and many other famous early African settlers are kept, and the Rhodes Scholarships, which have fostered luminaries from Robert Penn Warren to Bill Clinton (and, since opening its ranks to women in 1977, Naomi Wolf and Rachel Maddow). Less famous is the secret society for the expansion of the British Empire that Rhodes intended to found with the bulk of his untold wealth – though Rhodes's legacy retains an occultist flavour in the Masonic architecture of the Rhodes House building.

Rider Haggard was followed by a great many other novelists who used eastern and central Africa as a blank space in which to erect imaginary new societies. Ignatius Donnelly's 1890 dystopian novel *Caesar's Column* ends with the proletarian heroes fleeing a burning New York by airship to start afresh in Uganda, and of course Joseph Conrad's 'Mistah Kurtz' was to use the Congo as the location for his own theocracy. The popularity of these tales meant that the most widely read and captivating descriptions of eastern and central Africa available to English readers – and soon more widely through translations – were inventions with only the slightest basis in fact. It seems very likely that these fantasies played a key part in the series of darkly comic colonial episodes which took place in East Africa in the 1890s. Perhaps the most striking of these was the project by the 'Freeland Association' to set up a socialist paradise in East Africa, one of the many nineteenth-century political fantasies that could trace its roots to Thomas More's *Utopia* of 1516, the very same text that had partly inspired Shakespeare's story of an experiment in island rule in *The Tempest*.[18] Inspired by the science fiction novels of Austrian economist Theodor Hertzka – *Freeland* (1890) and its sequel *A Visit to Freeland* (1893) – a group of European idealists landed in Lamu in 1894 with visions of pastoral communities, free from private property, dancing in their heads. Rather uncannily like Allan Quatermain and his companions, their plan was to sail up the River Tana in search of a place to found their Utopia somewhere near the base of Mount Kenya.* Descriptions of the Association's members, led by an Englishman, Captain Dugmore (who joined the expedition for 'sport'), give a taste of their quality:[19]

GUSTAV RABINEK
Cashiered from Austrian Army for embezzlement – utterly dishonest – habitual swindler

AXEL STOCKERBYE (Lieutenant, Danish Navy)
Drunkard, but perfect gentleman even when drunk

PETER SCAVENIUS
Son of Danish Cabinet Minister – an intriguing agitator, bitterly hostile to British Influence

REINHARD GLEISERING
Drunkard and thief, lunatic with homicidal tendencies

FELIX THOMAS
Irreclaimably dishonest (expelled)

---

* A rather better-resourced (though not less fantastical) project was anticipated in Joseph Chamberlain's 1903–5 plan to found a Jewish homeland in the African interior, a plan which met with furious resistance from the growing community of European settlers. This plan was inspired by another utopian tract by the confusingly similar-named Theodor Hertzl. A full account of the East African project is given in Robert G. Weisbord's *African Zion*.

HANS SALNER
  Nickname – 'Sassy', drunkard, fanatic anarchist and supporter
    of the bomb-worker, clever chemist, wife a second Louise
    Michel.*

In the event, however, the Freelanders never got further than
Lamu, in large part because their provisions for transport up the
River Tana proved wholly inadequate – the river is only navigable
for a short distance and even then only after the rains. As novels
from Conrad's *Heart of Darkness* to Naipaul's *A Bend in the River*
suggest, rivers were central to the imaginative experience of colonialism, in part because they held out the promise of travel far into
the interior while keeping a safe distance from land in the
comparative comfort of a boat. East Africa, however, offered no navigable rivers like the Congo, Amazon or Yangtze; in fact, water
travel forms little or no part of the life of most inland East Africans, and many tribes even consider fish to be a debilitating
foodstuff.

  I am reminded of this hydrophobia by the fact that *most* of those
with me on the ferry to the mainland are being sick, even though
the seas are relatively calm. Even for many of the afflicted passengers, however, this seems to be a regular commute, and though
regular sea travel seems to have done nothing to cure them of their
nausea, it does at least seem to have made the sickness something
like a routine. I might perhaps have been worried by the number
of incapacitated, even convinced that there was an infection
running through the boat, if it weren't for the placidness with
which passenger after passenger lifts a bag to their face, only after-

---

* Louise Michel was an anarchist leader during the French Commune of 1871. Mrs
Salner was evidently proud of Dugmore's comparison, as when the expedition landed
at Lamu she gave a speech in which she declared herself the 'African Louise Michel'
(Beachey, "'Freeland'", p. 61).

wards to resume a conversation or settle back down to sleep. I remember a similar predicament when, reaching cruising altitude on a propeller-driven plane flying from Mexico to Cuba, I was alarmed by the mist that filled the cabin making it impossible to see anything more than a few feet away; my anxieties were dispelled, however, by the fact that the rest of the passengers didn't pause for a moment to notice the swiftly filling cabin, and blithely continued chattering on their mobile phones.

The Freeland Association, stranded in Lamu, used up their resources in three months doing little more than gaining a reputation for drunkenness, infighting and lascivious approaches towards the local Muslim women. Most of them returned to Europe and disappeared back into obscurity; a few remained as settlers, having been granted land by the Imperial British East Africa Company (IBEA). The IBEA (the *Kumpani*, as they were locally known) was bankrolled by the same Scottish shipping tycoon, William MacKinnon, who had paid for many of Henry Morton Stanley's explorations. In order to function efficiently, outfits like the *Kumpani* (and Rhodes's British South Africa Company) developed all the paraphernalia of modern European states: professional armies (occasionally with uniforms), contracts which defined the relationship between the Company and local tribal leaders and which formed a skeleton legal system, and even their own coinage.[20] Corporate nations such as the *Kumpani* exercised political influence by placing their economic and military power at the disposal of whichever local leader stood to further their cause most directly; and when it came to pass, as it did without exception, that these chieftains faced threats to which the Company's irregular troops proved unequal, the Company would appeal to its home nation to be given 'Protectorate' status, which allowed for the possibility of an occupying force from the regular army. The transition from Protectorate to Colony happened at some point afterwards (1920, in the case of Kenya), but was largely by that point a legal formality. Like Stanley's treaties with the chieftains of the Congo, the agreements with local leaders used the fantasy of a universal culture – this time a legal and political culture which could be assumed to be just as valid in Africa as it was in Europe – to assert dominion over a native population who were dressed up in the trappings of European civilizations, making them more like Haggard's lost tribes.

Given that Shakespeare's works were prominent in the attempts to demonstrate that there *was* such a thing as universal culture, it is ironic that many of these same plays show a fear that accepting foreign cultures might simply be a prelude to political domination. John of Gaunt's 'sceptered isle' death-speech from *Richard II* is one of the most famous expressions of English patriotism, but it is rarely remembered that the speech is prompted by a fear that the English love of Italian fashions is weakening them as a people:

GAUNT:
Though Richard my life's counsel would not hear,
My death's sad tale may yet undeaf his ear.

YORK:
No, it is stopped with other, flatt'ring sounds,
As praises of his state. Then there are found
Lascivious meters to whose venom sound
The open ear of youth doth always listen,
Report of fashions in proud Italy,
Whose manners still our tardy apish nation
Limps after in base imitation.
[. . .]

GAUNT:

This royal throne of kings, this sceptered isle,
This earth of majesty, this seat of Mars,
This other Eden, demi-paradise,
This fortress built by nature for herself
Against infection and the hand of war.
[. . .]
This land of such dear souls, this dear, dear land,
Dear for her reputation through the world,
Is now leased out – I die pronouncing it –
Like to a tenement or pelting farm.

Richard II (II.i.15–23, 40–44, 57–60)

England has 'made a shameful conquest of itself', allowing itself to be distracted by foreign fashions and poetry from the fact that it is undergoing a conquest by contract, a conquest it would have avoided had it been properly aware of its own cultural riches and uniqueness.

I will end this brief excursion into the prehistory of colonization with the story of my favourite fortune hunter drawn to Africa in the tide created by these fantasies: John Boyes, the Yorkshire urchin whose impossibly picaresque life climaxed in his rising to become 'king' of the Gikuyu.[21] This tribe, whom the colonizers found settled in Kenya's rich uplands, would eventually become the dominant economic and political force in the independent Kenyan nation, in part driven by the fact that the first president (Jomo Kenyatta) was Gikuyu. Boyes's autobiography relates his vagabond existence, from Midlands runaway to North Sea trawlerman, up the River Amazon and down the west coast of Africa, through the Transvaal as an engine stoker, and finally to Kenya to try his fortune as a trader. The charmingly bumbling manner in which

Boyes stumbles from one predicament to another puts me in mind of the response of E. J. Wayland, an early Ugandan geologist, when a publisher once asked him to write of his adventures: 'I had none,' he said, 'only incompetent people have adventures.'[22] Though written in a poor approximation of Rider Haggard's gruff and spare style, Boyes's memoir can be rather touching when his tales of high adventure falter and more intimate memories get an airing, such as the night he spent as a lad marooned in a sandspit bathing-hut in Rotterdam harbour, clutching the tobacco he had been sent ashore to purchase for his superiors. Boyes's story also involves encounters with some of the more prominent figures of the day, such as the following during his time serving in the Africander Corps in Matabeleland (modern Zimbabwe) when he encounters the founder of the Boy Scout movement:

> It was about this time that I first met B.-P. – now General Sir R. S. S. Baden-Powell, but then only Colonel – who had been sent up to take charge of the operations [. . .]. I was on water guard that day, to see that the natives did not poison the stream, when a man whom I took for a trooper came up and entered into conversation with me [. . .] and it was only when I got back to camp, after going off duty, that I found I had been talking to the officer in command of the expedition.[23]

Though it is of course possible that this is an entirely honest recollection of one of Boyes's treasured experiences, alarm bells may sound when the Shakespeare reader recognizes the similarity to a scene repeatedly used in the plays – that of having the disguised leader mingle with those under him. Perhaps most famously Henry V does this on the evening before Agincourt (*Henry V*, IV.i), though there is also a version of this device in *Measure for Measure*. Boyes does not, however, strike one as the type for

Shakespeare worship, and it would be tempting to put the echo down to coincidence, were it not for the fact that the next episode of his autobiography involves him falling in with a troupe of Shakespearean actors:

> Finding that funds were running out, I took to the sea again, and, getting a ship, worked my way around to Durban. Here I had to look around for something to do, and finding that a Shakespearian company was playing in the town at the time, I presented myself at the stage manager's office, and applied for an engagement. They happened to have a vacancy, and I was taken on for small parts. The company was at rehearsal when I was engaged, and I was told to take my place among the others on the stage. As far as I could judge, I was no worse than the other members of the company, and for a month I appeared nightly for the edification of the aristocracy of Durban.[24]

What we know of the Theatre Royal in Durban, where Boyes spent a season in 1898, confirms that it was very much the home of transient vagabonds like the future Gikuyu king. One of Boyes's fellow actors, a Mrs Render, was in that same year cited in a divorce action by Mrs Madore against her husband, and another 'handsome actress', Maybell Rogers (known professionally as May Bell), was arrested in Johannesburg, charged with stealing three diamonds which she claimed had been given to her by a male admirer.[25] The theatre booked a succession of touring theatre companies and orchestras, though Durban also saw smaller outfits; the impersonator Mr Henry Lee stayed on for six months in 1898 doing impressions of Joseph Chamberlain, the Pope, Rudyard Kipling, Charles Dickens and Henrik Ibsen. Impersonation, one suspects, must have been a somewhat less demanding craft before the age of movie reels or even radio.[26]

Following a hunch that Boyes's story about Baden-Powell and as a player of Shakespeare could not have been merely coincidentally similar, I later traced the Durban theatre season of 1898 through the pages of the *Natal Mercury*. The chronology of Boyes's stay in Durban is a little hazy, so it is hard to determine which of the two theatre companies that visited Durban that year he would have acted with. One of these, the Haviland–Coleridge Shakespearian and Old English Comedy Company, was resident at the Theatre Royal in Durban from May to June, and then again from October to November, and played *The Merchant of Venice, Hamlet, Othello* and *Romeo and Juliet* among their repertoire.[27] The chronology, however, makes it more likely that Boyes would have taken up with the rather more modest Holloway company, which visited between August and September and played *As You Like It* and *Richard III*.[28] While *Richard III* does gesture towards the trope of the 'disguised king', it is only in a single line about Richard's intention to 'play the eavesdropper' (V.iii.19), something he does offstage, and I am tempted to abandon the idea of Boyes's Shakespearean memory. But we crucially learn from the *Mercury* review that the Holloway company were playing an adapted text of *Richard III*. Although *Richard III* is a favourite play with today's audiences, Shakespeare's original had long been considered (as the reviewer reminds us) 'one of the least satisfactory of Shakespeare's tragedies'. As a consequence, it had for two centuries been performed largely through Colly Cibber's 1699 bowdlerization, a hotchpotch of Shakespearean history plays that shortens the original and significantly increases the gore by (among other things) staging the murder of the Princes in the Tower. Cibber also added a number of monologues to enhance Richard's part – including, in the night before Bosworth, a thinly disguised lift from *Henry V* of Richard secretly visiting his troops.[29] It seems likely, then, that Boyes did experience a visit from a disguised general during his time in Africa, with the slight caveat that it was a Shakespearean character and not General Baden-Powell. Once again, the anecdotes of African life being reported back in England were simply a false memory of the stories they were taking to Africa with them.

The appearance here of the 'disguised king' episode is interesting, because just as Trinculo and Boyes provide the burlesque counter-history of colonization, so this motif is the counterpart and reverse of the 'refused crown' motif that seemed to motivate Steere's simultaneous recoil from and attraction to the exercise of power. The refusal of a proffered crown – in *Julius Caesar* and *Richard III*, and in Steere's protesting preference for libraries over power – is a ritual which demonstrates the fitness, even destiny, of the ruler for rule: it is both right and natural that they are above all men, as they alone have the self-control to resist the allure of power. Ruskin, in his 1870 lecture on 'Imperial Duty', used the same motif to place his audience of Oxford undergraduates in the position of the reluctant and righteous rulers of the Globe: 'the refusal of the crown' of imperial dominion would be, he laments, 'of all yet recorded in history, the shamefullest and untimely'.[30] The mingling of the disguised king among his people – an episode which Shakespeare had inherited from medieval romance – had originally served the same purpose, as in *I Henry VI* where Joan of Arc is able to pick the disguised French king out from a crowd by sensing his kingly aura (I.iii). But for the most part when this happens in Shakespeare, it has the opposite of the desired effect: the king learns how little support he has from among his people (*Richard III*) and it becomes apparent that he is a man like any other, virtually indistinguishable from those over whom he is set to rule. This episode, then, suggests that sovereignty is nothing more than a collective delusion, consisting only of our willingness to believe in its existence; it proves, in effect, a perfect prelude not only to Boyes's own extraordinary feat of persuading the Gikuyu to elevate him to power, but also to the collective delusion which sustained belief in the justice of colonial rule for the half-century that followed.

It would be all too easy to write off these episodes pinched from Shakespeare as merely travellers' tall tales. The consistency with which these stories are lifted specifically from Shakespeare, however, suggests that there is something else at play here. In a funny way, these mirrorings are rather like the theological idea of *typology*, the doctrine that sees episodes from the Old Testament as foreshadowing and predicting those of the New: Abraham's near-sacrifice of Isaac, and the replacement of Isaac by a ram, is a premonition of God's sacrifice of his own son Jesus, the Lamb of God. This doctrine was later extended by Christian thinkers to suggest that episodes from the Old Testament were also predictions of *historical* events that had not yet come to pass: so Christian thinkers saw the tribulations of the people of Israel, and their eventual triumph, as a version of their own sufferings and a guarantee of their own future vindication. But just as Shakespeare and the Bible were two sides of the same coin for Allan Quatermain (and Bishop Steere), so the English travellers seem to have found in Shakespeare a way of thinking about the things that happened to them in the Dark Continent. Stanley's and Boyes's use of Shakespeare narratives is not a simple duplicity, a substitution of *facts* for something more compelling; it is, rather, evidence of a belief – perhaps unconscious – that certain scenes in life have an eternal form, a universal structure, which is captured by Shakespeare better than anyone else. The savage *must* be a devotee of fire and an enemy of the written word, because civilization *is* the containment of primal forces in the hearth and the primacy of written record; the great general *must* walk unknown among his troops, because he is the earthly equivalent of the God who walks among us unknown, the General of the Church Militant.

These stories from Haggard and Boyes confirmed once again the extraordinary impression that literature – and, more specifically, Shakespeare – was an integral part of the repertoire of early explorer and settler life, something which appeared almost automatically in every experience of the Dark Continent. The very oddity, even unbelievability, of Shakespeare blossoming in alien landscapes seemed to make his presence indispensable to these stories. Before long, however, there was a thriving and unmistakably *real* Shakespearean presence on the East African mainland, though (once again) this bardolatry would come from an entirely unexpected quarter.

4

MOMBASA

Shakespeare, Bard of the Railroad

The lunatic, the lover, and the poet
Are of imagination all compact.
One sees more devils than vast hell can hold;
That is the madman. The lover, all as frantic,
Sees Helen's beauty in a brow of Egypt.
The poet's eye, in a fine frenzy rolling,
Doth glance from heaven to earth, from earth to heaven,
And as imagination bodies forth
The forms of things unknown, the poet's pen
Turns them to shapes and gives to airy nothing
A local habitation and a name.
Such tricks hath strong imagination
That if it would but apprehend some joy,
It comprehends some bringer of that joy;
Or in the night, imagining some fear,
How easy is a bush supposed a bear!

A Midsummer Night's Dream (V.i.2–22)

H. Rider Haggard was not, of course, the first stranger to make East Africa the local habitation for his 'shaping fantasies', and Mombasa, my next stop, served as the anchoring point for a good number of these stories. As early as the fifteenth century, the Arabic geographer Abu al-Mahasin reported of Mombasa that 'the monkeys have become rulers . . . [who,] when they enter a house and find a woman, they hold congress with her'. 'The people', al-Mahasin laconically concludes, 'have much to put up with.'[1] The most persistent story that the earliest European travellers told of eastern Africa was that of Prester John, the mythical priest-king who ruled over a lost Christian tribe somewhere outside the bounds of the Christian world. Rumours of an actual Coptic Christian kingdom in Ethiopia may have led to the lands of Prester John being pinned down in Abyssinia during the late Middle Ages, and finding his kingdom was a central aim of the Portuguese mariners who pioneered the route around the southern tip of Africa in the late fifteenth century. The 'Abyssinia' over which Prester John ruled in the travellers' minds was not, however, tied to any one geographical location, and their eagerness to find it made them see signs of his kingdom everywhere.* An episode in the Portuguese national epic, *The Lusiads*, recounts how Vasco da Gama's search for a sea route to India nearly foundered at Mombasa, where a conniving Arab-Swahili guide draws them into an ambush using the long-sought Christian kingdom as a lure. As Captain Richard Burton's own translation has it,

---

* The currency of this myth in Shakespeare's time is demonstrated by the inclusion of the priest-king in the extended pilgrimage planned by Benedick to avoid having to speak to Beatrice: 'I will go on the slightest errand now to the Antipodes that you can devise to send me on. I will fetch you a tooth-picker now from the furthest inch of Asia, bring you the length of Prester John's foot, fetch you a hair off the Great Cham's beard, do you any embassage to the pigmies, rather than hold three words' conference with this harpy' (*Much Ado about Nothing*, II.i.230–35).

And eke he telleth, with that false intent
   whereby fell Sinon baulked the Phrygian race
   of a near-lying isle, that aye had lent
   to Christian dwellers safest resting place. [. . .]
Here too with every word the liar lied,
   as by his regiment he in fine was bound,
   for none who CHRIST adore could there abide,
   only the hounds who worship false Mahound, [. . .]
So near that islet lay along the land,
   nought save a narrow channel lay atween;
   and rose a city thronèd on the strand,
   which from the margent of the seas was seen;
   fair built with lordly buildings tall and grand,
   as from its offing showed all with sheen:
Here ruled a monarch for long years high famed;
Islet and city are Mombasah namèd.[2]

For all Burton's archly medieval spelling and Homeric register, the poem does draw directly on some of the earliest recorded European experiences of the East African coast. The poet Camões, who wrote much of this epic in a cave while shipwrecked near the Mekong delta in China, had himself sailed the southern route to India and so knew the locations of which he wrote intimately. At the close of this extraordinary scene, Camões has da Gama saved by the intervention of Venus and her ocean nymphs, a delightful fantasy in which the explorers are saved from the trap baited with an exotic myth by the protective force of a classical one.

The reasonable assumption that the legend of Prester John would evaporate as knowledge of the African interior became available proved false. H. Rider Haggard's East African novels are themselves variations on the Prester John legend, and something of this tradition of blissful inland kingdoms remained even in my childhood in the prurient gossip about goings-on at secluded up-country ranches which were a law unto themselves. As late as 1910, the celebrated novelist John Buchan's *Prester John* shows that the myth still had some power, though in a clever inversion of the usual narrative Buchan's hero rises to power – like Boyes and my other player-kings – by making a false claim to *be* the legendary priest-king. Buchan, who had lived in and travelled through southern Africa at the turn of the century, evidently sensed how stories had a curious way of turning themselves into facts on the Dark Continent.

I have come to Mombasa to follow leads I unearthed back in Cambridge which gave a glimpse of a vibrant culture of East African Shakespeare performance in the early years of the twentieth century. The Shakespearean actors of whom I have come in search arrived just as the construction of the railways changed the shape of the continent, driving any 'lost kingdoms' further and further inland.* Before the building of the railways, the East African interior was sufficiently vast, unknown and unstructured to allow ample space for the European imagination to run wild; as already noted, the lack of navigable rivers made inland travel unthinkable to all but the best-supplied ventures by seasoned expeditionaries. Victorian industrial innovation had provided a solution for this impenetrability in the form of an iron rivulet which would run uphill from Mombasa through the Taru desert and Tsavo to the Mau escarpment, and beyond to the great inland seas on which the kingdom of the Buganda sat. This kingdom, if

---

* When in his 1906 novel *Benita* Rider Haggard returned once more to his favourite storyline of wealth hidden in the African continent, he was forced south to the Zambezi for an uncharted territory in which to set his story. This novel, in which the treasure hunter mesmerizes an African boy in order to dredge from his memory the whereabouts of buried gold from early Portuguese travellers, gives some taste of the complex way in which European legends of Africa blended with occultist fashions in the *fin de siècle* imagination.

not magically white or Christian like those of the literary imagination, was at the very least rich, relatively developed and verdant. Importantly, it was also deemed strategically crucial for protecting the headwaters of the Nile, and hence Egypt and Suez and the passage to India, jewel in the crown of the British Empire. The railways created arteries where there were none before, and from these arteries were to bud depots which would grow into the first towns of the interior, just as port towns had grown up on the coast where the ships were accustomed to stopping. The railways also allowed for the transport inland of industrial hardware and troops, and of settlers who could arrive in coaches tricked out in dark cool wooden panelling, soft leather banquettes and lead-crystal glassware.

The East African Railway was still a major fixture during my childhood, though by then airports had once again reoriented the world, so that one arrived on the mid-continental plateau and took the train down to the coast, as we did for beach holidays over Christmas. The arrival of chartered flights and tarmacked roads had halted the refurbishment of the rolling stock in the middle of last century, and by the time of my childhood the once-luxurious railway carriages were lumpy and tarnished. They nevertheless at the time seemed to me the height of grandeur; indeed, the impression created by these decaying remnants was evidently so strong that I still have a hard time finding elegance in anything new. Yet for all that these trains were down at heel when I began to ride them, travelling in them still featured the little ritual absurdities and talismans which the early settlers had put in place to protect themselves. There were white-gloved stewards turning down starched sheets as the locomotive bottled its way through the pitch-black savannah, occasionally halting until a herd of buffalo moved off the track, and dinner was parcelled out in a sequence of courses served by swaying waiters in the dining car. There is still something unmistakably riverine about these night trains – in the gentle lilt of the coaches as they eddy back and forth, the feeling of coursing through rapids as the train goes down into the Rift Valley or towards the coast, and the mild resistance as the train climbs, as if pushing against the current.

The railways are important to the story of Shakespeare in East Africa because they created the first urban populations dense enough to make professional theatre possible. These are, of course, the same conditions which led Shakespeare to write the plays in the first place. For a professional theatrical culture to develop there must be enough people in the same place to replenish the audience day after day (or, as lighting developed, night after night), and preferably enough for two or more theatres, so that competition can drive productions to new levels. This critical mass in East Africa was not produced, however, by native Africans clustering at the rail depots or by European settlers, who only began to arrive in any numbers years after the railways were built. It came, rather, from the tens of thousands of Indian labourers, clerks and sepoys brought over to build the railway, and the inevitable caravan of followers who trailed after to service their needs. The use of Indian labour to build the railways was to have a profound effect upon the character of East Africa, inserting between the white colonial masters and the native Africans a middle class of shopkeepers and administrators. The Indian immigrant population made its first home at Mombasa, and it was to Mombasa that they returned during periods of furlough.

The task assigned to this workforce from 1896 onwards was to lay heavy steel rails and sleepers in a relatively straight line up the 5000 feet of the central African plateau, and the wilfully ungeometrical landscape required cuttings and bridges that made this an even more fraught business than usual. These labour parties suffered the same deprivation, malaria and tribal attacks which the

An unidentified group of Indian railway workers, from an uncatalogued photograph found in the archive of the Nairobi Railway Museum.

explorers had during their treks along the same routes, but their size and slow movement also created new dangers. A pair of man-eating lions besieged the railhead party for ten months in 1898 as they built a bridge over the Tsavo River, probably taking over 120 from the party and creating in their decimation a climate of crazed fear which a parade of sportsmen-hunters from Europe and America could do nothing to end. When the lions were eventually shot, each measured a monstrous ten feet from nose to tip of tail. (Their hides can still be seen today, stuffed and slightly moth-eaten, at the Field Museum in Chicago.) The railhead manager and successful stalker, John Henry Patterson, was celebrated by the workers in a lengthy Hindustani praise-song.

Bones, flesh, skin and blood, they devoured all, and left not a
trace behind them. [. . .]

On all sides arose weeping and wailing, and the people would sit
    and cry like cranes, complaining of the deeds of the lions. [. . .]
And after seeing what the animal had done, the Englishman
    spoke, and said
'For this damage the lion shall pay his life.' And when night came
    he took his gun and in very truth destroyed the beast.
Patterson Sahib is indeed a brave and valiant man, like unto those
    Persian heroes of old – Rustem, Zal, Sohrab and Berzoor [. . .]³

Though the poem truncates the siege into a matter of weeks, the
long-lasting reality left plenty of time for less affectionate feelings
to develop against Patterson Sahib, leading eventually to an
ambush and a mutiny which saw most of the workers on their way
back to Mombasa on a hijacked goods train.*

Although accounts of the railway's construction have tended to
focus on the many dangers faced by the work parties, I wondered
as I drove through Tsavo East whether their solitude among the
animals might also have had its consolations. The modern Tsavo
game reserve covers an area roughly the size of Wales or New
Hampshire, large enough for one often to encounter elephants
without a trace of human life on any horizon, as I did several times
during my drive. Anyone who has done this knows that it is an
experience with almost unparalleled spiritual resonance. The
massive solidity of the elephant and the otherworldly quality of its
skin, somewhere between stone and leather, combine with the delicacy and grace of its movements, and the profound stillness of the
eyes between its filament-like lashes, to deliver a silencing riposte
to human self-importance. There is nothing quite so calming as

---

* Patterson would go on, in the course of an extraordinary life, to lead the first Jewish
fighting force since biblical times into the Battle of Gallipoli, and to serve as godfather
to a future Israeli Prime Minister, Binyamin Netanyahu.

being faced with a thing for which your very existence is wholly trivial; both Lear and Hamlet are changed men after facing just such sublime grey objects – a storm for Lear and the sea for Hamlet. It is easy to see why the elephant-headed Ganesh might figure so highly in the Indian pantheon.

The Indian community brought with them the noises and tastes and patterns which became characteristic of East African urban life, and with which I became intimately familiar from the houses of my schoolmates and from the *dukas* of Nairobi, small goods stores which were almost without exception owned and run by Indians. The sacks of turmeric and cloves and cumin, shops with rolls of fabric like a parchment library, flour cooking in hot ghee, the translucence of paper bags holding oily samosas; the clatter of heated discussion in a palette of tongues and later raucous laughter, and later still the Bollywood showtunes on a battery-powered radio. But the Indian settlers also brought with them their love of Shakespeare – or rather, it should be said, their *two* loves of Shakespeare, each equally intense but not quite the same. The first of these, which would come to East Africa later, was a scholar's love of Shakespeare, which came about through long hours of intensive reading of the works and which led to a nineteenth-century cult of Shakespeare that placed him on a level with the Sanskrit poet Kalidas and saw him venerated by (among others) the Bengali poet and novelist Rabindranath Tagore. Whether or not this would have developed naturally on the subcontinent, where a culture of storytelling and respect for literary traditions might have made Shakespeare welcome, we will never know. As it was, knowledge of the works in India became for some a matter of survival after the Governor General of India, Hardinge, declared in 1844 that the highest places in the colonial service would be reserved for Indians who had distinguished themselves in the study of European literature – which, as we have already seen, meant Shakespeare above all else to the Victorian colonial class. This same idea was to make a home in Kenya Colony and in Uganda in the early twentieth century, but that belongs properly to a later part of this story.

The other love of Shakespeare, the theatregoer's love of his plots and characters, developed alongside the official culture in the popular theatres of northern India, beginning with the Parsi theatres in Maharashtra and accumulating (according to one commentator) 6000 different versions of Shakespeare plays in Indian languages. These productions were known, as one historian of Indian Shakespeare puts it, for their 'flamboyant manner of acting, grandiloquent speeches, loud and titillating music, gorgeous backdrops, dazzling costumes, and illusion-creating stage props'.[4] It was this Shakespeare that arrived with the travelling theatre troupes, which began including Mombasa and Zanzibar on an itinerary which had already included stops in other British colonial hubs such as Aden, for wherever the Empire went it took with it the blueprint of its Indian masterwork and (more often than not) the ready-trained personnel who worked there.

The story of the Indian settlers of East Africa is still surprisingly untold. Indians appear on the margins of European accounts of the region, usually as uninspiring functionaries who serve as comic bourgeois counterparts to the white aspiration for aristocratic primitivism in the African wild.[5] There have been some recent attempts to gather oral histories from now ancient early migrants, accounts which sway charmingly between minute personal details and vague truisms about major historical events and figures. Sadly no one alive now is old enough to remember the period in which I am interested, a period during the Great War when paranoia meant that every theatrical production was required to be licensed by the Protectorate authorities. Even these records are rather patchy, but a few spare and dryly bureaucratic lines in copies of the official organ of the administration, the *Kenya Gazette*, give some idea of the richness of this culture. In the eighteen months after February 1915, the *Gazette* records licences for at least *forty-three* separate productions of plays in a range of Indian languages, especially Hindustani and Gujarati.[6] These plays are given licences beginning at number 793, suggesting that hundreds of other productions had been licensed by the Protectorate since 1895 but not recorded in the *Gazette*. The sheer volume of plays, each of which was supposed to be 'passed' by a government censor as not having objectionable (presumably seditious) content, seems to have quickly defeated the Protectorate's will to control this flourishing culture, and the record of licences peters out abruptly after this. Similarly, the insistence that an English-language copy of each of the plays should be presented for inspection seems to have proved unrealistic, for while a few of the plays list English titles – *The Merchant of Venice, Richard III, Hamlet* – the vast majority of them are poorly transcribed versions of their titles in Indian languages. Providing as it does only misspelled words in a wide range of tongues, the list required some decoding; but blended in with the tales of Persian heroes (like those to whom Col. Patterson was compared) are at least *fifteen* separate productions of Shakespeare plays in this eighteen-month period. This made these Indian communities in those years a considerably more concentrated centre of Shakespeare performance than London's West End, and not too far behind Shakespeare's birthplace in Stratford-upon-Avon, home of the Shakespeare Memorial Theatre (which would one day become the Royal Shakespeare Company). It is also clear that, while the first performances were given by touring theatre troupes, the Indian settlers eventually established their own companies, such as the Eastern Art Theatre Company, the Indian Amateur Dramatic Society and the Mombasa Shakespeare Group.[7]

Among these productions was an anonymous adaptation of *Othello* (*Saubhagya Sundari*), a play of such fame in India that one of the most celebrated actors of the age (Jayshankar Sundari) took the stage name Sundari (Desdemona) for his trademark performance of that role, a role that according to his autobiography made him both a pattern for women's fashion and an object of women's desires.[8] The largest number of the Shakespeare translations performed in Mombasa, however, came from the pen of the most revered playwright of the age, Agha Hashr Kashmiri, who translated at least five of Shakespeare's plays and had been honoured as the 'Indian Shakespeare' at a public ceremony in Delhi. Licences were issued in 1915 for Agha Hashr's *Saidi Havas* (a play that blends *Richard III* and *King John*), and his versions of *King Lear* (*Sufed Khun*) and *Macbeth* (*Khwabe Hasti*), as well as for a *Hamlet* likely to be the *Khun Nahaq* of Mehadi Hasan, whose *Twelfth Night* (*Bhul Bhuliyan*) also features on the list.[9]

The vast body of Indian translations is a treasure trove for the aficionado of Shakespeare, showing the plays richly refracted through the eyes of a place and time wholly alien to the Swan of Avon. In part this is the thrill of seeing Hamlet look for the ghost of his father on Mughal battlements, or Juliet's sleeping draught replaced by a snake; the pleasure is like that of watching someone you love in costume, newly beautiful but still the same. Some of these changes also make interesting links in the mind – a Mughal version of Hamlet makes him blur into Othello, and snakebitten Juliet edges closer to the Cleopatra she might have become if there had been men after Romeo.

Unlike early Indian critics of these plays, however, I am more interested in the versions that change Shakespeare's plots than those that slavishly imitate the master. This is in part because the changes, irreverent as they are, pick up on mysterious loose ends in the original and provide their own readings of hidden undercurrents in Shakespeare's writing. The Marathi version of *Romeo and Juliet* (*Mohana-Tara*) senses that something is amiss when

Romeo's first love, Rosaline, is passed over for Juliet and then simply disappears from view, and so it resurrects her, marries her to Romeo's nemesis Tybalt, and has her to blame for Romeo's failure to receive Friar Lawrence's message that Juliet's death is fake.[10] The change so economically repairs two odd fractures in the play by fitting them together that one is tempted, like Burton correcting the *Sonnets*, to rewrite this part of the play.

Eyewitness accounts of Mombasa's rich theatrical culture in this period are not easy to find. As is so often the case, in the rush to record what seemed important at the time much that must have given the fledgling city its flavour was simply treated as unimportant and ephemeral, leaving future ages with a somewhat sterile version of the lives lived by these early settlers. The visitor to today's Mombasa can still find traces of each of its historic cultures – Arab, Portuguese and Indian, as well as the coastal African tribes – laid out as if an archaeological dig on its side, each stratum a little further from the seaward edge of the estuary island occupied by the town. At that end, overlooking Port Tudor, is the Lusitanian Fort Jesus, built at the behest of Elizabeth I's chief rival, Philip, where Renaissance sailor graffiti abuts on the markings made by prisoners who were interned here when it was repurposed by the British colonial regime. Working inland from this, there is a slim band of Arabic streets like those in Stone Town, which are kept pristine for the docking tourists who are nowadays unlikely to venture further into the town than this before heading back out to the private beach resorts strung along the coast on either side. Beyond this is a wide swathe of Mombasa which once would have been the preserve of the colonial elite, with the small-gauge local tramway moving past grand institutions, from the Metropole and Castle Royal hotels to the law courts and Mackinnon Market. Now the tramway and the white colonials are gone, and the genteel repose of this part of town buzzes with *tuktuk* rickshaws moving past Indian *dukas*, shops where the age-old dried goods in sisal sacks sit next to wall-racks of mobile-phone accessories. At the top of the island, at the point where the railway crosses Kilindini Harbour, the residential districts give way to a modern industrial zone, which looks across a narrow strait to where, atop a teetering landfill, the poorest residents of Mombasa watch the trains enter from the mainland. In this palimpsest of history, where each subsequent age squeezes out the one before it, destroying all but the most robust of structures, there seems little chance of recovering the flimsy world of working-class evening entertainment.

In another of the common ironies of history, however, the fullest picture of Mombasa's Shakespeare that we are able to piece together comes not from admirers of the Indian stage but from occasional (usually unsympathetic) reviews in the English-language newspapers of the day. The *East African Standard* of 22 August 1908 contains one such report from a bemused English witness of a *Merchant of Venice* put on by the Shah Company at the New Indian Theatre in Mombasa. Though much of the article is given over to titillating the English reader with stories of transvestite actors and gently mocking the fact that the handbill actually read 'The Merchant of Venus', we also learn a good deal about the production. The three-and-a-half-hour performance was accompanied (as was standard) by drums and a harmonium, and acted out (as was also conventional) against a backdrop featuring full-length portraits of King Edward VII and Queen Alexandra. We are able to identify the specific translation as another of Agha Hashr's, *Dil Farosh*, by the reviewer's mention of a 'drunken brother' for Bassanio, an addition by Agha Hashr who provides comic and unsuccessful competition for the hero while 'indulging in wine and women and coarse songs to the glory of "English Brandy" with his boon companions.'[11] We also learn that *Dil Farosh* played to a full house, consisting of '96 people in the gallery at 50 cents, 162 in the pits for a rupee, 72 in the second stalls at 2 rupees and 42 in the first stalls for 3, making 372 people and 478 rupees in total, a princely sum when one considers that the unskilled railway labourers were only receiving 15 rupees a month in wages. The proprietor of the company, a Mr Yakubaly Jumlay, also reports that he spent a year at Aden and a month in Zanzibar before arriving in Mombasa, where he planned to stay a month and expected to play to sell-out crowds every night.

Though Jumlay and other Indian theatre impresarios evidently made efforts to attract Europeans to their productions, inviting reviewers and offering gala nights specially reserved for white audiences, these seem to have been for the most part rebuffed. Another review in the *East African Standard* (6 June 1914) seems surprised to find that two Indian theatrical companies – the Rising Star Company and the New Indian Opera and Theatrical company – have been performing in Mombasa for some time and 'commanding full houses'.[12] The Rising Star Company, which the reviewer visits, is resident in a galvanized-iron building with terrible ventilation and acoustics, causing the players to bellow in a way which the reviewer compares to Victorian music hall parodies of Shakespearean actors. The musical accompaniment to the play is assessed by the reviewer in terms which manage to be dismissive of not one but two cultures, all while asserting his open-mindedness: 'To the European ear these interminable Indian melodies become as monotonous as an African n'goma, though, of course, it must be classed as music – music of an arrested development.' The assessment of the acting is similarly belittling:

> Most of the acting is melo-dramatic and the elocution a rant, giving no place to the softer inflections of the tongue, which enable it to portray the subtleties of the human passions, or to give lightness, spirit, and dynamic force to dialogue. Passion and character

are thus dwarfed, and it may be safely sworn that these Indian players could not delineate Shakespeare's characters.

The reviewer was invited back a week later to see another play –
Agha Hashr's *Khubsurat Bala*, a version of *Macbeth* – which he
dismisses with equally magisterial lack of understanding.[13] The
very failure of these performances to appeal to the European
reviewers is, however, in one sense encouraging. Unlike those
studying Shakespeare to pass exams for the Colonial Service, these
Indian troupes were performing Shakespeare's plays without any
encouragement or hope of reward from the colonial masters;
although they seemed to think that they might be offering the
Europeans something in an idiom they would understand –
enough to merit one evening a month for 'European night' – this
seems to have been of slender importance to them, and the white
settlers' failure to sense what they were missing did nothing to
diminish this popular love of Shakespeare. In fact, the use of Indian
titles in the licensing applications suggests that often these troupes,
like the Zanzibari villagers performing Steere's version of *The
Merchant of Venice*, were unaware that what they were performing
was Shakespeare. In a way, their confident act of taking over a
foreign culture is rather like Shakespeare's own. If Shakespeare's
John of Gaunt is worried that the English love for Italian fashions
might open the way to foreign conquest, Shakespeare himself
showed no hesitation in borrowing from foreign cultures, and he
based many of his own works on stories derived from the Italians
and French as well as from classical Latin and Greek culture. Just
like the popular Indian performances, however, Shakespeare did
this with a blithe lack of reverence for the original texts, and he was
also roundly mocked in his day for this arrogance, and dismissed
by his fellow playwrights as an 'upstart crow' with 'small Latin and
less Greek'.[14]

For all that these performances attracted audiences of 400 or more every evening, amounting to tens of thousands over these years, the fact that they were performed in lean-to theatres of ribbed galvanized iron – *mbati*, as it is known locally – gives some idea of the difficulty involved in reconstructing their feel (or even the whereabouts of the theatres) a century later. I am lucky enough to have the Indian equivalent of the 'bush telegraph' activated on my behalf, awakening conversations over cappuccinos and pakoras which stir the buried memories of a theatrical culture now all but lost. The few trails I am able to follow are provided by the descendants of these actors, some of whom are able to pull photographs of these productions from attics and cupboards. A historian of the Indian diaspora, Neera Kapur, digs out for me photos of her grandfather's 1930 production of Mehadi Hasan's version of *Hamlet*, *Khoon ka Khoon*. The images capture the frenetic glory of this theatrical culture: overloaded motor cars and shoulder-borne floats, advertising the coming production, push slowly through crowds of onlookers; they are all eager for the splendour that the stage will bring, as in the image of Hiralal Kapur, majestic in sword and sash and turban. This same play was, five years later, filmed as the first 'talkie' version of *Hamlet* in any language.[15] Heartbreakingly, no copy of this film can be found. The many days I spend in *tuktuks* – motorized rickshaws – following leads in Mombasa teach me little more than to cherrypick rickshawmen without sunglasses. It is not so much the glazed eyes of the *khat* chewer that should be of concern – consumption of the narcotic is near-universal, and besides gives the drivers' insouciant disdain for risk to their passengers something very much like charm. The more worrisome thing that I found the sunglasses to hide, on more than one occasion, was dual cataracts so unctuous as to prevent the driver's actions from bearing any relation to the world in front of him.

Given the difficulty of following these leads in the present day, it is our great good fortune that we do not have to rely entirely on the *East African Standard* reviewer's opinion of the musical performances that he heard that day, because versions of these same songs are among the very first Indian sounds to have been recorded for posterity. In a canny attempt to break into the potentially enormous Indian market for gramophone machines and records, Gramophone Typewriter Limited sent agents, beginning with their principal sound engineer, F. W. Gaisberg, in 1899, on missions to return with recordings of local music that might create a generation of Indian consumers. They began with the dancing and singing girls of Calcutta's theatres, outcasts in the most literal sense, having lost caste through their disreputable profession. Gaisberg's account of the trip makes clear his amazement, not only at the alien aesthetic of Indian music and its easy familiarity with Shakespeare, but also with the studied indifference of the Anglo-Indians to the culture that surrounded them.[16] Among those songs recorded during these first visits, from 1899 to 1909, were ones from Agha Hashr Kashmiri's immensely popular Shakespearean plays, including *Dil Farosh* (*The Merchant of Venice*), which drew the ire of the *Standard* reviewer in 1908, as well as *Bhul Bhuliyan*, a version of *Twelfth Night* by Mehadi Hasan.[17] Only a few of these exquisite amber-caught moments of turn-of-the-century Indian music survive, though even these survivals are astounding when one realizes that these recordings were not made on the wax or metal discs common at the time – which have endured relatively well – but on discs made from shellac, crushed beetle-shell.

When I later went to listen to the two surviving recordings from these songs at the British Library sound archive, I was giddy with the thought that I was hearing the same sounds that would have rung out of the ramshackle theatres onto the Mombasa streets, the love songs of Hindustani Shakespeare, preserved in the carcasses of beetles which had once footled around the forests of Bengal. The

Indian nautch girl.

song from *Bhul Bhuliyan* is a duet, 'Bar Tar Saroor Mein Tujhpaar Nissar' ('All that is beautiful in this world is devoted to you'), sung by 'Miss' Acheria and 'Miss' Subashi (so titled following Western stage traditions).[18] The music is, it must be admitted, initially monotonous – even enervating – to my untrained ear, but as I listen over and over again in my booth the song, which jumps into life after an initial section damaged beyond repair, reveals a web of erotic longing it weaves through its lines of clipped, repeated words, each one only changing the last but a little, until it blurs into a strange mixture of flirtation and chant. It is, in fact, a perfect evocation of those famous opening lines of the play, in which the spurned lover Duke Orsino imagines gorging on love-music until such time as his body revolts:

> If music be the food of love, play on.
> Give me excess of it that, surfeiting,
> The appetite may sicken and so die.
> That strain again, it had a dying fall.
> Oh, it came o'er my ear like the sweet sound
> That breathes upon a bank of violets,
> Stealing and giving odor. Enough, no more!
> 'Tis not so sweet now as it was before.

Twelfth Night (I.i.1–8)

Perhaps the most touching thing about Hasan's *Bhul Bhuliyan* being performed in Mombasa in 1915 comes from the changes he made to the original plot. Shakespeare's second wondrous 'twin play' – the first being *The Comedy of Errors* – opens with a shipwreck on the Illyrian coast which sees Viola separated from her twin, Sebastian, forced to dress as a boy, and thrown into a love triangle which only the reappearance of Sebastian can square to end the play happily. Hasan's play transposes these events to Tartary, where the Princess of Baghdad (Dilara) and her brother, Jafar, are driven from their country by the armed and unwanted suit of the King of Bokhara. The most striking change, however, is the replacement of the shipwreck in Shakespeare's version. In the original play, this merely sets up the events of the play and is the subject of only a few dozen lines; in *Bhul Bhuliyan*, however, it is a disaster which takes up much of the first act of the play, as we can see from a 1905 English summary of the play printed in the Parsee Orphanage Captain Printing Works in the Parel suburb of Bombay:

ACT I

[...]

SCENE III

Being defeated in the battle Prince Jafar and his sister run away from their home, by a railway train.

SCENE IV

A railway train is seen passing, in which Dilara and Jafar have taken their seats.

SCENE V

A railway Bridge is seen. Heavy rains with thunder and lightning burst forth. Lightning destroys the bridge. The train (in which Jafar and Dilara have taken their seats) coming up, falls dashing in the waters below.

ACT II

[...]

SCENE II

A passenger of the lost train has saved Dilara and landed her on the shores of Tarter.[19]

Few members of the Mombasa audience would not have known or been related to at least one of the 2498 men who died during the construction of the line which ran from the coast to Lake Victoria. Little trace has been left of these men, and other than those with the dubious fortune to fall prey to the man-eating lions of Tsavo, even their manners of death only merit occasional mention among the drifts of paper mouldering in a shed in the Railway Museum in Nairobi. We do know, however, that many of them died in the collapse of railway bridges during times of heavy rain and flood, when the pioneering work of construction in the sandy soil of the savannah took its toll. This Shakespearean fantasy, then, of a survival which is turned to victory, must have resonated very deeply with the audiences packing the flimsy and overheated Mombasa theatres. And it is these very liberties taken with Shakespeare's texts, the liberties which so dismayed the reviewers from the *Standard*, that meant Shakespeare was a living voice to these audiences, and not being watched simply to venerate some lifeless idol.

It also makes perfect sense that Shakespeare's plays appealed to that audience. Shakespeare, the glover's son who moved to London in his mid-twenties to join a theatre scene for which he had no obvious qualifications, is (after all) the poet of new beginnings. Unlike the French and Spanish dramatists of the day, Shakespeare and the Elizabethan theatre he helped to create did not produce plays in which, following classical models, a long history comes home to roost on a character at the end of their story. Instead, Shakespeare's most popular plays involve characters entering a new world or a new phase of life, and these plays are about facing what lies in wait there. The pasts these characters do have are quickly suppressed, surviving only in garbled fragments. We learn that Romeo had a first love, Rosaline, but she plays no part in his life; Lady Macbeth speaks as a mother of children who are nowhere to be seen. What happened to the mothers of Imogen, Cordelia, and Miranda? No one knows. The most awkward moment in *Hamlet* is the appearance of the prince's schoolfriends, Rosencrantz and Guildenstern, remnants of a past that he has no desire to recall; Hamlet famously sends them on to England and death without him, protesting that they 'are not near my conscience'. Shakespeare's plays are often about people with no apparent past, a feat which often requires sweeping what *has* happened under the carpet. In being so, they perfectly suited themselves to the world that inherited Shakespeare. Unlike the Elizabethan world in which

Shakespeare himself grew up, the world in which his works grew famous constantly thought of itself as at the beginning of a new age and not at the end of time. This was certainly the case in the Mombasa theatres, where a community clung to the side of a continent in which everything remained to be done.

I was thrilled later to find evidence that, although the traces of Mombasa's Indian Shakespeare scene have now largely vanished, this culture did not peter out but rather provided another route for Shakespeare to make his way into eastern Africa. During her travels through the coastal region in 1913 studying Bantu languages, the linguistics expert Alice Werner was presented with a manuscript by an African teacher from the mission at Ngao near the River Tana. As she reports in the journal *Folklore* in 1915, the manuscript contained a version of *The Merchant of Venice* in Swahili – *The Story of the Flesh of the Thigh* – in which a wife saves her husband from a moneylender by employing Portia's trick, allowing him the flesh he is due as long as he does not take any blood.[20] *The Flesh of the Thigh* is, moreover, not just an anecdote snatched from Shakespeare's original, but contains much of the cross-dressing, female resourcefulness, and dramatic tension of the play. The presence of Shakespeare in Swahililand, Werner points out, should not be that surprising, given that Steere's Shakespearean schoolbook was a staple of classrooms in the region. Crucially, however, the teacher affirmed that he heard the story at Kipini on the north Kenya coast from a 'Banyan' – an Indian merchant – and that he believed the story to be 'from one of his own Indian books' rather than from a European one. This, then, was further evidence that Shakespeare's presence in East Africa had Indian as well as English roots. Whatever some European travellers might have done to keep Shakespeare separate from the Dark Continent, his writings were no longer their sole possession; they would make their way in the world without fanfare or even the protection of his name.

Like any well-structured drama, my time in Mombasa is drawn to a close by a looming deadline. A few weeks before my arrival a grenade attack had killed several people at a popular bar where people had gathered to watch the Euro 2012 England–Italy match, and during the tension that followed a radical Islamist preacher had been killed. Although embassies had issued travel warnings to their citizens advising them to steer clear of Mombasa, I had been told at a cocktail party at the US embassy in Nairobi not to worry. The reassurance seemed believable in large part because the physique and grooming of the man who gave it were greatly at odds with his humdrum official title (Liaison for Agricultural Standards, or some such thing). But now I had been told that there were riots expected after Friday prayers had finished at the mosques, and that the police would most likely be barricading routes on and off the island. Finally, then, after some weeks of coasting, I was headed inland, paralleling the route taken by the Indian-built railroad, though off in bush which would have been more like the unspoilt grassland which they were expected to pioneer.

5

NAIROBI

Expats, Emigrés and Exile

SHYLOCK:

What judgment shall I dread, doing no wrong?
You have among you many a purchased slave,
Which like your asses and your dogs and mules
You use in abject and in slavish parts
Because you bought them. Shall I say to you,
'Let them be free; marry them to your heirs!
Why sweat they under burdens? Let their beds
Be as soft as yours, and let their palates
Be seasoned with such viands'? You will answer,
'The slaves are ours.' So I do answer you:
The pound of flesh which I demand of him
Is dearly bought. 'Tis mine, and I will have it.
If you deny me, fie upon your law:
There is no force in the decrees of Venice.
I stand for judgement. Answer! Shall I have it?

The Merchant of Venice (IV.i.89–103)

The railways provided for the mass transportation of people and goods into the East African interior, a change whose most striking effect would be the transformation of the Kenyan highlands into industrial farms of a quasi-mythical richness, which would be jealously guarded by the European settlers who staked their claims in the early years of the twentieth century. As anyone knows who has spent time in the Kenyan uplands, the soil is more forcefully present there than is believable on first acquaintance. The red murram dust coats everything in the dry season, silts into shoes and under windows and powders dogs; and in the wet season, when rains are announced by the rising scent of wet earth long before any drops are heard or felt, the same clay makes everywhere ochre-coloured sculptures out of the doughy mud, with tyre ruts and shoeprints baked hard by the soon returning sun. The soil is also dauntingly fertile, sprouting with deep green at every pore, and making a pitiful mess of any tarmac laid over it.

The brute forces of soil and steam transportation may have transformed East Africa, but it was the way in which the railway allowed decadence to blossom in the wilderness which most caught the imagination of the world outside. Evelyn Waugh wonderfully captures this fantastical realm in his account of his short stay in 1930. After leaving Mombasa on the night train, he writes:

> It was a novel sensation, after so many weeks, not to be sweating. Next morning I changed from white drill to grey flannel. We arrived at Nairobi a little before lunch time, I took a taxi out to the Muthaiga Club. There was no room for me there, but the secretary had been told of my coming and I found I was already a temporary member. In the bar were several people I had met in the [ship] *Explorateur Grandidier*, and some I knew in London. They were drinking pink gin in impressive quantities. Someone said, 'You

mustn't think Kenya is always like this.' I found myself involved in a luncheon party. We went on together to the races. [...]

Someone took me to a marquee where we drank champagne. When I wanted to pay for my round the barman gave me a little piece of paper to sign and a cigar.

We went back to Muthaiga and drank champagne out of a silver cup which someone had just won.

Someone said, 'You mustn't think Kenya is always like this.'

There was a young man in a sombrero hat, trimmed with snake skin. He stopped playing dice, at which he had just dropped twenty-five pounds, and asked me to come to a dinner party at Torr's. Raymond and I went back there to change.

On the way up we stopped in the bar to have a cocktail. A man in an orange shirt asked if we either of us wanted to fight. We both said we did. He said, 'Have a drink instead.'

That evening it was a very large dinner-party, taking up all one side of the ballroom at Torr's. The young lady next to me said, 'You mustn't think that Kenya is always like this.'

After some time we went on to Muthaiga.

There was a lovely American called Kiki, whom I had met before. She said, 'You'll like Kenya. It's always like this.'[1]

Even Waugh, the portraitist *par excellence* of London's Roaring Twenties, was impressed by the bohemian grandeur of the so-called Happy Valley set, of whom Raymond de Trafford (mentioned here) was a key member.

The most famous accounts of this world, however, come from the pen of Karen Blixen, who arrived in 1913 from Denmark to join her soon-to-be-ex-husband, Baron Blixen, and to set up a coffee farm, within the grounds of which I grew up. Blixen's coffee farm was plagued by problems (starting with being planted in the wrong area) and she left in 1931 after it fell into bankruptcy. There was tender irony, then, in the fact that some of her coffee bushes could still be found in our garden, resilient against the regrown forest in the way that they had not been for Blixen. Though not quite as remote from Nairobi town as when Blixen was in residence, the area named 'Karen' after her was still relatively wild when I grew up there: our house was a fair drive down a steep dirt track from the potholed Mbagathi Ridge road on which Blixen's farmhouse sits, and was regularly only accessible on foot during the rains. The breeze-block bungalow, which was a palace for me from the moment that we arrived to find it overrun with lizards, clung to one side of a valley densely wooded on either side, still the habitat of Sykes monkeys, miniature suni and duiker antelope, the occasional leopard, and the tree hyraxes that scream at night like a strangled child. At the bottom of the valley the Mbagathi River seeped through a sedge of papyrus swamp and eucalyptus groves, though at times it broke free of the swamp and made rills where we caught crayfish and built childish dams. The eucalyptus leaves, tough and green like scales of oxydized copper, clattered together and mingled with the river sound to make a noise only describable by one of Homer's greatest descriptive turns, when he calls Mount Pelion 'εινοσιφυλλον', 'ashiver with leaves'.[2] Herodotus had a tale about the tribes who lived near the cataract of the Nile and who were so inured to the deafening roar of the river that they could not hear it any more. He didn't, perhaps, consider that the same people would hear its absence anywhere else.

Neighbours were reached by a quarter hour's walk through the rocky scrubland beyond the edge of the forest, fields where I served as my brother's assistant and carried the bags containing the harvest of snakes and lizards we would bring back to the house, to join the tortoises and turacos of our menagerie. I suppose I thought of them as pets at the time, though there was little real boundary between the house and the world around it, and these animals mostly came and went with little regard to how we felt about the matter. The lack of boundary between our world and theirs was underscored when our Jack Russell, 'Tumbili' ('little monkey') was killed by a python from the swamp, and our trigger-fingers were restrained during its slow and immobile digestion as an early lesson in not begrudging animals their wildness. The snake was caught in and killed by a water-pump downstream during its next venture into the human periphery a few weeks later.

Though Blixen's farm was a dismal failure financially, she found fame on her return to Europe through her account of settler and plantation life, *Out of Africa*, even though the book is quite discreet about the passionate affair with the Great White Hunter, Denys Finch-Hatton, which became the focus of the Sydney Pollack film of the same name. Blixen and Finch-Hatton, along with Berkeley Cole and the godfather of the settlers, Hugh Cholmondeley (pronounced 'Chumley'), third Baron Delamere, were among a select first wave of highland settlers, from whom the Happy Valley set would later take the flame in the twenties. Though this first group were serious farmers who never quite managed the cocaine-fuelled orgies of the Happy Valley set, they did not run their vast fiefdoms without a certain amount of self-indulgence. Among the favourite habits of Hugh Delamere, who breakfasted on gazelle chops and blancmange to the sound of his gramophone blaring from the verandah, was to head into Nyeri town of a Saturday night and end his binges by trashing the bar of the hotel he himself owned. It is said that he always faithfully paid the bill for damages.[3]

It came as no surprise by this point to find, upon reading the great profusion of memoirs and diaries and letters left by this group, that these settlers followed Burton and Stanley and Roosevelt in making Shakespeare a central totem in their culture. Yet while there was a flourishing culture of amateur Shakespeare performances among the humbler settlers, including an annual

Shakespeare Festival at the Railway Club, which ran from 1933 until the 1950s, the colonial elites were more interested in the explorers' fantasy of Shakespeare in the wilderness.[4] Just like Berkeley Cole, who 'when he stayed on the farm, had a bottle of champagne out in the forest every morning at eleven o'clock' and insisted on the best glasses, they immersed themselves in Shakespeare in precisely those moments when he might most seem out of place. Blixen's writings and letters are littered with quotations from Shakespeare, and her library at her home in Rungsted on the north Danish coast holds eleven editions of the *Works*, most of them heavily annotated and marked by remnants of her life – four-leafed clovers, dried flowers, water damage on an edition used as the pedestal for a vase. In one copy she has written over Shakespeare's name the rather excellent anagram 'HE'S A SPEAKER'. These kinds of markings were long ignored by scholars, considered to be meaningless additions to (or even desecrations of) the text itself; only more recently have these things been recognized for what they truly are – evidence of the part these books played in their readers' lives, of where they were read and what daydreams they provoked. She later commented that

> Books in a colony play a different part in your existence from what they do in Europe; there is a whole side of your life which there they alone take charge of; and on this account, according to their quality, you feel more grateful to them, or more indignant with them, than you will ever do in civilized countries. The fictitious characters in the books run beside your horse on the farm, and walk about in the maize fields.

Among her Shakespeare volumes are those she kept from Denys Finch-Hatton's collection, which he stored at her house when he could not take them on safari – his schoolboy edition, purchased at Eton in 1905, his mother's volume with her schoolgirl notes, the inscribed volumes that his mother gave to his father.[5] New arrivals in Kenya proved themselves to be of the 'right sort' by showing Blixen their devotion to the works, as did Edward Grigg, Governor of Kenya Colony from 1925 to 1930:

> it is always pleasant to meet Grigg [. . .]. He is such a great devotee of Shakespeare, so we always talk very enthusiastically about him, – also very well up on the Old Testament, two interests that often go together, although not where I am concerned, for I can get nothing whatsoever out of it and think they were a lot of scoundrels . . .
>
> Letter to Ingeborg Dinesen, Sunday, 14 September 1930[6]

Grigg was later to remark that Shakespeare was losing out to Robert Burns in the British colonial expansion: whereas Burns's statue had been erected around the world by proud Scots, the English were too sheepish to rear their standard in strange lands.[7]

What one can reconstruct of these conversations from Blixen's writings, however, suggests that Shakespeare was not, for Blixen and Finch-Hatton, used as an amulet to keep them from 'going native', as it had been by Burton and the members of the Emin Pasha expedition. Rather, during the resistance she staged to the administration's 'reforms' of the local Gikuyu way of living, Shakespeare allowed Blixen to frame their plight in a manner not so easily dismissed by the other colonists. So, when the buyers of Blixen's bankrupt estate determined to evict the Gikuyu residents from her land as 'squatters', and the administration deemed their desire to stay together when moved to the Gikuyu Reserve unnecessary, Blixen turned to Lear's unparalleled defence of the part played by the impractical in human dignity:

'Oh reason not the need,' I thought, 'our basest beggars are in the poorest things superfluous.' – and so on. All my life I have held that you can class people according to how they may be imagined behaving to King Lear. You could not reason with King Lear, any more than with an old Kikuyu, and from the first he demanded too much of everybody; but he was a king. [. . .] The old dark clear-eyed Native of Africa, and the old dark clear-eyed elephant – they are alike; you see them standing on the ground, weighty with such impressions of the world around them as have been slowly gathered and heaped up in their dim minds; they are themselves features of the land. Either one of the two might find himself quite perplexed by the sight of the great changes that are going on all around him, and might ask you where he was, and you would have to answer him in the words of Kent: 'In your own kingdom, Sir.'[8]

Well-intentioned though it may be, Blixen's romantic reduction of Africans to picturesque and bestial features of the landscape is a little hard to stomach nowadays; I suppose we do well to remember that we will (with any luck) fall as far short of future standards of compassion as Blixen does of ours. But Blixen's support for the Gikuyu demands *despite her failure to see them as rational* is part of the point, and it is here that Shakespeare's stunning observation on the nature of dignity comes into play. King Lear, we remember, resigns his kingdom to his elder daughters at the beginning of the play, only to find them chipping away at the few privileges he retained, deeming them unnecessary for a man in his dotage.*

---

* It is fascinating that *Lear* should provide the text of Blixen's act of empathy, just as *The Tempest* served as inspiration for the colonizers' fantasies. The two texts are, after all, mirror-image reversals of one another: Lear's failure to control his daughters finds an outlet in his railing at a storm, a confrontation which encapsulates his powerlessness; Prospero begins *The Tempest* by controlling a storm, though it later becomes clear that this is mostly in service of controlling the marital choices of his daughter. The stories are essentially nightmarish and wish-fulfilment versions of the same rela-

Realizing what is going on, Lear's mind is raised to a point of furious clarity that enables him to make a moral and political argument centuries ahead of its time – namely, that *dignity is only dignity* when it is allowed to define its own terms. Deciding what is or is not important or valuable or appropriate for someone else deprives them of the most fundamental part of personhood, and it is only in defending those values that seem confusing to us that we demonstrate our belief in dignity.

An episode in my own childhood has always served to bring home to me the weight of Lear's observation. One Sunday afternoon, walking with my father and brother in the same Ngong hills from which the Gikuyu residents of Blixen's farm were evicted, we rounded a corner and came upon a group of young men lying in wait for us. Anyone who has been in this situation knows the leaden steps taken towards a fate from which one knows it useless to run. We were pinned to the ground and my father took a beating, and a few of the things we had on our walk were taken from us – a wallet, my father's leather sandals, a bone-handled fishing knife given to me by my grandfather. We were lucky that my father had the presence of mind to throw the keys to our car into the bushes as they approached, and that the path was popular enough for these desperate men to choose not to linger long. I remember that, walking back along the dusty path to the car, my strongest impression was of my father's bare feet. This, it seemed to me, was a matter of shame and the greatest defeat that had been visited on us that day. Dignity, as Blixen and Lear knew, must be allowed its own terms. Doubtless many of the young men who attacked us were themselves lacking shoes.

---

tionship as they occur to Shakespeare, father of daughters. But, as Blixen and the colonizers saw, they were also two narratives about political power. In the earlier of these, Lear the tyrant comes to understand the dehumanizing effects of arbitrary power upon the ruled.

The part played by Shakespeare's works in Blixen's conversation did not merely confine itself to exchanges with Finch-Hatton and with other colonists. A memorable episode in *Out of Africa* recounts an occasion on which she tried to explain the plot of *The Merchant of Venice* to Farah, the Somali servant who was at her side during her whole African stay and with whom she formed a close personal bond. Having received a letter from a friend in Denmark about a production of *The Merchant*, Blixen recalls that 'the play became vivid to me, and seemed to fill the house, so much that I called Farah in to talk with him about it, and explained the plot of the comedy to him'. Much to Blixen's apparent befuddlement, however, Farah sides with Shylock, insisting that he should not have forgone his claim to 'an even pound' of Antonio's flesh, to which he had a claim under law after Antonio defaulted on his loan. When Blixen points out that Shylock would face death if he shed a single drop of blood in the process of cutting the flesh from Antonio, Farah responds with practical advice:

> 'Memsahib,' said Farah, 'he could have used a redhot knife. That brings out no blood.'
>
> 'But,' I said, 'he was not allowed to take either more or less than one pound of flesh.'
>
> 'And who,' said Farah, 'would have been frightened by that, exactly a Jew? He might have taken little bits at a time, with a small scale at hand to weigh it on, till he had got just one pound. [...] he could have taken small bits, very small. He could have done that man a lot of harm, even a long time before he had got that one pound of flesh.'[9]

The problem here, Blixen explains, is that 'Coloured people do not take sides in a tale; the interest for them lies in the ingeniousness of the plot itself.' The very cultural differences, then, that were to

Illustration of Shylock from the Swahili translation.

be respected in the Gikuyu demands for land on which to keep their cattle and stay together are the same differences which mean that, for Blixen, the African will never understand Shakespeare. Farah has failed to understand what Blixen believes to be the point of the play, the triumph of the good man Antonio over the villain Shylock. I wonder, though, whether Farah doesn't have a point: as Shylock has been deprived, like Lear, of the right to define his own standard of dignity, it behoves him to stand upon whatever rights he does have in the law of his oppressors, even if that means staining himself with blood. The first African politicians, as we will see, became expert in using the colonial law against their masters.

Interestingly, stories like Blixen's appear (with variations) quite frequently in travellers' and settlers' tales of their lives in Africa and other exotic places. Perhaps the most famous version of this 'explaining Shakespeare to savages' episode was told by Laura Bohannan in her 1966 article 'Shakespeare in the Bush' for *Natural History* magazine, an article that is still regularly given to first-year anthropology undergraduates to illustrate the fundamental differences between cultures. Bohannan relates how, during her field trip to study the Tiv people of Nigeria, heavy rains forced her to spend much of her time in one of the elders' huts, where it was customary to retire during the wet season to drink the local brew and to tell stories. Although she postpones her own turn as story-teller as long as possible, eventually the audience will brook no further delay, and she decides to tell the story of *Hamlet*, a copy of which she has brought with her for her stay in the bush. Bohannan's attempt to tell the story faithfully and in great detail descends into chaos as she encounters the barriers between the two cultures: the Tiv do not believe in ghosts, and it is customary among them that a man marry his dead brother's widow, so the apparition of Old Hamlet to condemn Claudius's marriage to Gertrude makes no sense; Hamlet is wrong, in Tiv culture, to scold his mother, and instead of seeking revenge himself should have consulted a man-who-sees-all about the truth of his father's death before referring the matter to his father's age-mates for justice. Ophelia could not have drowned herself as only witches can drown people; Hamlet could not have *forged* a death warrant for Rosencrantz and Guildenstern, because written things are unexceptionably trust-worthy. In the end, the Tiv elders produce their own, more satis-factory versions of the story, including a rewrite of Hamlet's relationship with Ophelia and her brother Laertes:

> Polonius knew his son would get into trouble, and so he did. He had many fines to pay for fighting, and debts from gambling. But he had only two ways of getting money quickly. One was to marry off his sister at once, but it is difficult to find a man who will marry a woman desired by the son of a chief. For if the chief's heir commits adultery with your wife, what can you do? Only a fool calls a case against a man who will someday be his judge. Therefore Laertes had to take the second way: he killed his sister

by witchcraft, drowning her so he could secretly sell her body to the witches.[10]

Bohannan's objections and attempts to salvage the situation fall on deaf ears: she is told, 'We believe you when you say your marriage customs are different, or your clothes and weapons. But people are the same everywhere; therefore, there are always witches and it is we, the elders, who know how witches work.'

Both Blixen's and Bohannan's stories are amusing attempts to prove that even great Shakespeare is not universal – indeed, Bohannan's story even features as its antagonist a pompous old Oxbridge don whose belief that Shakespeare transcends cultural differences is triumphantly disproved.[11] We should, however, be cautious in accepting these stories at face value. After all, one needn't go as far as Nigeria or Nairobi to find someone to whom parts of Shakespeare's plays don't make sense – indeed, many members of Shakespeare's original audience would have been uncomfortable (for instance) with the idea of ghosts. On the other hand, eloquent proof that Shakespeare's works *were* open to under-standing by vastly different cultures was being furnished even then by the readers of Steere's Swahili Shakespeare and the culture of Indian performances which spread to Nairobi in the 1920s.* Both Blixen and Bohannan, I suspect, *set out* to demonstrate that the Africans with whom they are conversing need to be understood on their own terms, and this requires dispensing with the notion that there can be any kind of story which makes sense equally to all mankind. In an early version of multiculturalism, a threatened culture is defended against an invasive one by insisting on their

---

* Indeed, Old Hamlet's ghost ironically makes *more* sense within a Gikuyu context, where the spirit of the father is kept in existence by the remembrance of his male children, but is not accessible after death by female relatives (just as Gertrude cannot see Old Hamlet's ghost). See Kenyatta, *Facing Mount Kenya*, 15.

fundamental incompatibility, and thus the need to keep them apart to prevent the unique features of the threatened culture being lost. Blixen and Bohannan's retellings focus on elements of the plays – belief in ghosts, the righteousness of revenge – which were hardly universal for Shakespeare's original audience, and certainly weren't believed in by Bohannan and Blixen themselves; they rely, for their amusing anecdotes, on a confusion about the nature of the stories they are telling. The Tiv believe that Bohannan is telling them a true story, which must therefore play by the rules of the world as they see it; Farah, on the other hand, does not understand that he is being told a moral fable, and so concentrates on inconsistencies in the plot. The fact that both Blixen and Bohannan were misleading their readers in a good cause – to deliver a rebuke to Western cultural complacency and to demand that the Gikuyu and Tiv be understood on their own terms and not in terms of some supposedly 'universal' standards – makes one a little more sympathetic to them. It is a curious result of these well-intentioned attempts to stick up for other ways of doing things that they actually erect barriers between cultures where they needn't have been.[12]

Perhaps I am so quick to forgive Blixen because I remember with some regret my own attempts to keep cultures separate. For all that I don't remember having bigoted thoughts as a child, my life in Kenya was lived mostly among whites and those of Indian descent, a segregation effected more by means of wealth than skin colour; sadly, the social and economic history of post-independence East Africa meant that this led to fairly thorough separation. The school I attended did have black African students, but they were a noticeably small minority compared to the white and Asian populations, each of which made up about half the school. My interactions with black African children, then, were most often in the form of brief friendships struck up with local youngsters while on safari, and of interactions with the children of our household servants. As was usual then – and is now – the servants lived in purpose-built quarters in the grounds of the house. This will understandably strike many as a deeply paternalistic arrangement, though the many affectionate master–servant relations in Shakespeare's plays remind us too that there are also intimacies to these situations. The families of the resident staff mostly lived elsewhere, back in the ancestral village, to which they would return with their earnings on days off and during longer periods of leave. Occasionally, though, their children would come to stay with them for long stretches, and this was the case with the son of our cook Memli, whom I spent one summer failing to induct into the mysteries of baseball.

European and American friends of mine are often shocked to learn, when they ask about my exotic African childhood, that their lives – of suburban malls and theme parks – were every bit as much a part of my fantasy world as exploring jungles may have been of theirs. Every two years my father's work allowed for a paid and extended period of 'home leave' – leave which presumed that Europe or America remained forever 'home' – and for these trips I would plan feverishly in the months that led up to them. That summer I had visited my father's American relatives and had returned obsessed with baseball. Though I retain the passion to this day, my mature mind has come to justify my interest as residing in the finely orchestrated duel of pitcher and batter through a series of three-strike crescendos; my immature passion, however, probably had more to do with the oiled baseball mitt I had brought back, the perfect bone-whiteness of the ball with its faultlessly even red stitches, and the smooth perfection of my Louisville Slugger bat. I can now see the irony in the fact that these things, which I valued for the pristinely manufactured condition lacking in almost everything made in Africa, were made not from plastic but from the same natural materials – leather, wood – out of which local products were made. I still struggle to think of anything as truly desirable unless it is made from these things.

Not understanding this little fetish – or perhaps understanding it all too well – my mother determined that I should spend the rest of the long summer months out from under her feet and honing my skills at the game I professed to love. As Nairobi is a vastly spread-out place, and visits between schoolfriends were rare (even when they were in Nairobi during the long vacation), she suggested to Memli that I should pass the days teaching her son to play baseball. We duly retired to an area of dust and scrub which was the emptiest patch in our heavily forested compound; it sloped sharply upwards to an old abandoned water tank, in which during another summer my brother and I would attempt to make moonshine from apple juice and baker's yeast. In retrospect, our little league takes on an absurd aspect: I am sure that William had better things to do – though for all I know he was earning pocket money for entertaining the *bwana kidogo*; and I was caught in my own lie, falling deeper in despair with each blemish inflicted by the thorns and dust on my tooth-white ball.

The experiment was, of course, a failure. Despite being my age-mate, William was embarrassingly superior to me in athletic ability, and his easy mastery of the skills I was trying to teach only deepened my unhappiness. We kept it up for a fair few sessions, but only because I didn't want to give the impression that I didn't think the servant's boy good enough for me, or admit that I was only interested in the paraphernalia of the sport; and presumably he didn't feel he *could* throw over the sullen little *mzungu* with whom he had been saddled. That I remember this episode with almost as much interest as shame is down to the fact that my reaction was conjured by something other than a feeling of superiority: I certainly didn't think him *not good enough* to play baseball, or to play baseball with me; I simply liked to keep these two parts of my life separate. Each seemed diminished when mixed with the other, like Blixen's Shakespeare and her beloved Africa with whom she refused to share it.

Though Blixen and other defenders of native rights often gave in to their temptation to romanticize Africans, to think of them as part of an oral culture that could only be harmed by the introduction of literacy, they nevertheless had some sense of the way the wind was blowing, and Blixen herself set up a school for the Gikuyu on her farm. The writings of Blixen and other settlers, however, show very little sense of quite how sophisticated the political opposition to colonial dominance already was in the new urban environment. Nairobi was still little more than a rail depot when Blixen arrived in 1913, with planned neighbourhoods being marked off in the surrounding swampland ('Nairobi' coming from a phrase meaning 'cold water' in Maasai). Conditions were so poor (at least for those not largely concerned with racecourses and country clubs) that the local prison was widely known as the *Hoteli ya Kingi Georgi* ('The King George Hotel') because the amenities it provided were so superior to those available to most in town. A member of the Indian community dryly remarked in that year that the new Indian residential location, 'situated on the plain near to or where now is the Somali village', 'would be an excellent location as the drainage difficulties are not insuperable'.[13] Yet it was not long before a group of young men-about-town began to emerge as the voice of this fledgling urban community, and what set them apart was literacy. Known as the *Athomi*, or 'Readers', these young agitators were mission-educated and were to supply the first generation of Kenyan politicians. Among these *muthamaki* ('one who draws men to him with words') was Harry Thuku, who worked as a type-setter at *The Leader* newspaper in the 1910s and was to lead the first non-tribal political group, the East African Association, until his arrest and exile to Somalia in 1922. The path from literacy to political self-consciousness was not entirely smooth – and Thuku recalls in his autobiography a risibly poor fraudulent cheque for which he was arrested in 1911 – but it was clear at the time that the British had created something they could no longer contain. As Thuku writes:

> The Catholic policy was only to teach Africans religion, but no fuller education. . . . When there were political troubles in Nairobi in 1922, they thought this showed their policy had been right. For they wrote in their mission newspaper published in Nyeri, 'You British people, you have made a mistake. You sharpened a knife which is now cutting you.' They meant the knife of education.[14]

As Thuku implies, those educated by the Protestant missions had a much broader syllabus available to them than the catechism – including, of course, language teaching through texts including Steere's *Hadithi za Kiingereza* – and, along with the printing press that Steere had also introduced to East Africa, this gave them the rudimentary tools of their own insurrection.*

Another graduate of the mission schools and member of the *Athomi*, Johnstone Kamau, was to set up the first vernacular newspaper (the Gikuyu *Muigwithania*, or 'Reconciler') and act as General Secretary to the Gikuyu Central Association, a successor to Thuku's East African Association which commemorated annually his rising in 1922 and awaited his return from exile.[15] During these years Kamau's name changed to Kenyatta (after the brightly

---

* At the same time in Tanzania, members of the earliest native political organization (the Tanganyika African Civil Servants' Association) were strongly resisting 'the current pre-occupation in British colonial thought with "adapting" educational systems to the mentality and culture of Africans', sending Martin Kayamba to the Advisory Committee on Native Education as a 'consistent opponent of any proposals to compromise standards of English literary education'. See Austen, 'The Pre-history of Tanu', *Makerere Journal* 9, 2.

coloured belt he habitually wore), the name by which he was to be remembered as the first President of an independent Kenya.

Although Kenyatta was to develop a vision for his country formulated entirely in African terms, he did so only after a period of residence in Europe convinced him that the *Muigwithania* mission of reconciling *kikuyu karinga* (authentic 'Gikuyu-ness') and Western ways was futile. During his seventeen years of living in England, Kenyatta was courted and rejected in turn by the missionaries, the labour movement and the communists, all of whom despaired at his refusal to renounce tribal social structures and customs (including female circumcision) in favour of one or other brand of righteousness. But while the image he left to history was that of a tribal elder, carrying a flywhisk and with an animal-skin cloak covering his Western suit, his earlier life was a much more hybrid affair, as suggested by the British wife (Edna Grace Clark) he left behind on his return to Kenya in 1946, the (lost) satirical novel he began about an African student in Britain, and the volumes of Shakespeare which, though studiously ignored in his published writings, were (according to his daughter, Margaret) his favourite books, from which he often recited.[16]

Though the story of future African leaders in the West during the early twentieth century is a neglected one – ranging as it does from the residence of 'King Freddie of Buganda' (Mutesa Edward II of Uganda) at Magdalene College, Cambridge, to Kwame Nkrumah's stay in the United States before returning to serve as the first African President (of newly independent Ghana) – it was very much part of the popular consciousness of the time, as I was reminded when reading *The Story of Babar* to my son. As many a parent (or former child) will remember, Jean de Brunhoff's cherished picture book of 1931 centres on a young elephant who escapes to the town after his mother is shot by a hunter; luckily, upon his arrival in the town, 'a very rich Old Lady who has always been fond of little elephants understands right away that he is longing for a fine suit'. She underwrites his predilection for cream cakes and spats as well as providing him with a sports car and a tutor, in return for which Babar provides companionship and regales her dinner guests with stories of the jungle. Upon Babar's return to the jungle, the elephant elders are unanimous in their view: 'He has just returned from the big city, he has learned so much living among men, let us crown him king'.[17] In later instalments, Jean de Brunhoff's elephant obligingly builds a European city in the kingdom of the elephants, complete with a theatre that produces classical French plays, introducing civilized ways and rooting out the 'laziness' that comes naturally to wild animals. De Brunhoff's colonial fable comes eerily close to some of the realities of fashionable support for young African visionaries in the 1930s and how they were perceived by contemporaries, right down to the implied sexual edge of the elephant's relationship with its society hostess. The same note of scandal is seen in intelligence reports, such as those on Kenyatta's relationship with the American shipping heiress and civil rights champion Nancy Cunard, who Special Branch recorded in 1933 had 'recently been associating – apparently with considerable satisfaction to herself – with Johnstone Kenyatta'.[18]

A more detailed, though hardly less pessimistic, account of this period is given in the *roman à clef* by the South African novelist Peter Abrahams, *A Wreath for Udomo*. Under a thin veil of fiction, Abrahams recounts in the first half of the novel the residence in London of his close friends of the 1930s and '40s, friends who included the future Ghanaian independence leader Kwame Nkrumah, the leading pan-Africanist George Padmore, and Johnstone (now Jomo) Kenyatta. Abrahams gives us some insight into the human side of the heady years during which the pan-Africanism that would dominate politics on the continent for the next three decades was forged in student dorms and at house

Captain Richard Francis Burton, who read Shakespeare extensively with his future nemesis John Hanning Speke during their expedition to find the source of the Nile.

Henry Morton Stanley in a *carte de visite* portrait staged at the London Stereoscopic and Photographic Company (1872), with his servant Ndugu M'hali, whom he re-named 'Kalulu'.

MR. STANLEY,

N THE DRESS HE WORE WHEN HE MET LIVINGSTONE IN AFRICA.

Stereoscopic Co.   *Copyright.*

Teddy Roosevelt with members of his 1909–1910 East African hunting safari, including his son Kermit (seated, right). Roosevelt clutches a book from the fifty-five-volume 'pigskin library' that accompanied him on his expedition.

Edward Steere, third Missionary Bishop of Central Africa. Steere's press on the island of Zanzibar produced many of the first volumes printed in Swahili, including the *Hadithi za Kiingereza* (a translation of Charles and Mary Lamb's *Tales from Shakespeare*).

A procession announcing a performance of *Khoon ka Khoon*, a translation of *Hamlet* by Mehadi Hasan, winds through the streets of Nairobi around 1930; and Hiralal Kapur (seated left, below) in his costume for this production. The photos are provided by his granddaughter Neera Kapur-Dromson.

Karen Blixen in the first photo she sent back to Denmark of her household near Nairobi. Farah, with whom she recounts discussing *The Merchant of Venice*, is seated second from left.

Apollo Milton Obote, the future first President of Uganda, in the title role of the 1948 production of *Julius Caesar* at Makerere University. Cassius, kneeling, is played by A. F. Mpanga, who would become legal adviser to Obote's government.

A production of *Coriolanus* staged at Makerere University in 1951, with Assiah Jabir in the role of Volumnia.

Julius Kambarage Nyerere, the first President of Tanzania, photographed in 1960 during the struggle for independence from British colonial rule. Nyerere's Swahili translations of *Julius Caesar* and *The Merchant of Venice* were undertaken during his first five years in office.

Che Guevara in disguise, crossing Lake Tanganyika to fight in the Congo. Che spent several months recovering from his Congolese expedition in a secret room at the top of the Cuban embassy in Dar es Salaam.

Emperor Haile Selassie I parades the streets of Addis Ababa with his entourage in 1971.

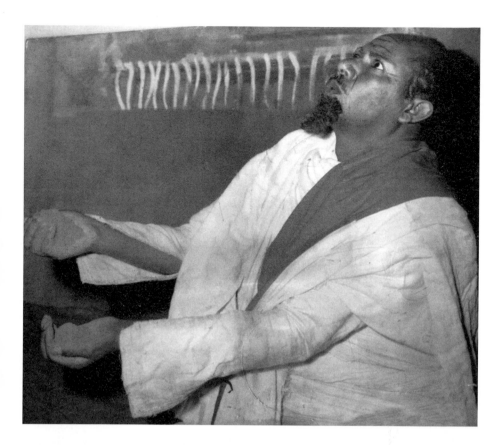

Images from productions of Tsegaye Gabre-Medhin's *Otello* (1963, top) and *Hamlét* (1967, above). In the upper picture, Othello is played by Awelaččaw Däjäné; in the lower, Täsfäye Gässäsä (standing, with prominent shoulder clasps) plays Hamlet.

Standing over the bodies of Imogen and Cloten in the Juba Arabic production of *Cymbeline* staged at Shakespeare's Globe in 2012.

parties in London and across the United Kingdom. The novel focuses on Udomo (immediately recognized as Kenyatta by Abrahams's first readers), whose growth to political consciousness is complicated by his erotic encounters with English women. The love affairs of these independence leaders with English women – and through them with Englishness – fundamentally compromise their commitment to the independence movement. The second half of the novel deals with the slow decline from idealism after these same men became leaders of independent states, descending into a saga of internecine struggles, betrayals excused by political necessity, and trade deals which all but give the power back to the old colonial masters.

These insights into the early emotional life and character formation of Jomo Kenyatta are all the more tantalizing given the fact that Uhuru Kenyatta, his son and the heir to his political legacy, is a regular at the Aero Club of East Africa which I make my home while in Nairobi. Settler life in Nairobi often migrated between the poles of private members' clubs, from the elite Muthaiga Club, where Waugh had stayed and where the liaisons of the Happy Valley set had taken place, to the Railway Club, which had, in the pre-independence years, served as a downmarket alternative. The Aero Club served the needs of bush pilots who, like my father, swarmed in and out of the private Wilson airport on their way to destinations only reachable by light aircraft, and its walls are a gallery of those East African aviators – including Beryl Markham, the first pilot to cross the Atlantic flying westwards – who have made it their home over the years. The club is unremarkable in appearance, merely a bungalow and a compound fenced off from the parade of Cessnas and de Havillands landing outside; but the Members' Bar has a mythic quality, an unmistakable affinity to Falstaff's Eastcheap tavern that is made all the more uncanny by the presence of Kenya's Prince Hal, Uhuru Kenyatta. This has only partly to do with the slender legs and generous paunches of your average bush pilot, or the endless chits that disappear behind the bar for some later reckoning, or the list of members excluded for non-payment, or the endless panegyrics to strong drink, which makes the blood 'course from the inwards to the parts extreme' and 'illumineth the face, which, as a beacon, gives warning to all the rest of this little kingdom, man, to arm' (2 *Henry IV*, IV.ii.97–9). It is, rather, the way in which the stories of *derring-do* expand into the room as the teller warms to his theme, calling across the bar for some expert witness to corroborate the fact that such-and-such a landing strip (landing strip? D' y' reckon *that* was a landing strip?) was then by no means the novice's training run that it is now – even now, when it is mostly rocks and no one to chase away the buffalo – and the crosswinds, *believe me*, man ('What, art thou mad? Art thou mad? Is not the truth the truth?'), and cursing this bad world in which manhood is forgotten, to the gales of laughing drinkers returning to their conversations. Uhuru Kenyatta realized the hope and expectation of the time by becoming the fourth President of Kenya during the writing of this book, and I would lay money that there is a drinker or two at the bar who thinks he has forgotten them.

Peter Abrahams's *A Wreath for Udomo* is all the more astonishing for the fact that it was written in 1956 – before any of these countries had won independence and decades in advance of the political defeats he predicts with such accuracy. The story is, in a sense, another version of Blixen and Bohannan's multiculturalism, a warning of what lies in wait for Africa if it does not effect a full separation from English culture. For all the starkness of its warning, though, Abrahams's novel is not a battle cry but rather a deeply ambivalent account of the complex emotional ties between the powerful and the disempowered, between the servant and the master, and in this respect it is deeply Shakespearean. Shakespeare was himself a servant – one of the Lord Chamberlain's 'Men' and then one of the King's. Much of the force of this fact is lost on us today because we think of actors and playwrights as people of great prestige and cultural power. But in Shakespeare's England such 'players' were barely distinguishable from vagrants – indeed the law treated them as the same in many respects – and the only way that they could stay on the right side of the law was to take the livery of a powerful person, becoming, in effect, their servants. Remembering this draws our attention to the over-whelming presence of servitude in Shakespeare's plays, a feature that is often forgotten in a modern world so uncomfortable with a relationship that blends the power to command with such intimacy. The most famous expressions of love in the English language, after all, are Shakespeare's sonnets to the 'master-mistress of his passion', the unnamed patron who is both master and lover.

Shakespeare's plays have a similar obsession with master–servant relations, and (what's more) one that evolved as Shakespeare the servant himself became more wealthy and successful. The early plays feature fantasies of the master and servant switching places – as Tranio and Lucentio do in *The Taming of the Shrew* – and of servants who 'marry up', as Viola does in *Twelfth Night* and Helen does in *All's Well That Ends Well*. The portrayals of 'marrying up' in Shakespeare's early plays, however, stay inside the bounds of what was acceptable to his society by having only *women* enter into sexual relations with their social superiors. When men try to do this – as when the steward Malvolio conceives a passion for his mistress, Olivia, in *Twelfth Night* – they are exposed as upstarts and roundly mocked. In this respect not much had changed between Shakespeare's society and the twentieth century; it's hard not to think that *My Fair Lady* was a popular comedy and *Lady Chatterley's Lover* was a scandal in part because women having sex across social boundaries was fine and men doing it was threatening. By the time of the later plays, however, Shakespeare was himself a part-owner of his theatrical company, a landlord with significant holdings and even the possessor of a coat of arms, a status symbol which entitled him to be addressed as 'Master', and for which *he* was mocked as an upstart by many of his contemporaries. Two of these late plays are centrally concerned with *men* who attempt to marry above themselves. In the first of these, *Cymbeline*, the heir apparent to the throne marries 'a poor but worthy gentleman', prompting her father to exile him and set in motion the events of the play. The other play, *The Tempest*, delves more deeply into the fear of upstart men by adding race to the mix. As the play opens we find the native Caliban in a state of slavery, though it becomes clear that his relations with Prospero were not always this way: Prospero claims at first to have treated Caliban 'with humane care, and lodged [him] / In mine own cell' (I.ii.346–7). This intimacy is cemented by Miranda's desire that they should have a shared language and culture as well as shared lodgings:

> When thou didst not, savage,
> Know thine own meaning but wouldst gabble like
> A thing most brutish, I endowed thy purposes
> With words that made them known.

The Tempest (I.ii.354–7)

Caliban has been degraded to the status of a chained slave, whose labour is compelled by pain rather than encouraged by reward, because he presumed to cast a desiring eye on Prospero's daughter. Caliban, however, does not accept this judgement lying down, and turns the tools of his master against him:

You taught me language, and my profit on't
Is I know how to curse. The red plague rid you
For learning me your language!

Blixen and Bohannan hoped that by demonstrating African imper-
viousness to Shakespeare they would slow the progress of Western
culture and its claims to be universal. But for Udomo, as for
Caliban, it is too late: whether or not the culture of the master had
any claims to be universal, it is clearly dominant, and it is now
indelibly part of their heritage too. Caliban, however, shows that
accepting this is not the same as letting the master have his own
way in everything. Caliban, like Harry Thuku, knew that education
could be a tool that the teacher sharpened against himself.

In one of the little ironies of history, Blixen's late-life fame
inspired a number of projects to track down her servants and hear
their side of the story about her years in Kenya. One of these, by
the photographer Peter Beard, led to the houseboy Kamante entering into a correspondence with Jacqueline Kennedy Onassis; I met
the author of another, Tove Hussein, on the terrace of the Muthaiga
Club, where Blixen had first stayed on arrival in Kenya almost a
century before. During our conversation I am reminded that one
of the last things Blixen wrote before she died was an adaptation of
The Tempest, in the form of a short story called 'Tempests'
published in 1958 in a collection called *Anecdotes of Destiny*. This
tale sees Malli Ross, the abandoned daughter of a Scottish seaman,
join a troupe of coasting Nordic actors whose impresario casts her
as Ariel in his long-dreamt-of production of Shakespeare's play.
The production is sidelined, however, when the troupe are shipwrecked during a storm off a Norwegian fishing port. Though the
rest of the actors make it to shore safely, Malli is left on board ship,
only to win herself an almost mythical status when she (like Ariel)

steers the craft to the safety of a nearby island. There Malli's path changes from that of Ariel to that of Miranda; she falls in love with the island's most eligible bachelor. After a brief period of bliss, however, she absconds. She explains in her parting letter what she now understands: that she braved the storm because it was nothing but a stage effect to her, and her free spirit with which he had fallen in love was in fact a part of her disengagement from the world. This, she sees, is the magic of Prospero, who can control the world because it is nothing but a stage play to him. Falling in love has removed her power because she now sees the world as others do, with a deep-seated fear of loss.

The figure of Caliban is noticeably missing from Blixen's retelling of *The Tempest*. Perhaps this was because, like Malli and the storm, she could no longer lightheartedly treat matters about Africa – and indeed she would never write about Africa in her fiction. Perhaps, though, it was because Caliban *is* the island-dwelling man with whom Malli falls in love.

6

KAMPALA

Shakespeare at School, at War and in Prison

Then the whining schoolboy with his satchel
And shining morning face, creeping like snail
Unwillingly to school. And then the lover,
Sighing like furnace, with a woeful ballad
Made to his mistress' eyebrow. Then a soldier,
Full of strange oaths, and bearded like the pard,
Jealous in honor, sudden and quick in quarrel,
Seeking the bubble reputation
Even in the cannon's mouth. And then the justice,
In fair round belly with good capon lined,
With eyes severe and beard of formal cut,
Full of wise saws and modern instances,
And so he plays his part.

As You Like It (II.vii.145–57)

The truncated account of the seven 'stages' of life given by 'melancholy Jaques' in *As You Like It* is funny in part because of the cutting accuracy with which it reduces each age in men's lives to a few commonplace attributes. Men – and it is specifically *men* here – are entirely simple and predictable, even though their experience of these life stages is as of things newly discovered, emerging from unique and powerful passions. Jaques is being cynical, suggesting that man's life is no more than a series of parts and therefore of no more worth than a stage show. But as is so often the case in Shakespeare, Jaques is being played for a fool: what he takes to be the triumph of nihilism, proof-positive of life's absurd lack of meaning, is in fact a gesture to a compelling affirmation of life. Perhaps life *is* worth no more than a stage play, giving us mere outward show and performed parts, and requiring from us an infinite suspension of disbelief; but can't a stage play, like the one you are experiencing even now, be filled with passion and significance and wonder, all the more beautiful in that it has been conjured from nothing by make-believe and sleight of hand? This trick is everywhere in Shakespeare. Macbeth dismisses life as a 'poor player, a walking shadow / That struts and frets his hour upon the stage, / And then is heard no more' (V.v.23–5), but the very speech he is speaking is still being heard four centuries later, and even now refutes the idea of him as a mere 'shadow'. Hamlet scorns 'actions that a man might play' (I.ii.84), but is later inspired by a player to some of his most powerful and immortal lines – themselves, of course, part of a play. In part Shakespeare's genius lies in his ability to capture the paradoxical thing that Jaques misses – the experience of the universal as something particular. Romeo and Juliet are *every* pair of young lovers and Lear is every 'foolish, fond old man', but Shakespeare never assumes that common experience is commonplace; for them, as for each of us, our most profound and overwhelming experiences are almost always ones widely shared in some form or other. So reading Shakespeare is often like hearing Jaques's speech: we recognize, sometimes with astonishment, how perfectly he has captured stages of life through which we have passed, and gives us some sense of those that are to come. And because Shakespeare's plays are among the only works to which we still return at various stages of our life, reading them can be something like an ongoing revelation: each time we return to them, we find some new truth that wasn't there the last time we looked.

One of the most striking things I found as I followed Shakespeare on his travels through East African history was the fact that the works were present at every stage of life in the region during the very period when the region was struggling to free itself from colonial rule. The plays were set as compulsory reading at school, yes, but they were not dispensed with after that as nothing more than rote learning. Many – even *most* – of those who would go on to become post-independence political, social and cultural leaders went on to study English literature at Makerere University, where the emphasis was heavily on the reading and performance of Shakespeare's plays. And though this odd fact in itself was the result of a curious set of historical circumstances, these readers of Shakespeare did not simply shake off their reading after graduation as so much colonial propaganda. Instead, they took Shakespeare with them out into the world, and he was woven into every part of the fabric of African life, into the speeches of politicians and lawyers, but also into the folklore of rural villages. Shakespeare even followed in times of crisis, into riots and guerrilla warfare and into concentration camps. Yet any temptation to write this love of Shakespeare off, as merely a self-loathing attempt to be like the colonial masters even as they overthrew them, is quickly dispelled as the trail is followed: these are wholehearted commitments to reading Shakespeare, and ones as likely to Africanize his works as to preserve him as a pristine European fetish. Intrigued by what the ongoing revelation of Shakespeare would have been like for people in such extreme circumstances, I headed for Makerere University in Kampala, where African cultural and political life converged in the middle years of the last century.

I arrive in Kampala sick as a dog, and Kampala is not the place to be sick. I remember thinking even as a child that Kampala was an uncanny and rather forbidding town, and my swimming head and cold sweats do nothing to shake this impression. The chief Ugandan city is perched, like a tropical Rome, on a series of dark-green hills a little way inland from Lake Victoria; the mid-continental air is heavy and humid, and the town is overrun with marabou storks, massive and funereal scavengers which stand on every avocado tree and telephone pole, like morticians in need of work. Travelling around the city means swooping from hill to hill via the gullies in between, constantly swarmed by the motorcycle taxis which serve as the main mode of transport. Kampala is where the early missionary and colonial settlements chose to make their base in order to set themselves apart from the royal Buganda homestead at Entebbe. When the centre of power shifted from the Kabakas (kings) to the European settlers, local tribes gathered around the Kampala missions, converting long-standing tribal enmity into enmity between Catholic and Protestant converts, who fought 'religious' wars here in the late 1880s and early 1890s. Kampala was to see darker days still after independence; my mother was here studying and teaching at Makerere in the 1970s when the first President, Milton Obote, was overthrown in a military coup by Idi Amin, and the Makerere campus still bears the scars of the fighting. Amin had spent his childhood working as a kitchen boy for the British Army, and between that and his Scottish missionary education developed a violent dislike for the English. He promoted a climate of fear in Uganda, starting with the expulsion of Asian residents and proceeding to the torture and execution of his political opponents, as well as to rumours of cannibalism which Amin himself delightedly encouraged.

After a day of sitting in a clinic waiting room, my paranoia not helped by the outbreak of Ebola virus in Uganda the previous summer, I learn to my relief that I do not have malaria, but rather a double bill of tonsillitis and dysentery, brought on (I imagine) by the acacia gum that I shared with a Maasai guide while *bundu-bashing* (bush-walking) a few days previously. And though I know it is probably down to my delirium, the oddity of Kampala still dogs me. When I came here as a child, I was given a thick roll of banknotes for my pocket money, only to discover that this would scarcely buy me one of the freshly bootlegged Michael Jackson tapes which were sold on every street corner. The disconcerting singularity of Uganda impresses me now as well. A taxi driver proudly tells me that the Queen has visited Uganda more than any other African country, and drives me to a clock and a luxury hotel erected for her visit; but he does so with such fanaticism as to be vaguely threatening. The feeling of an alien land is further exacerbated by the fact that I don't speak the language. There was an attempt by the colonial authorities to make the coastal Swahili that their officials already spoke a *lingua franca* here, but it met with only moderate success: the Buganda had a long, proud history, and weren't about to drop their tongue for a mongrel merchant *patois*. Luganda is an odd language, with long words and too many vowels, and the few words I can say make me feel like I am speaking in tongues.

Half-crazed and weak as I am, I have limited time in Kampala, and so I drag myself unwillingly to the Makerere University Library in search of the Shakespeare that East Africa's freedom fighters came to love here as students. Makerere is draped across one of Kampala's hills, descending from where the Italianate palazzo of its

Main Building, with its red-tiled roof and bell tower, gives way to the more practical concrete structures of its post-independence heyday. The whole, however, seems always on the point of being overwhelmed by plant life, and the early accounts of students here feasting on the campus avocado trees bears a touching similarity to the original 'Academy', where Aristotle learned from Plato under the trees of a sacred olive grove. The university once had the greatest library in eastern Africa, but it had been rifled and left to rot under Idi Amin, and is only now slowly beginning to recover. I do manage to track down copies of the college magazine, and from this a picture of these crucial pre-independence years begins to emerge. Literature played little part in the curriculum during the first years after the foundation of Makerere College in the 1920s, with the focus being largely on providing practical education to Africans as farmers and minor functionaries. A precise date for the rise of a literary culture on campus is hard to give, in part because the wartime paper rationing meant that no college annual was printed between 1941 and 1946, the years during which future Shakespeare translator and first President of Tanzania Julius Nyerere was studying there to be a teacher. But by the time the annual resumed there seems to have been a flourishing culture of Shakespeare reading under the tutelage of a newly arrived English lecturer, Margaret MacPherson. The 1947 issue of *Makerere* notes public readings of *Julius Caesar*, *As You Like It* and *Hamlet*, and there appears to have been a pseudo-Shakespearean skit (*The Two Gentlemen of Soho*) performed that year as well. The real watershed, however, came in the summer of 1948, when MacPherson and the English department began producing an annual full-length Shakespeare play. MacPherson clearly had an extraordinary eye for charisma, and her casting over the succeeding years predicts with astonishing accuracy the vanguard of independent East African life. The title role of the 1948 *Julius Caesar* was played by none other than Apollo Milton Obote, who would become the first President of Uganda.[1] The next year's production, *Richard II*, was led by an 'outstanding performance' as the weak king by Geoffrey Kariithi, who would go on to become the head of the Kenyan Civil Service. The role of Falstaff in the 1952 *Henry IV Part II* was taken on by James Rubadiri, who (as David Rubadiri) would later become one of Africa's leading writers and intellectuals and a leader of the Malawian resistance against the eccentric dictator Hastings Banda. And, since Makerere began admitting female students in 1945, these productions featured performers of both sexes. A review in the annual notes a brilliant performance of Volumnia in *Coriolanus* by a Zanzibari girl, Assiah Jabir, though Margaret MacPherson notes elsewhere that her fellow Islamic islanders forbade her to act in a Sheridan play. MacPherson suggests that this distinction was made because Sheridan was not part of the course, though Sheridan's status as an outlaw – outside the course as well as the pale for Islamic students – most likely had something to do with the raunchiness of his plays (something that wouldn't have been a problem with the sexless Volumnia).[2] The Ugandan theatre was to have a long reign in testing the boundaries of East African sexual culture: when the future journalist and activist Yasmin Alibhai-Brown took the female lead in a 1960s school production of *Romeo and Juliet* she was disowned by some of her family for her stage affair with a black Romeo.[3]

The expat lecturers who write the performance reviews in the Makerere annual are convinced that these actors are coming to Shakespeare for the first time, but by now I am primed to spot this obsessive tendency on the part of English travellers to think that they are introducing the Genius of Shakespeare to the benighted natives. In fact, though the teaching staff of Makerere might have insisted on thinking of their students as parochial, most of these students represented the African social elite, and they came to

Makerere from exclusive boarding schools such as the Alliance High School in Kenya and Tabora Boys' School in Tanzania. James Ngugi, who came to Makerere from Alliance in 1960, spoke bitterly during the culture wars of the late 1970s (under his re-Africanized name Ngugi wa Thiong'o) of 'Shakespeare in Colonial Trousers', though he later recalled with more affection the annual all-male Shakespeare productions at Alliance. Ngugi remarks that even as a schoolchild he mapped the Shakespeare he was watching and reading onto contemporary African politics, imagining that the band of woodland exiles in *As You Like It* were the Mau Mau rebels with whom his brother was encamped in the northern highlands.[4]* Ngugi's first major piece of writing, the play *Black Hermit*, was put on at Makerere in 1962, and was written in response to the dominance of Shakespeare on the East African stage.

The Makerere Shakespeare productions were not, however, the naïve productions that the English lecturers imagined them to be. The review of Milton Obote's performance as Caesar is rather dismissive, saying that he 'did not achieve sufficient dignity except in his last speeches to the senate', and that his murder was 'clumsily managed', 'drawing laughter from some of the audience'.[5] We further learn that the most satisfactory performance was given by the 'crowd', who played both the Roman rabble and Brutus's army, in which guise several of them appeared dressed as members of the King's African Rifles. But photographic evidence, found for me by the University Archivist, tells a different story. A striking and little-known image shows Obote, instantly recognizable by his distinctive coiffure, sitting on a dais in front of the Italianate main university buildings, as a traitor kneels before him. The moment is

---

* Ngugi's recollections, in the second volume of his memoirs *In the House of the Interpreter* (1950–53) are echoed by many other major East African novelists, such as Abdulrazak Gurnah (*Desertion*, pp. 146–7 and 214–15, and *By the Sea*, p. 177) and M. J. Vassanji (*The Book of Secrets*, p. 246).

instantly identifiable as the one in which Caesar, 'constant as the Northern Star', protests his steadfastness to the treacherous men who are about to murder him. This image seems prescient of the momentous things that were stirring even as the production was rehearsed, and of which the reviewer was unaware when he dismissed it: at the same time as learning Caesar's lines, Obote was forming a political organization to stage protests against the Ugandan Lukiko elite as puppet-tyrants for the colonial overlords. In the light of these events, which would grow into the Ugandan independence movement, it is not surprising that the murder of the tyrant Caesar at the hands of a mob of deserting African soldiers drew a laugh from the crowd. And in a moment of supreme historical irony, the tables were soon to be turned on the reviewers of the student *Caesar*. As the protests heated up on campus, the faculty members resorted to wearing helmets and shields to protect themselves from the stones hurled by Obote's protesters, the very ones that had been fashioned from oil drums to serve as legionaries' costumes in *Julius Caesar*.[6]

The Makerere Shakespeare productions were, then, a cultural centrepiece at the beating heart of East African intellectual life, in a period when the students and faculty counted among their numbers not only future independence leaders but also leading African public figures and international celebrities who would take the African Question to the wider world. The leading Kenyan historian Alamin Mazrui and the future theatre director Okot p'Bitek became members of the faculty in the 1950s, and they were joined by the American novelist and travel writer Paul Theroux early in the 1960s, who overlapped with the future Nobel Laureate V. S. Naipaul during his period as writer-in-residence there in 1966. In an age when the greatest challenge facing African independence was the need to develop inter-tribal solidarity and overcome the divide-and-conquer tactics of the colonial administration, it is thrilling to note that the Makerere Shakespeare productions, which seem to have acted as a breeding ground for political figures and movements, were truly pan-African. The reviewer of the 1949 *Richard II* notes that over twenty different tribes were involved in the production; this trifling 'stage play', then, would have given many emerging leaders their first experience of organization along national and international lines, even as they played at killing tyrants. The colonial authorities clearly also recognized the capacity of theatre to foster political organization, and when they took over the Gikuyu schools from the native administrators at the beginning of the Kenyan independence movement they immediately cut performance from the syllabus.[7]

Though the students at Makerere were drawn from the East African elite, the reach of these Shakespeare productions was by no means restricted to a small audience of university students. The review of the 1949 *Richard II* notes that the play was chosen because it was on the 1950 Cambridge Examinations syllabus, and that 2000 schoolchildren saw the play during the course of its five performances. Their familiarity with these school texts would have a profound effect on East African cultural life; *Richard II* was, incidentally, the text on which I also sat my end-of-school exams, and I can testify that one never gets to know any other text quite as fully and intimately as these. The vast majority of these witnesses did not, of course, go on to be leading public figures. But they did fan out across the region and through them Shakespeare trickled down into the groundwater of East African life. Back at the Aero Club in Nairobi the great Shakespearean actor John Sibi-Okumu had told me over dinner that he first heard the plot of *Julius Caesar* as if it were a local legend, recounted to him by his Uncle Daniel, who had returned to their small village from boarding school. Abasi Kiyimba, a professor at Makerere who works on Ugandan folklore, confirms that this is a common experience: he remembers how as

144

a schoolchild he and his peers would contribute to evening story-telling sessions by adding their own versions of stories learned at school, from the Lambs' *Tales from Shakespeare*. Shakespearean narrative, he tells me, blended easily with the traditional folklore of the older generation: the moving Birnam Wood that comes to defeat Macbeth was just another version of the traditional *Kibate* stories of forests that come to life; and Portia's triumph over Shylock found a ready audience in a culture rich in trickster tales. There is even a similar one, in which the moneylender is duped into receiving stones (*ejjinja*) when he believes he will be paid in a particular town (Rejinja). *Lear* made its way into Buganda folklore, as a traditional narrative in which the apparently prodigal child is revealed to be the most reliable one; and *The Taming of the Shrew* was cited by the elders as proof that even the Europeans were departing from their traditional ways in allowing women greater liberties. Shakespeare was not alone in this – Abasi tells me that Chinua Achebe's groundbreaking 1958 novel *Things Fall Apart* circulated more widely by word of mouth than as a printed text during his childhood – but he does seem to have been pre-eminent. In a culture where memory is communal and is shared orally, these evening storytelling sessions represented nothing less than Shakespeare entering the fabric of East African life, blending irreversibly with traditional stories and the world as understood by them.

Many of the leading figures in the East African independence movements, then, had a primarily literary education, and their first experiences of intellectual debate and community organization came through discussions and productions of Shakespeare's plays. Following the story of these figures from their school days into the fray of revolutionary politics, it becomes clear that they were forced to use the tools they had at their disposal, to turn what they had received as the totem of British civility into a weapon all the more dangerous for its closeness to the British heart.[8] I've come across dozens of instances of this in the archives from the independence days of the early 1950s and 1960s, such as when the first African member of the Kenya Legislative Council, Eliud Wambu Mathu, used *The Merchant of Venice* to put the injustices of the colonial government in their own language. Mathu was one of the first Kenyan Africans to be educated to secondary level, and he went on to be the first African master at the elite Alliance High School before leaving for further study at the University of Exeter and at Balliol College, Oxford (supported by none other than the Rhodes Trust); while in Britain he spent his weekends in London staying with Kenyatta and associating with the leaders of George Padmore's International African Service Bureau. His fifteen years on the Legislative Council after his return to Kenya, where he was driven by the conciliationist ideas of his idol, Booker T. Washington, have led many historians to characterize him as a puppet of the colonial administration, a piece of window dressing which allowed the pretence that the African population was being consulted to continue. But it is evident from the transcripts of the debates in the Legislative Council that Mathu was intent on embarrassing the colonial government on its own terms. During a 1955 session in which the colonial administration attempted to renew a tax that disproportionately affected the Gikuyu tribe by asking them for money while restricting their ability to work – its real intention being to drain the financial resources of the Gikuyu Mau Mau militant group – Mathu responded by turning the white man's mantras against him:

MATHU: . . . Sir, I am afraid of this [legislation] because I do not want the Government and this legislature to be accused of being like Shakespeare's Shylock, the Jew, and Bassanio in *The Merchant of Venice*.

Here we are making a bond in the way of an Ordinance for 1956 and the Jew, in this case the government, is going to demand before 31st December, 1956, a pound of flesh in the form of the tax. The question is this: Antonio is not there, so who is going to pay? Because the cargo is delayed, because the ship cannot come in to shore on time, and that is just the point here. Now the cargo is being waited for and the cargo, in my opinion, which is going to come in order to pay Shylock, the Jew, the pound of flesh, is the opportunity for earning a decent and legitimate livelihood by these people. The question is who is our Bassanio, Sir, and who is Portia to give the judgement. (Applause)

THE MINISTER FOR AFRICAN AFFAIRS: Mr Speaker, I do not propose to bandy Shakespeare with my hon. friend . . .⁹

Mathu's clever analogy, between the moneylender who hopes his creditor will default so he can have power over him and the government that lays a trap for its subjects by instituting a tax it knows they cannot pay, evidently struck a powerful chord with those who were listening. The time Mathu spent in Britain was likely enough to convince him that the British could not stand being shown their own villainy as reflected in one of their most cherished morality tales. Like Caliban cursing Prospero in his own language, Mathu and other political agitators became adepts at using the colonials' cultural totems against them.

While the public demonstrations which led to nationalism in Tanzania and Uganda were largely peaceful affairs, not all the struggle took place in Legislative Councils and courtrooms. The rising of the anti-colonial Mau Mau Gikuyus in Kenya, at its height between 1952 and 1956, made a reality of the worst nightmares of the colonial administration, and their reaction was swift and brutal. A state of emergency was declared, and the Mau Mau practice of using traditional oaths to bind members to revolutionary solidarity was outlawed; in the imagination of settlers and Europeans back home, these native forms of affiliation were recast as superstition, witchcraft and a regress to savagery from the 'modern' forms of the colonial period. Over the coming decade a million Gikuyus were held in concentration camps and enclosed villages, where they were subjected to physical torture and psychological warfare in the name of 'retraining'. The scale of British wrongdoing during the Emergency is only now coming to light, as reams of previously classified documents come into the public domain.[10]

Heartbreaking as the stories from inside the camps and prisons are, there are also a number of inspiring stories of detainees refusing to be bestialized by the conditions in which they were kept by colonial and apartheid regimes in Africa. The most famous case of this is perhaps on Robben Island, a penal colony off Cape Town, where in the late 1970s Nelson Mandela and thirty-three other political detainees marked their favourite Shakespearean passages in a copy of the *Works* that was passed around among the prisoners and became known as 'The Robben Island Bible'.[11] The passages chosen by the prisoners are often from the Roman plays and the history plays, marking out sections in which some parallel to their own political struggle and imprisonment can be seen; but there are also selections that turn entirely away from the circumstances of captivity, that find in Shakespeare a total escape from the prison island and its daily routines. Mandela signed his name on 16 December 1977, fifteen years into his three-decade detention, next to Julius Caesar's famous lines on the resilience of the brave:

Cowards die many times before their deaths;
The valiant never taste of death but once.
Of all the wonders that I yet have heard,

It seems to me most strange that men should fear,
Seeing that death, a necessary end,
Will come when it will come.

Julius Caesar (II.ii.32–7)

It is extraordinarily moving that Shakespeare's pithy distillation of classical stoicism should have been given voice by the most famous and triumphant survivor of racial oppression in Africa. One cannot help but feel that, whereas the prisoner in monochrome garb most likely felt himself uplifted by Shakespeare's venerated words, the blessing is in fact the other way around: the love for Shakespeare of Mandela and other African political prisoners in some way purifies the works, removing from them some of the taint of their use as a tool of psychological warfare and cultural colonization.

The very power of dramatic writings to mingle with the thoughts of those speaking them, however, made them a more sinister tool in the hands of those charged with 'rehabilitating' the Mau Mau detainees in the Kenyan camps. If great lines of verse can give expression to feelings that might otherwise be difficult – or danger-ous – to articulate, they can also be forced upon people, putting words in their mouths in hopes that these will stick in their hearts and minds. This is an idea as old as rote-learning and catechizing, and everyday language provides plenty of instances of how what we say and what we think are often seen as interchangeable: a 'creed' is both our belief and the specific form of words we must learn to express that belief, and to 'sing from the same hymn sheet' or to 'be on the same page' is not merely to be experiencing the same words but also to be taking them into us and making them part of how we view the world. This was one of the main reasons why Steere and his fellow missionaries were determined to be the first to produce standardized, authoritative writing systems for native languages; he who wrote the hymn book would hold a powerful sway over the minds of those singing from it.

The colonizers would not, however, have everything their own way. As we have all experienced, from childhood onwards, what sticks with us most powerfully from songs, poems and speeches is not so much the specific words as the non-semantic elements of language – rhythm, syntax, rhyme. We have all, I am sure, inserted new words into famous lines and felt how the power of the original carries over into the dubbed version; this was a common phenomenon even in Shakespeare's day, when popular songs were rewritten to have political or spiritual messages, piggybacking on the fact that the verses already had a place in the popular memory. The native African political movements availed themselves of this power by altering the words of Christian hymns and colonial anthems in native languages to become their first expressions of resistance, doubtless revelling in the fact that their fervour could not only be expressed in the open in front of uncomprehending colonial officials, but would even be mistaken for expressions of piety and nationalism.[12] They might, indeed, have echoed Shakespeare's powerful formulation on how song can reverse the polarity of power:

> . . . our cage
> We make a choir, as doth the prisoned bird,
> And sing our bondage freely.

> *Cymbeline* (III.iii.42–4)

The central Mau Mau practice of 'oathing' similarly blended the ancient tribal rituals that bound the individual to his age peers with the legal and spiritual forms of swearing that had been brought to Africa by the colonizers.

So when the colonial government rounded up tens of thousands of suspected Mau Mau fighters in October 1952 they were concerned not merely to put anti-government forces out of commission but to reverse their loss of power over the things that were spoken in Kenya Colony. In addition to separation from families, physical brutality and forced labour, the detainees were subjected to mass 'confessions' of having taken part in the 'oathing' process, replacing formulas of allegiance to Mau Mau with formulas of penance and repudiation. In a bizarre turn of events, the very people who had been responsible for transforming Christian hymns into songs of Mau Mau protest were now ordered by the rehabilitation teams to recast them again as anti–Mau Mau propaganda.[13]

Language, though, is a slippery thing, and will not always behave as we want it to. If being forced to repeat words can sometimes instil belief in the speaker, it can also draw our attention to the fact that there is more going on than what is being said. Agreeing to 'play our part' means falling into line and doing what we are told, but it also alerts us to the fact that we are merely *playing a part* – play-acting rather than doing for real. Hamlet has often been seen to represent a breakthrough in human thinking about selfhood, in many ways not because he says anything groundbreaking about what it is like to be a person but rather because he suggests we *can't* say anything about the important parts of selfhood. Everything that *can* be performed – speech, gesture, emotion – is necessarily open to fabrication, and so the authentic part of us must be something that cannot be performed. Hamlet, more than anything else, has 'that within which passeth show', and his attitude to everything external is tinged with that kind of ironic distance with which modern audiences find it so easy to identify. Yet this insight into the distance between what we say (or do) and who we are releases Hamlet to be Shakespeare's most theatrical character, one who not only spends much of the play pretending to be mad (which he thinks of as putting on an 'antic disposition', or playing the part of a theatrical fool), but who is also – in his additions to the 'play-within-a-play', *The Mousetrap* – the only playwright character in Shakespeare.

This may help to explain the fact that the rehabilitation programme not only failed to end the antipathy of the detainees to white colonial rule, but also gave rise to some of the first theatrical writing in East African languages. This drama was, to be clear, mandated by the camp wardens and was in itself meant to be part of the rehabilitation programme, intended both to test the extent to which the detainees had repudiated their former views and to re-stage history, forcing the audience to watch their confederates revile Mau Mau with the same lips that once sang its praises. Although it is impossible to weigh one form of persecution against another, to say whether this brainwashing was worse than the physical brutality to which the inmates were subjected, there seems to be a particular darkness to the British using theatre in this vindictive manner. In Shakespeare's day there was a popular apho-rism expressing this bleak kind of fall from grace: *corruptio optimi pessima* ('the corruption of the best is the worst'). There is, they recognized, a kind of special defilement in making your most cher-ished things the engine of evil.

Some consolation may be taken from the fact that this part of the programme also seems to have failed dismally. Gakaara wa Wanjaū, one of the authors who had been tasked with rewriting his own anti-colonial hymns and with producing pro-British propa-ganda plays, recounts joyfully the performance of his play in front of successively smaller and more authoritative audiences – first for the detainees and prison guards, then for the Commandant of the camp, and finally for a group of Special Branch officers.[14] The play, *Let the Guilt of His Crimes Weigh Heavily on His Conscience*, centres on a prison camp ringleader (Zakayo) who learns from a visiting priest that his family is falling apart in his absence – his former business partner has denounced his older wife to the authorities, exiled his son from the family shop, and taken up with the younger wife. Zakayo is broken by this knowledge, and his confession to the camp authorities allows him to return and salvage some of his former life, with his older wife returning from the Kamiti prison and his younger wife revealing that she has been hiding money away against his return. Had the play ended there the authorities might have been satisfied with it as a morality tale demonstrating the benefits of acquiescence and evidence of Gakaara's change of heart. But the climactic ending of the play turns the preceding narrative on its head by having the business partner, Labani, return at the moment of reconciliation and collapse at the sight of his one-time friend whom he thought to see die in prison. The 'guilt' announced in the title is not the guilt of the Mau Mau resistance fighter but rather of those who have collaborated with the colonial authorities. 'I was under the impression, from the demands for extra performances', the playwright comments with delicious irony, 'that everybody was deriving a lot of pleasure from my play.'

The camp authorities had made a mistake in choosing an inveterate rebel to write their propaganda for them: Gakaara had, as a young man, been expelled from the Alliance High School for taking part in a protest against the removal of sugar from the students' daily rations, and later agitated from within the British Army against the slave-like treatment of the black soldiers who were shedding their blood for Britain in the East African Campaign. He was, however, at Alliance long enough to have his first introduction to theatre through the school's heavily Shakespearean drama and reading programme, and it is hard not to see in his play's conclusion an echo of those Shakespearean plays – *The*

Tempest, Measure for Measure, Cymbeline, Macbeth – that end with a central villain collapsing under the weight of their guilt.

For all that the colonial authorities did little to bring the Gikuyu around to their way of thinking, their campaign against the Mau Mau uprising did succeed in sowing discord among the many different constituencies who wished for an end to British rule, revealing stark differences in how each group saw Kenya's future and its place in the world. One of the most fascinating episodes of the Emergency saw two of these contending visions come face to face during the trial of Jomo Kenyatta, where the authorities employed as their Gikuyu translator none other than the celebrated fossil-hunter Louis Seymour Bazett Leakey. The trial was, in effect, a shock-and-awe campaign by the British government intended to nip the independence movement in the bud. Although Kenyatta had aspirations for a political route towards African independence that set him apart from the Mau Mau militants, he refused to accede to British demands that he publicly denounce the Mau Mau. In order to avoid making the trial a focus of anti-colonial sentiment, it was held in remote Kapenguria on the Ugandan border, thirty miles away from the nearest communications and drinking water.

Despite the fact that they were seated on opposite sides of the bar in this desert tribunal, Leakey and Kenyatta had up to this point led uncannily parallel lives. Although he was white, Leakey had been born and raised in Gikuyu country and had been inducted as a member of his Gikuyu age group a few years after Kenyatta himself had undergone the ritual; Leakey always considered himself a 'white Kikuyu', and later nominated Gikuyu as one of the languages in which he would be examined while at Cambridge. (The scarcity of Gikuyu speakers also led briefly to his being appointed his own examiner.) It is even said that he maintained throughout his life and everywhere in the world the idiosyncratic walk of the African bush, where one foot is placed in front of the other to walk the tightrope of the thin savannah paths. Kenyatta's wife had been educated at the mission school run by Leakey's sisters, and both men had written ethnographies of the Gikuyu tribe in the 1930s; there was even a confrontation between the two at a seminar Kenyatta gave at the London School of Economics, where they engaged in a heated discussion about female circumcision which, being held in Gikuyu, was wholly lost on the rest of the audience.

Their shared tribal loyalties could not, however, prevent them from formulating vastly different visions for the African future after this. Kenyatta for his part put away his former identities, including that of Shakespeare-loving English novelist, and began to mould his image as a fully African politician with no room for compromise with the culture of the colonial oppressor: he would be Jomo, not Johnstone, and his robe and sceptre would be the leopard skin and flywhisk of a Gikuyu chief. In essence Kenyatta had reached the same conclusion as Blixen in her own thinking on the Gikuyu. For African societies to grow independent and strong they must assert themselves as incompatible with the ways of their colonial masters; there could be no universal political system or set of ethical standards, and by extension no shared culture.

Leakey's thinking seems to have gone in a very different direction, though it was by no means the case that he was sympathetic to (or even quiet about) the colonial regime, for all that he was by training a palaeontologist and that he worked with the authorities against the Mau Mau. He had come in for a barrage of criticism from British reviewers when a 1936 book declared that Kenya would never be a 'white man's country', and throughout his career he would furiously refute public slights against Africa and its people with his own beliefs in African superiority. And though his career was dedicated to the ostensibly objective arena of hard science, of data collection and analysis, his chosen field of early human evolution had always been hopelessly entangled with contending beliefs about what it means to be human. This fact had been forcefully brought to the public's attention in the same year as the Kenyatta trial with the debunking of Piltdown Man, the most notorious palaeoanthropological forgery of the twentieth century. The Piltdown 'fossils', which had emerged between 1908 and 1915 from various gravel pits in East Sussex, were claimed by their discoverers as evidence not only that *man* (as distinct from various earlier evolutionary forms) had first emerged in Britain, but also that the crucial leap was a change in brain size.[15] This discovery not only promised to allow British archaeologists to claim precedence over their counterparts on the European continent, who had recently uncovered enviable specimens of Cro-Magnons and Neanderthals in France, but it also bolstered the cherished claim that it was intellectual capacity which sorted the sheep from the goats in evolutionary terms. As had once been suggested using the example of Shakespeare, the distinguishing mark of humankind was British Genius. Piltdown Man had, from the very beginning, prominent detractors among the archaeological community – including Leakey – and it was finally exposed in a 1953 *Time* article as the fraudulent assembly of a medieval human skull and an orangutan jaw.

But if Leakey was outspoken in his protests against the shoddy archaeology and wishful inferences in the Piltdown affair, there was more than a touch of ideological zeal in his own conviction that he would uncover the earliest evidence of man in East Africa. He retained a prominent strain of his parents' missionary faith alongside his scientific training and, like the Jesuit Father Teilhard de Chardin, who was involved in the Piltdown discoveries, he argued that evolution was compatible with the Christian creation story (by imagining the 'days' of God's work as millions of years). His popular accounts of human prehistory always gestured to the biblical stories on which he was raised, from *Adam's Ancestors* to his never-performed play about man's East African genesis, *Eve's Children*. There is even an unmistakably biblical air to the salt flats and desert gullies from which Leakey's revelations about man's past emerged. The overwhelming impression given by visits to these sites – Olorgesailie, Baringo, Olduvai – is of an apocalyptic landscape, flashbulb-bright and bare, the anxiety of the top crust giving way underfoot only made worse by the occasional flamingo carcass preserved in the salt.

That Leakey's claims about man's earliest ancestors living in East Africa's Rift Valley appear to have been right should not distract from the fact that his firm conviction arose in part from the same desire as the Piltdown forgers – to lay claim to mankind's origin and thus to give his East African homeland a kind of authority in the matter of what it means to be human. Even the names given to these discoveries are evidence of an attempt to bend the history of man towards Leakey's own vision: *Kenyapithecus africanus*, the Kenyan-African Man; *Homo habilis*, the man who triumphed not by his intelligence but by his handiness, his ability to survive in the bush. Leakey was always fairly frank about the political implications of his work; on the occasion of being presented with an honorary degree by the newly installed President Julius Nyerere of Tanzania, he used part of his speech to make explicit the part that palaeoanthropology could play in the fight against the apartheid regimes in South Africa and Rhodesia:

> People frequently ask me why I devote so much time to seeking out facts about man's past. . . . The past shows clearly that we all of us have a common origin and that our differences in race and colour and creed are only superficial.[16]

Louis Leakey's son Richard with the skulls of *Australopithecus* and *Homo habilis*, and Laurence Olivier as Hamlet with the skull of Yorick.

Like Steere's belief that a shared God must make a shared culture possible, palaeoanthropology offered a way past the brutal nationalism of the middle of the twentieth century by suggesting that we were, at heart, all the same. If languages and cultures could truly speak to each other, this would have to be through a shared root; but now it was not so much a divine master-language as a common genetic predecessor who gave us a similar physiological makeup. Leakey opposed to Kenyatta's stance on cultural uniqueness a vision of a shared humanity, though one which East Africa has a right to define by virtue of priority. And for all that this seems a very long way from Shakespeare, these were in essence the two visions of Africa along which the culture wars following independence would be fought – one which believed in a universal human culture to which Africa should and must stake its claim, and one which felt that such claims were mere extensions of the colonizers' power over their former subjects.

7

DAR ES SALAAM

Shakespeare in Power

BRUTUS:

Remember March, the ides of March, remember.
Did not great Julius bleed for justice' sake?
What villain touched his body, that did stab,
And not for justice? What, shall one of us,
That struck the foremost man of all this world
But for supporting robbers, shall we now
Contaminate our fingers with base bribes,
And sell the mighty space of our large honours
For so much trash as may be graspèd thus?
I had rather be a dog and bay the moon
Than such a Roman.

Julius Caesar (IV.iii.18–28)

On my first evening in Dar es Salaam I meet a teenage prostitute with the unlikely name of Agrippina. I am staying at a hotel recommended by a local friend, who probably only knows the bar for its popular weekend happy hours; during the week, however, the bar evidently serves as a place for tourists to meet local girls. It is too late for me to go anywhere else, so I sit alone at a table and try to avoid the glances of women who would not even notice me back at home. I have seen this all before – perhaps first becoming aware of it in Havana, where the achingly beautiful local girls make eyes at slovenly European men wearing money belts and floral-print shirts – but it never fails to make the throat tighten. The sad scene is only made worse by the speakers blaring Tom Petty and Bruce Springsteen songs about young couples in industrial America fighting uphill battles against poverty and low expectations. Sex tourism plagues East Africa these days, though it is little seen by the average visitor, restricting itself to particular spots reserved only for those purposes.

My attempt to read *Julius Caesar* in my copy of the *Works* is (understandably enough) seen as a pitifully thin cover-story, and after several near passes without success Agrippina sits down at my table and asks for a light. (That smoking provides entrées for prostitutes was not among the main reasons I gave it up soon afterwards.) She tells me her name and that she is nineteen, though it is obvious from her limbs that she has not yet grown that far into womanhood. Between my awkward attempts to be polite, my intrigue at her name and her tenaciousness, we speak for a little while. She is from Zanzibar and has a brother studying in Texas. In response to a question I tell her that I am married, and she laughs to hear that my wife and I are childless after three years. She tells me that she will not marry until she is forty-five, as marriage is when you have to say 'it is over'; and that she has four children – two boys and two girls – the first of whom she had when she was eleven. She can't tell me much about how she came to have such a name – the name of a Roman empress (Nero's mother and Caligula's sister), as well as of the daughter of the Agrippa who defeats the lovers at Actium in *Antony and Cleopatra*; her father, she thinks, was interested in Roman history. There is, however, an excruciating fitness to the name, which means 'born through pain'.

I am torn between desperately wanting to keep her from going about her business and feeling guilt for occupying her time when I have no intention of coming to terms with her. After a few minutes I make my excuses and return to my hotel room, refusing her offer to help me with my reading. The bar is rather empty that evening, and she is evidently deflated by the fact that her attempt has failed. The experience is, in the truest sense of the word, abysmal.

I have come to Dar on the trail of Julius Nyerere, the first President of Tanzania, who translated *Julius Caesar* and *The Merchant of Venice* into Swahili in spare evening moments during the very years that he was taking his country from British colony to independent nation and then to grand experiment in African Socialism. Biographies of Nyerere – as *Baba wa Taifa* ('Father of the Nation') – tend to be hagiographical affairs, even more so now that there is an active campaign by the large community of Tanzanian Catholics to have him canonized by the Vatican.* So although accounts of Nyerere's life routinely mention the Shakespeare translations among his achievements, and gesture proudly to their status as canonical texts in Swahili literature, there is little detail to be found on the extraordinary circumstances of their origin.

---

* At the time of writing, the Vatican has awarded Nyerere the title of 'Servant of God', which represents the first step on the road to canonization.

The fact that Nyerere found time to render more than 5000 lines of dense Shakespearean verse into Swahili is itself astonishing, given that he was at the time also negotiating the transition to independence, drafting and redrafting constitutions, setting up the Organization of African States, and spearheading pan-African efforts to end colonialism on the continent and drive Apartheid from the south. Even these activities were ones he took on in addition to the day-to-day business of running the country, and in doing so of formulating and moving towards a kind of African Socialism which he hoped would add economic independence to the new political freedoms. Nyerere came late in life to politics after a career as a teacher, and he was from early days known by the affectionate title of *Mwalimu*, 'teacher'. The endearing image of the scholar-statesman, however, does little to explain what it would have meant to translate Shakespeare of an evening while spending the days forging a new nation. Why had he chosen these specific plays, and what do these readings by a brilliant man in a unique position at a watershed moment in history reveal about the Shakespearean texts we think we know so well? He would have known these plays intimately, as perhaps only a translator can, after considering how best to preserve the dense meaning of each word and phrase as they are delicately transferred to a foreign tongue. How, then, did Shakespeare's profound treatment in these plays of tyranny, insurrection, friendship and the role played by money in our lives colour his experiences during the years he was overthrowing the colonial state and crafting a new form of African society with which to replace it? And how did it all go wrong – how did the path from *Julius Caesar* lead to the Tanzania I found today, with its Agrippinas and its endless traffic jams snaking through the slums between the main roads?

Kambarage Nyerere was born on a rainy day in April 1922 in the small village of Butiama, a little way inland from the shores of Lake

Victoria; he did not take the name 'Julius' until the age of twenty-one, when he was baptized into the Catholic faith to which he had been converted during his schooling by the missionary White Fathers.[1] He delayed his baptism until after the death of his father, a minor local chieftain who would not have approved of his son's departure from the polytheism of his ancestors. Nyerere was one of the chief's twenty-two children by one of his many wives. Following the custom of the Zanaki tribe, the wives' houses were arranged in circular wings extending away from the chieftain's house around a central *boma* enclosure, with odd-numbered wives on the left and even on the right. As the child of the chief's fifth wife, Julius Nyerere would have grown up on the left-hand side of his father's house. Life in this kind of extended family is hard to imagine for those to whom the nuclear family has come to seem almost inevitable. Ngugi wa Thiong'o writes touchingly of his childhood in a Gikuyu homestead of four wives and twenty-four children, where the children were identified by their biological mother but raised by all the mothers in a strict matriarchy.

After a largely tribal childhood, Nyerere was sent at the age of twelve to the Native Authority School in Musoma, and then (after displaying outstanding promise) to the elite Tabora Boys' School, described at the time by the visiting naturalist Julian Huxley as 'the Eton of Tanganyika'.[2] The young Nyerere was considered exceptionally bookish by boys at a school which had absorbed the sporting ethos of the English public school; in order to avoid the bemused surveillance of the other boys, he set up a study in a nearby cave, as a private retreat in which he could read undisturbed. One wonders if, even at so young an age, he would have sensed the Shakespearean significance of mixing caves and books. He later returned to Tabora as a teacher at another school (St Mary's), after taking a degree in education at Makerere College across Lake Victoria in Uganda.[3] A letter written in 1946 for the college annual, *Makerere*, upon his return to Tabora gives some flavour of the fiercely humble young man and the strong sense of duty he felt to his yet-unborn nation:

> I wonder whether it has ever occurred to many of us that while that £80 was being spent [by the government to educate] me (or for that matter on any other of the past or present students of Makerere) some village dispensary was not being built in my village or in some other village. People may actually have died through lack of medicine merely because eighty pounds which could have been spent on a fine village dispensary was spent on me, a mere individual, instead. Because of my presence at the College, (and I never did anything to deserve Makerere) many Aggreys and Booker Washingtons remained illiterate for lack of a school to which they could go because the money which could have gone towards building schools was spent on Nyerere, a rather foolish and irresponsible student at Makerere. My presence at the College therefore deprived the community of the services of all those who might have been trained at those schools, and which might have become Aggreys or Booker Washingtons. How can I ever repay this debt to the community? . . . The educated man is not important in himself; his importance lies in what he can do for the community of which he is a member.[4]

After a few years as a teacher Nyerere was sent on a government scholarship to the University of Edinburgh, where he studied politics, philosophy and economics, and where he mixed with the pan-Africanist circles around George Padmore, the same circles in which Kwame Nkrumah and Jomo Kenyatta had forged their strategies for independence and self-government.

Although Nyerere briefly continued teaching upon his return to Tanganyika, he soon turned to full-time involvement in politics, first as the president of the Dar branch of the African Association, and then in 1954 as the founding President of the Tanganyika African National Union. The success of TANU was an astonishment to all who witnessed it. While even the more progressive of colonial administrators were envisioning a move to self-government in a matter of decades, the explosive growth of its membership led to the transfer of power being repeatedly brought forward. In a speech to the UN in December 1956, Nyerere showed his considerable skill in framing the Tanzanian independence struggle for an international audience. At the same time as giving the movement deep roots and drawing on postwar anti-German sentiment by locating the genesis of nationalist sentiment in the 1907 Maji Maji rebellion against German colonial rule, Nyerere distances TANU from the revolutionary struggles led by the Mau Mau in Kenya:

> There was no nationalist movement, no nationalist agitators, or subversive Communists who went about the country stirring up trouble against the Germans. The people fought because they did not believe in the white man's right to govern and civilize the black. They rose in a great rebellion not through fear of a terrorist movement or a superstitious oath, but in response to a natural call, a call of the spirit, ringing in the hearts of all men, and of all times, educated or uneducated, to rebel against foreign domination. It is important to bear this in mind, madam, in order to understand a nationalist movement like mine. Its function is not to create the spirit of rebellion but to articulate it and show it a new technique.[5]

As might be expected, Mwalimu Nyerere's pamphleteering and speechmaking used Shakespeare quotation prominently to prick at the colonial opponent, as when he paraphrased *Julius Caesar* in a pamphlet entitled *Barriers to Democracy* to remind the colonial masters that 'men at some time are masters of their fates' (I.ii.140).[6]

The momentum of TANU was initially checked by the counter-manoeuvring of the Governor, Sir Edward Twining, who attempted to divide and conquer by promoting a rival party (the multi-racial United Tanganyika Party) and by summoning a convention of chiefs (themselves colonial appointees with a history of working for the British), as well as closing branches of TANU.[7] A moment of crisis arose when Nyerere seemed headed to prison for refusing to pay a fine after a court charged him with libelling a British District Commissioner; the fact that Tanzania did not follow the bloody path of Kenya can be attributed in part to Nyerere's resistance to being made a martyr in this way, and in part to a realization in the British administration that the time for temporizing had passed. Twining was replaced by Sir Richard Turnbull, and despite Turnbull's fearsome reputation as the 'Hammer of the Mau Mau' he and Nyerere struck up a working relationship based on what seems to have been a genuine mutual respect.

Charles Meek, a colonial official who was at the table during the transfer of power (and who later became Nyerere's Permanent Secretary), records the lightning pace at which things progressed from this point on:

> We moved from ministerial government to semi-responsible government, full internal self-government and then independence within the amazingly short period of three and a half years. We seemed to shed constitutions every six months like a kind of political striptease.[8]

Nyerere was appointed Chief Minister of a caretaker government on 1 September 1960; in December 1961 Tanganyika declared independence with Nyerere as its first Prime Minister; he became President of Tanganyika when a republic was declared exactly a year later, and President of the new country of Tanzania when Tanganyika merged with Zanzibar in 1964.

It was during these pivotal days in 1961 that the Father of the Nation began retiring from the day's work to complete his monumental Swahili translation of *Julius Caesar*, sending it to be published by the Dar branch of Oxford University Press in 1963. Scanty as they are, all sources are in agreement that Nyerere's *Caesar* was the occupation of solitary evenings, when perhaps he sought to recapture the privacy of his schoolboy cave. Meek recalls how 'In those days [Nyerere] was apt to be beset in the evenings by his political associates', and how he would often seek to escape from the hubbub of his official residence at Meek's own house. 'Inevitably we would talk over the problems of the day, but we were just as likely to discuss *Julius Caesar*, which at the time it was his diversion to be translating into the mellifluous Swahili of which he was a master. I recall a long discussion about how best to render Shakespeare's pun about "Rome and room enough".'[9]* Contemporary accounts are also largely in agreement that Nyerere's aim in making the translation was to demonstrate Swahili's capacity to serve as a great literary language, though one commentator also suggests that Nyerere was determined to make a Tanzanian contribution to the quatercentennial celebrations of Shakespeare's birth in 1964.[10] Nyerere's attempts to adapt Shakespearean blank verse met with a mixed reception, with some heralding it as a liberation from the fetters of traditional Swahili rhyme, while others saw it as a tragic abandonment of the indigenous poetic aesthetic.[11]

The most intriguing question, however, is why Nyerere should have chosen *Julius Caesar* as the play with which to spend his

---

* The pun, which is dependent on 'Rome' and 'room' being homophones in early modern English, is part of Cassius's attempt to paint Caesar as constricting Rome by reducing it to one man's fiefdom.

evenings and with which to make an argument for Swahili as one of the world's great tongues. The immediately obvious connection, between the name of the title character and of the translator, can quickly be dispensed with as a motive: Nyerere was, after all, not named after the Roman tyrant, but rather after one of the Catholic saints of the same name (as the baptismal ritual required). It is also unlikely that Nyerere would have felt much affinity with Shakespeare's character, who is the tyrant and not (like Nyerere) the tyrant-slayer. Caesar is, in more senses than one, not the hero of his own play: the assassination of this weak, vain and affected man before the half-way point of *Julius Caesar* gives way to the real heart of the play, as the battle for the hearts, minds and bodies of Rome takes place between the patriotic rebel Brutus and the cunning politician Mark Antony. The momentous course that East African history was taking at the time also does not offer any easy explanations: not only did the first reviewers deny any link between *Caesar* and the events of the day, but later attempts to read Nyerere's translation as a political allegory rely heavily on him being prescient of events that occurred *after* he published his version.[12]

The key to understanding Nyerere's choice of *Julius Caesar* lies, I think, in looking past the intrigue and assassination in the first half of the play to the conclusion for which these events prepare.[13] Like three of Shakespeare's four 'high tragedies' – *King Lear*, *Hamlet* and *Macbeth* – *Julius Caesar* is centrally concerned not just with the tragic events themselves but with living with the consequences of past upheavals: the murder of Old Hamlet, Caesar and Duncan, the disavowal of Cordelia.* In a moment that serves in

---

* Indeed *Hamlet* is *so* concerned with consequences that almost nothing happens – and almost everything that does happen does so by mistake (the deaths of Polonius, Ophelia, Laertes and the Queen, and of Rosencrantz and Guildenstern). *Othello*, like *Romeo and Juliet*, is a tragedy in which the mistake is so great that there can be no living on after it.

many ways as the emotional climax of *Julius Caesar*, Brutus, the leader of the insurrection, accuses his friend and co-conspirator Cassius of using their new power to enrich himself. Each man stands upon his dignity, Brutus disdaining to discuss the matter further with a fallen man and Cassius astonished to be turned upon by his closest friend. After a fraught scene of charge and counter-charge the men are reconciled, though it is obvious that the wound has been covered rather than cured: friendship, which is evidently central to the value the two men place on life, has been irremediably polluted by power. During the negotiations with Governor Turnbull over the transfer of power to the independent nation, Nyerere shared his premonitions that the same fate might await him. Drawing upon the experiences of his childhood, when he and his companions would break away from herding or from schoolwork to hunt small birds, Nyerere spoke of a 'certain pattern':

> When hunting there is no problem. . . . Problems start when the animal has died, that's when fighting starts, because this one wants that piece and another cuts another piece, and that's when people start to get their fingers cut.[14]

Nyerere, like Brutus, fears that he will have to choose between his friendship and his honest dealing with the country he loves. In lines that rang with Nyerere's commitment to *wakulima*, the peasant farmers of Tanzania, his Brutus said:

> Naapa ni afadhali niufue moyo wangu
> Uwe fedha, na kutoa moyo wangu uwe pesa,
> Kuliko kuikamua mikono ya wakulima
> Vitakataka vyao kwa njia ambayo ni mbaya.

By heaven, I had rather coin my heart
And drop my blood for drachmas than to wring
From the harsh hands of peasants their vile trash
By any indirection.

Julius Caesar (IV.iii.72–5)

Nyerere, who as a young man had translated the cost of his university education into the lives it could have saved, was keenly aware of the real price paid for luxuries like learning and friendship.

It is easy for us today to forget that friendship, that powerful bond inspired by shared tastes and values (and cemented by shared weaknesses), is by no means a phenomenon that has existed in the same way at all times in history and in all places.[15] While pre-urban cultures formed more binding relationships than we do, most of these were based on kinship or economic/institutional relations (master–servant, client–patron, membership of guild or parish). Friendship in a sense comes to replace these, when migration and residence in the anonymizing city mean that people begin to lose their ties to family, place of origin, or shared occupations. The idea of friendship, that one might owe one's loyalty to someone else purely on the basis of a shared set of ideas about the world, was one introduced in many ways to the modern West by Renaissance humanists, and with which Shakespeare himself was intensely concerned. A great many of Shakespeare's plays are about the very logics and limits of what (largely male) friends owe each other – Valentine and Proteus in *The Two Gentlemen of Verona*, Leontes and Polixenes in *The Winter's Tale*, Claudio and Benedick (and Hero and Beatrice) in *Much Ado about Nothing*. Shakespeare's society was one defined by fairly rigid social divisions, however, and the most powerful of these considerations of friendship deal with what happens when there is a power imbalance between the friends that threatens the ideal of a relationship based on shared values: Hal and Falstaff in the two parts of *Henry IV*, Antony and Enobarbus in *Antony and Cleopatra*, the speaker and the addressee in the Sonnets, and Hamlet and Horatio (as well as Hamlet and Rosencrantz and Guildenstern). Renaissance humanist ideals of friendship derived (as so much of the Renaissance did) from a classical pedigree, and the Roman Brutus shows himself to be a true devotee of friendship when, at the beginning of the plot to assassinate Caesar, he refuses to allow the conspirators to take an oath of loyalty:

> No, not an oath. If not the face of men,
> The sufferance of our souls, the time's abuse –
> If these be motives weak, break off betimes,
> And every man hence to his idle bed.
> So let high-sighted tyranny range on
> Till each man drop by lottery. But if these,
> As I am sure they do, bear fire enough
> To kindle cowards and to steel with valor
> The melting spirits of women, then, countrymen,
> What need we any spur but our own cause
> To prick us to redress? What other bond
> Than secret Romans, that have spoke the word
> And will not palter? and what other oath
> Than honesty to honesty engaged
> That this shall be or we will fall for it?
> Swear priests and cowards and men cautelous,
> Old feeble carrions, and such suffering souls
> That welcome wrongs. Unto bad causes swear
> Such creatures as men doubt, but do not stain
> The even virtue of our enterprise,
> Nor th'insuppressive mettle of our spirits,

To think that or our cause or our performance
Did need an oath, when every drop of blood
That every Roman bears, and nobly bears,
Is guilty of a several bastardy
If he do break the smallest particle
Of any promise that hath passed from him.

Julius Caesar (II.i.113–39)

Brutus refuses to let the bond of their shared values become cheapened by being reduced to a legal or ritual obligation, such as might be contained in a contract or a sacrament: all Romans who share the same noble beliefs are friends. They are linked by bonds as close as family ties, and betrayal will exclude them from these ties as if they were bastards.

There existed, in a sense, a direct equivalent of this friendship in the custom common to many East African tribes of ritually cementing the union between members of the same age group, forming a set whose shared identity was the product of shared experiences and not of blood ties. These bonds always exist in an uneasy relationship with the notion of family: they are always acts of voluntary association that claim a different type of allegiance from the individual to kinship, but, like the many childhood friendships I attempted to seal with blood or spit, they always reach towards the language of family relations – shared fluids and the threat of bastardy. There is more than a touch of Brutus's discomfort with this reliance on ritual in Nyerere's conscious attempt to distance himself, in his speech to the UN, from the ritual oath-swearing of the Mau Mau ('[The Tanganyikans] rose in a great rebellion not through . . . a superstitious oath, but in response to a natural call, a call of the spirit, ringing in the hearts of all men, and of all times, educated or uneducated . . .'). As

Nyerere translated *Julius Caesar*, he was experiencing, as almost no other reader of the play ever has, the core elements of Shakespeare's play: both the crucial importance of friendship and its fragility in the turbulent crucible of power from which a new state emerges.

Nyerere was right about the challenges he would face after winning the battle for independence. In part this was down to his refusal to engage in a witch-hunt against all non-Africans as vestiges of colonialism, preferring instead a conciliatory approach inspired by his other great literary idol, the black American civil rights campaigner Booker T. Washington (and mirroring the forgiveness of Brutus for those of Caesar's party). On the eve of independence, when Nyerere should have been riding a wave of popularity as liberator of his people, he was instead angrily defending to the National Assembly his Citizenship Bill, which allowed for white and Asian citizens as well as black. As Meek reported, Nyerere argued that 'his ideology he could change, his religion he could change, the one thing he couldn't change was his colour, and he rubbed his skin as he spoke. No man should be treated differently because of the one thing he could not change. He would rather resign than accept a racially defined citizenship.'[16]

Once in power, Nyerere continued to distinguish himself from many other post-independence leaders by not using his new powers to enrich himself or to consolidate power. He refused to live at the official residence, Government House, and instead built himself a relatively humble home on the beach. And though Tanzania was to be a one-party state (avoiding the tribalization which might result from many parties, as well as attempts by outsiders to play one party off against another), he was determined that it would be a participatory democracy.[17] Nyerere's main concern, however, was to develop a programme for Tanzanian society that would prevent traditional African communal ties from being eroded by rampant capitalism. As early as his Makerere days Nyerere had written passionately in the editorial pages of the *Tanganyika Standard* insisting that while the 'European tendency is to be as individualistic as possible', the African is 'naturally socialistic'.[18] The young university student's ideas were strikingly precocious, and seem to predate by some years the doctrine of 'African Socialism' as formulated by mature political thinkers. First and foremost among these was Léopold Sédar Senghor, the poet-philosopher who led Senegal to independence and became its first President. Like Senghor, Nyerere sensed that Africa did not need to follow the Marxist route to a fairer society. In large part this was because the nuclear family, which Marx saw as a bulwark of patri-archalism and private property, had never formed any part of African society. African Socialism, the theory went, would attempt to bypass the revolutionary overthrow of capitalism by simply institutionalizing the traditional, socialistic structures of the African community.[19]

As the first independent East African state and as a laboratory for progressive Africanist politics, Tanganyika was a magnet to revolutionaries from across the continent and the wider world.[20] While many of these, such as the Committee of Nine, who coordi-nated anti-colonial and anti-Apartheid struggles across the conti-nent, were in the country at Nyerere's instigation, others were not. Indeed, Nyerere was probably not even aware that the world's most wanted man – sought after by both comrades and enemies – spent his 'lost year' right under Nyerere's nose in Dar es Salaam. After helping Fidel Castro to overthrow the Batista regime in 1959, the Argentinian doctor Ernesto 'Che' Guevara quickly tired of his new establishment post (as Minister for Industry), and quietly left Cuba in April 1965 in search of new revolutions to support. His first choice was the Congo, where he joined the guerrilla forces of Laurent Kabila in their attempt to overthrow the violent dictator

Mobutu, who had himself recently ousted the independence leader Patrice Lumumba.* There followed seven months of dismal waiting, during which Che languished in the jungles of the eastern Congo, unable to stoke Kabila's troops to action (and even, increasingly, to lead his own hundred-man Cuban column effectively). Eventually he abandoned his plan to die as a martyr to violent revolution in the Congo, and allowed himself to be secreted back across Lake Tanganyika, debilitated by dysentery and with a broken spirit.

Che spent the next five or six months (October 1965 to February/March 1966) in a secret two-room apartment on the top floor of the Cuban embassy in Dar es Salaam, held in limbo as Fidel Castro tried to prevent his comrade-in-arms from having another shot at martyrdom in his native country of Argentina. (Che eventually settled on Bolivia, where he received his desired death at the hands of CIA operatives in 1967.) He spent the first few months of his confinement dictating his memoir of the Congolese campaign to the embassy's cryptographer, Colman Ferrer, calling it the 'history of a failure'. In an attempt to keep him in Dar longer, Fidel flew Che's wife, Aleida, to Tanzania, and from January to March the couple had a second honeymoon in their Dar safe house; in her later memoir, Aleida recalled the curious reunion in costume that greeted her in Tanzania:

> Che was waiting for me there, transformed into another character I almost didn't recognize. He was clean-shaven, not wearing the olive green uniform he always wore in Cuba. I, too, was incognito, extremely nervous, full of doubts. [. . .] In order to travel, I had

---

* The interest of the Cuban revolutionaries in the eastern African struggles was long-standing, as suggested by the fact that their guerrilla strike-force was nicknamed 'the Mau Mau'. See Anderson, *Che Guevara*, p. 384.

disguised myself with a black wig and glasses that made me look much older than I was. So two apparent strangers met in Tanzania, but our feelings for each other could not be disguised.[21]

Though Aleida had been spirited from landing strip to embassy, and later regretted not having seen the storied safari parks of eastern Africa, she remembered fondly the programme of reading they undertook together, with Che setting the syllabus and the two of them discussing what they had read each evening:

> Our accommodation was not particularly comfortable, but that hardly mattered. We had a single room in which we ate, slept, and studied, and a bathroom, where Che developed some of the photographs he had taken with his professional quality camera. We also returned to our regular routine. After breakfast, I would read, always with Che's guidance, and he would read or write.[22]

Che's leading biographer notes that the small library Aleida brought from Cuba in the diplomatic pouch was 'curiously apolitical': 'The Greek tragedies of Aeschylus, Sophocles, and Euripides, as well as Pindar and Aristophanes; the *Histories* of Herodotus, a manual of analytical geometry, the dramatic works of Shakespeare, and Dante.'[23] Like many African travellers before him, Che saw in the otherworldly environment of the Dark Continent the ideal location to immerse himself in high European culture. Despite his revolutionary temperament, he even brought with him the same library recommended by Burton, Roosevelt and other early travellers: the Greeks, Euclid, Dante, Shakespeare; but like Nyerere, Che hoped these books would show him the path to socialism in the Third World.[24] One cannot help but wonder whether, during his romantic African house arrest at the hands of his former comrade turned politician, Che was haunted by two of the plays that unstoppably rose to the surface in the African mid-century: *Julius Caesar*, in which the bonds of friendship are melted in the forge of nation-making, and *The Tempest*, in which the just man sequesters himself in the wild, with the books and the woman he loves, to await the day of his righteous return.[25]

During the first five years of his presidency, Nyerere was refining his programme of African Socialism, a programme that he launched in the 1967 Arusha Declaration, which outlined his plans for the nationalization of the farming industry and its redistribution among the newly fashioned communal farms which would be the bedrock of his progressive-traditional state. He was also translating his second Shakespeare play, *The Merchant of Venice*, which was published in 1969 as *Mabepari wa Venisi*. This time, Nyerere left no doubt about the motive for choosing this particular play as his second contribution to the Swahili canon. Even in the title, Nyerere's choice of 'Mabepari' (the Gujarati-derived word for 'bourgeois') to translate 'Merchant' hints at his interest in a Marxist-inspired look at the economic roots of society's ills.[26] As Marxists, Nyerere and Che would have believed less in the possibility of a universal culture and more that similar economic systems produced similar cultural forms. Shakespeare was the poet of emerging capitalism – the joint-stock companies like the East India Company (which may have performed his plays in idle moments) were an early form of this new world order – and he was perfectly placed to chart the world it created, including friendship, which was forged by its economic migration and threatened by the wealth it created. But he was also a poet of its discontents.

In one respect, there was nothing particularly groundbreaking about Nyerere's choice of a Shakespeare play to draw attention to the role of capital as the root of evil. After all, Marx himself was a declared fan of Shakespeare; his favourite play was the little known economic fable *Timon of Athens*, in which the *bon viveur* Timon is abandoned by his erstwhile parasites when the money runs out, precipitating a descent into a barking, cynical madness in which Timon recognized wealth as, in the words of Marx, 'the alienated ability of mankind'. *The Merchant of Venice* had proved the most popular of Shakespeare's economic fables, and it was often among the first plays to be translated into other languages; as we've seen, the *Merchant* was not only among the tales chosen for Steere's *Hadithi* (translated there as *Kuwia na Kuwiwa* or 'Mercy and Judgement'), but was also performed in Agha Hashr's translation in Mombasa (*Dil Farosh*) and was discussed at length by Karen Blixen and her servant Farah. Although interest in this play has recently revolved around whether or not the depiction of Shylock is anti-Semitic, the lack of a Jewish presence in East Africa makes it likely that these audiences' rancour was directed at the figure of the moneylender rather than the figure of the Jew – as, indeed, may have been the original intention of Shakespeare, who himself most likely had little acquaintance with actual Jews.[27]

But while Nyerere was almost certainly drawing on this general distaste for those who make vast profits off the desperation of others, I wonder whether he did not also see in Shakespeare's play a deeper affinity for his programme of *ujamaa*, or 'familyhood', through which he was attempting to steer Tanzania away from the inequalities of unbridled capitalism. After all, it easily escapes attention that the title of Shakespeare's play identifies as the *main* character neither Shylock, the moneylender, nor Bassanio, the amorous young man on whose behalf the loan is secured and whose romantic mission to woo the heiress Portia forms the focus of the play. Rather, the 'Merchant' of the title is Antonio, a rather reclusive figure who stands as guarantor of the loan and whose 'even pound of flesh' looks to be forfeit after he defaults on repayment. Antonio is a mystery in a number of ways. On the one hand, he seems like a superfluity: why not have Bassanio take out his own loan, allowing Portia to save *him* from the threat of the forfeit flesh? This would remove the awkward third wheel that is Antonio, who (as both facilitator of Bassanio's wooing and recipient of Portia's heroic aid in saving him from Shylock) seems very much to make this couple into a crowd. Modern criticism, with its propensity to think along a single track, has often identified a sexual motive for Antonio's actions: he consistently plays a part in Bassanio's love life because he can't bear to let go of him. Antonio's opening speech of the play is seen by many as a veiled reference to this unsatisfied romantic longing:

ANTONIO:
In sooth, I know not why I am so sad.
It wearies me, you say it wearies you,
But how I caught it, found it, or came by it,
What stuff 'tis made of, whereof it is born,
I am to learn;
And such a want-wit sadness makes of me
That I have much ado to know myself.

The Merchant of Venice (I.i.1–7)*

Yet though Bassanio later gives away his beloved Portia's ring to show his love for Antonio, it becomes clear that the relationship between the two is not erotic but a particular form of intense friendship that was held in the highest esteem during the

---

* Antonio is one of many middle-aged men in plays from this period of Shakespeare's career who express a similarly inexplicable *ennui*, a group that includes Hamlet (in his 'I have of late lost all my mirth' speech) and Jaques in *As You Like It*.

Renaissance. The Gascon essayist Montaigne went to great lengths to set this *amitié* apart from other forms of emotional attachment; although the special quality of this love was hard to put a finger on exactly, it was best captured by the feeling that between the two friends 'souls are mingled and confounded in so universal a blending that they efface the seam which joins them together so that it cannot be found', a feeling that Bassanio speaks of as being 'infinitely bound' to Antonio.[28] Antonio's discontent, then, stems from an economic motive, from the inability to do anything which will truly live up to his friendship with Bassanio. Montaigne similarly demonstrated the qualities of this *amitié* with a counterintuitive economic fable, about a dying man who bequeaths to his two great friends the right to look after his mother in her old age and to provide a dowry for his daughter. Though this sounds like madness to the common ear, Montaigne says, those who know true friendship will recognize that the man did his friends a truly great service in giving them the means to express their love. Antonio similarly experiences a profound satisfaction at the moment that he is able to throw off trade and speculation in order to do something for a fellow human being to whom he is linked by no other bonds than those of friendship. At the moment when Antonio believes that the court will uphold Shylock's right to his flesh, and that he will die as a result, he speaks the following words to Bassanio:

> I am armed and well prepared.
> Give me your hand, Bassanio; fare you well.
> Grieve not that I am fallen to this for you,
> For herein Fortune shows herself more kind
> Than is her custom: it is still her use
> To let the wretched man outlive his wealth,
> To view with hollow eye and wrinkled brow

An age of poverty, from which lingering penance
Of such misery doth she cut me off.
Commend me to your honourable wife:
Tell her the process of Antonio's end;
Say how I loved you; speak me fair in death,
And when the tale is told, bid her be judge
Whether Bassanio had not once a love.
Repent but that you shall lose your friend
And he repents not that he pays your debt;
For if the Jew do cut but deep enough,
I'll pay it instantly, with all my heart.

The Merchant of Venice (IV.i.259–76)

As he prepares to die, Antonio finds a peace that has previously eluded him, a peace produced by the marvellous ability of Shylock's bond to transform money from 'the alienated ability of mankind' into something right at the core of the experience of living. In short, it has meant that Antonio can give to his friend Bassanio something much more *real* than money; the gift of his actual heart's blood is a glorious release from the various metaphors for worth in which humans normally deal. Brutus was only speaking poetically when he said that he would 'coin my heart / And drop my blood for drachmas', but Antonio has found a way to make the metaphor real. My guess is that this is what Nyerere the translator saw in the *Merchant*: a cure for bourgeois *malaise* in the form of shared blood, a 'familyhood' that reverses the discontents of capitalism.

Nyerere's utopian and pacific vision of the African future was not without its critics. Elsewhere were voices warning that political independence by no means meant freedom from outside control. One of the most powerful expressions of this, directed in part against Nyerere and his ilk, was a version of Shakespeare by another black poet-statesman, the playwright Aimé Césaire from Martinique. Césaire's 1969 play *Une tempête* stays close to the plot of Shakespeare's *Tempest*, but radically recasts the meaning of each of the actions: Prospero's 'magic' is revealed to be no more than navigational skill, even if he believes he has created this New World with his compass and maps. They are to him '*terres pressenties par mon génie*', lands both made present and presented to him by his skill. The party arriving from Naples, moreover, is not there entirely by chance: they are there to expand their usurpation of his dominions by taking over the island. Stefano and Trinculo become revolutionaries who, like the Freelanders and Che Guevara, are attempting to plant the international anti-authoritarian project in foreign soil. For all that Césaire's recasting of Shakespeare might be thought to have been inspired by his island home, and the West African–derived populations of the Caribbean, it is clear that the East African independence struggles were at the front of the playwright's mind. Caliban retains some traces of the language he had before Prospero 'taught him to speak', and prominent in this language is the Swahili word *uhuru* (freedom), the battle cry of anti-colonialism in East Africa. Among these new visions of Shakespeare's characters, Ariel represents the figure of the intellectual – men like Nyerere and Kenyatta – forever counselling patience to the native population and living in hope of a peaceful co-existence in which the colonizer learns the error of his ways. The men who once had been pilloried and imprisoned as agitators were now under siege from the other side for a conciliatory stance that was seen by many as dangerous appeasement. Césaire's single major change comes at the end of the play. Caliban predicts that Prospero's plans to depart the isle to go back to Europe are illusory, and that he will never abandon his 'vocation' in the New World. Prospero, protesting that Caliban's plans to rid the island of the 'white toxin' do not constitute a platform for rule, and furious that the savage's ingratitude at his liberation has made him doubt himself for the first time, decides to remain on the island and give over the rest of his life to his civilizing project. There is, then, to be no easy escape for Caliban.

8

ADDIS ABABA

Shakespeare and the Lion of Judah

RICHARD II:

For heaven's sake let us sit upon the ground,
And tell sad stories of the death of kings:
How some have been deposed, some slain in war,
Some haunted by the ghosts they have deposed,
Some poisoned by their wives, some sleeping killed,
All murdered. For within the hollow crown
That rounds the mortal temples of a king
Keeps Death his court; and there the antic sits,
Scoffing his state and grinning at his pomp,
Allowing him a breath, a little scene
To monarchize, be feared, and kill with looks,
Infusing him with self and vain conceit,
As if this flesh which walls about our life
Were brass impregnable; and humored thus,
Comes at the last and with a little pin
Bores through his castle walls – and farewell, king.

Richard II (III.ii.150–65)

Of all the African scenes in which Shakespeare's words were spoken, Ethiopia was perhaps the one in which they required least adaptation. Here, after all, as late as 1974, was an absolute monarchy of the kind that offered Shakespeare and his fellow playwrights an endless dramatic gift, intensifying human folly and fragility by investing it for a time with unlimited power. As in Shakespeare's time, this mode of government produced a court in which courtiers vied for attention, with its promise of favour and patronage, through a complexly choreographed programme of intrigue and alliance, mingling flattery with duplicity and supported by the silent languages of costume and gesture. And, as in Shakespeare's time, the fragile equilibrium of this bizarre arrangement was held in place by a Christian church that both attested to the Godly and ancient nature of kingship and wrote this social structure into the daily life of the humble through a range of ritual practices. It should, then, be unsurprising that it was here that Shakespeare's East African adventure in a sense reached its climax, with translations of *Othello*, *Macbeth* and *Hamlet* by the Ethiopian poet laureate Tsegaye Gabre-Medhin forming a backdrop to the decadent reign and violent overthrow of Emperor Haile Selassie I, and earning their author extremes of adulation and condemnation, from state-mandated editions to censorship and imprisonment.

But it is also here in Ethiopia, among the people with a most natural affinity for them, that Shakespeare's plays become most estranged from Western ways of reading them, and this is what has drawn me into unknown territory. Ethiopia is outside of the Swahili-speaking former British colonies where I spent my youth, and so in some senses beyond the scope of this history; but because of its ancient traditions and its history clear of any real colonization, it was at the centre of thinking about what it meant to be African after colonialism. The decision by Nyerere and other pan-Africanist leaders to found the Organization for African Unity in Addis Ababa in 1963 was richly symbolic: here was a proud nation with a continuous history of sovereignty and a cultural legacy untarnished by occupation which could serve as a guiding light for the enterprise. This meant that Ethiopia was the natural place for ideas about what it meants to be African to make their own contribution to global conceptions of what it means to be human. As Haile Selassie recognized, quoting Pushkin in the year after the OAU's foundation, this meant making Shakespeare their own: 'After God Almighty', the Emperor pronounced after having been presented with a ceremonial copy of the *Works* by the British Council, '[Shakespeare] was the greatest creator of mankind.'[1] Ethiopia's centrality to Africa's future in the 1970s is also the reason that it is one of the fountainheads of my own African experience – it was here that my father arrived from America to be a student at Haile Selassie I University during the last years of the Emperor's reign, full of hope for the African future, and fell in love with an area that he has never really left.

Ethiopia seems always to have provided a dreamscape to the world outside, a space characterized by both the wish-fulfilment and the strange distortions of the somatic. While it is true that the medieval legends of Prester John, the mythical priest-king in whose realm unicorns roamed, were only occasionally and incidentally associated with Ethiopia, it is also true that fuller European knowledge of these lands did little to make stories about the region less extraordinary. Travelling through Ethiopia today it is easy to see why this is. There is the intense and peculiar religiosity which keeps alive a widespread belief that the Queen of Sheba once ruled these lands, that its rulers are direct descendants of the son she bore King Solomon, and that the Ark of the Covenant may still rest here.* There is the ancient Julian calendar, which means Ethiopia is seven years behind the standard European (Gregorian) date and has a thirteenth month, and the mesmerizing Amharic script, a unique and ancient lettering system which feels to the illiterate like a queer blend of Hebrew and runes. This is, then, a culture with Christian heritage that developed over a thousand years without contact with Western Christendom. The result is a spectacular and uncanny world of things at once familiar and foreign, from religious icons in illuminated Bibles to curse-scrolls and the intricate geometric tracery of the crosses. More recent history has made further additions to this strange collage. There is the vague presence of Rastafarianism, whose largely Caribbean faithful from the 1930s set up Haile Selassie as a god under his birth name 'Ras' – Prince – Tafari; the idea is usually met with polite scepticism from those who actually lived under the Emperor's rule. There are the rusting fleets of Russian-made Lada taxis, ghosts of the Soviet-backed military regime that overthrew Selassie, caught in limbo like the Cadillacs which have remained unretired in Cuba since the fall of Batista. The trained eye might spot amongst the Ladas a few of the last blue-and-white Fiat taxis, relics of the Italian wartime occupation which were the main mode of transport during my father's youth here. Each of these taxis advertises its ferocious allegiance to an English Premier League team, and I am repeatedly forced to spontaneously fabricate strongly held opinions in hopes of not being a disappointment to the driver. (To be fair, I do this in England as well.)

---

* Ethiopian tradition has it that Makeda, Queen of Sheba, was tricked into bearing Solomon's child in the following manner: Solomon made her swear a solemn vow not to take anything belonging to him, before serving her with a richly spiced banquet; during the night she drank from the pitcher of water placed by her bedside, and the watching Solomon, claiming breach of contract, had his will of her. Of this incident was born Menelik, called 'Ebna Hakim', 'Son of the Wise'.

The first substantial European reports of the region were written by Francisco Álvares, a priest who accompanied Dom Rodrigo de Lima on his 1520 Portuguese embassy to Lebna Dengel, the *negusa negast* ('King of Kings') ruling over central modern-day Ethiopia. Álvares's *Verdadera Informaçam das Terras do Preste Joam* ('True Relation of the Lands of Prester John') describes the course of their six-year stay in Lebna Dengel's kingdom and provides a detailed (if idiosyncratic) account of the country and its culture. It is fair to say that Dom Rodrigo's mission did not get off to the most auspicious start: after landing at Massawa (now in Eritrea) accompanied by the Armenian monk 'Matthew' (who had arrived in Goa a few years previously declaring himself to be an emissary from the Prester), the party were stranded for months in various coastal monasteries waiting for the 'Barnagais' (*Bar Negus*, 'King of the Shore', or coastal governor) to provide them with porters. Setting off inadvisedly during the rains to the roving tent-city that served Lebna Dengel as a capital, the party suffered robberies, stonings and mutinies, as well as the constant diversionary tactics of local governors; their guide and diplomatic contact Matthew also died, which was probably just as well, as it transpired that he wasn't an ambassador from Lebna Dengel after all. The party were often shadowed on the road by 'tigers' (though it is obvious from context that Álvares must mean hyenas). Reaching the court did not improve matters for the Portuguese: Lebna Dengel thought the gifts they had brought him woefully insufficient, and he was mostly interested in learning of developments in the doctrine of Western Christendom since the Council of Nicea in 325, posing questions that the humble priest Álvares was ill equipped to answer. It also became apparent that the Prester had a custom of forbidding the departure of outsiders who arrived at his court. They found at the court an assortment of European adventurers who lived in comfortable captivity, known locally as the 'Franks'; among these was the Venetian painter Niccolò Brancaleone, who had been there for forty years and whose work is thought to have had some influence on the later course of Ethiopian art.* It is clear from the ambassador's increasingly anxious petitions for licence to depart that he feared the same fate.

Yet if the 'Lands of Prester John' (as Álvares insisted on continuing to call them) were not the mythical cornucopia Álvares might have expected, nor the wealthy ally against the Turk the Portuguese might have hoped, they were nevertheless an endless marvel. Among other wonders, he records a staff of gold hanging in the air without support (recorded by other witnesses as late as 1700), a delicacy made of half-digested grass from a cow's stomach, the use of salt and pepper as currency, and the giant obelisks of Axum, carved in the style of arcaded buildings. At the top of one of these, he notes, 'are five nails, on the side looking south, nailed to the stone in the shape of a cross. When it rains the rust from these nails running down the stone from the nails for a span is like congealed blood.'² Though Álvares is no poet, he is often driven to striking metaphors to capture the strange sights of Abyssinia. He speaks of camels that 'squealed as though sin was laying hold on them', and 'an infinite quantity of apes in herds . . . very large, the size of sheep, and from the middle upwards hairy like lions' which 'promenade' on the flat ground and 'scrape the earth so that it looks as though it was tilled'.† The party enjoyed brief local celeb-

---

* Brancaleone is said to have caused a scandal by portraying the infant Jesus cradled in the Virgin's left arm, as opposed to the superior right arm, in his mural at the Atronsa Maryam. He left Venice in around 1480, when the Venetian Renaissance was flourishing under the inspiration of Andrea Mantegna and Giovanni Bellini, and in the year after Gentile Bellini left for his important residence at the Ottoman court. As Brancaleone never returned to Europe, he was unable to act as a similar conduit for cultural exchange.

† This is the first European reference to the Gelada baboon, notable for its habit of plucking grass for grazing, which Álvares mistakes for cultivation. Álvares either did

rity when their prayers appeared to drive off a swarm of locusts that yellowed the sky with their arrival and left the earth 'as though it had been set on fire'. Álvares also speaks with awe of the quails and monks so numerous they cover the earth; of the latter, he says laconically that 'From their age and from their being thin and dry like wood, they appear to be men of holy life.' As a priest Álvares is mainly interested in (often minor) differences in religious practice, and he speaks at length about their stone church bells, the fifty days of Lent they observe, and the churches at Lalibela hewn out of the living rock by a king named for the swarm of bees which covered him as a child.*

Álvares's account, and the accounts of travellers after him (Pedro Páez in the 1560s, and then Jerónimo Lobo in the seventeenth century and James Bruce in the eighteenth), was to stock the European imagination with a store of reasonably accurate but nonetheless baffling ideas about Abyssinia. Following in their wake would come a line of chancers and dreamers who hoped that Abyssinia would tear the veil of bourgeois *ennui* which had settled over their lives in the West. Prominent among these was the French poet Arthur Rimbaud, who at the tender age of nineteen cast off his role as *cause célèbre* of the Symbolist movement to run Remington rifles to Emperor Menelik, a supply that may have contributed to Ethiopia being the only African army ever to defeat a modern European force, when Menelik triumphed over the Italians at Adwa in 1896. (Souvenirs of the Battle of Adwa are still among the prized merchandise of Addis Ababa's antique shops.) Evelyn Waugh, who found himself an accidental expert in things Ethiopian after blagging his way into covering Haile Selassie's 1930 coronation, records

---

not notice, or omits to mention, the onanism which is the Gelada's other uncommon characteristic.

* The name Lalibela means 'the bee has recognized his grace'.

among other things in his travelogue *Remote People* a conversation with the Bishop of Harar, Haile Selassie's tutor, who remembered his friend Rimbaud as having a bad leg and a native mistress, and being 'very serious and sad'. Waugh the 'expert' was sent back in 1936 to cover the occupation of Abyssinia by another dreamer, Benito Mussolini, who hoped to revenge the shame of the Battle of Adwa and in doing so to set up Fascist Italy as a colonial power. Waugh produced two thinly veiled satires of his stumble onto the African political stage in his early novels *Black Mischief* and *Scoop*, novels that allowed him to replace his (now little remembered) novelist brother Alec in the public's affection.

Italy's long and tempestuous relationship with the region has left its mark on Ethiopia, and before the overthrow of Haile Selassie one was sure to find Italian restaurants and car mechanics in the most distant reaches of the country, the legacy of Italian prisoners-of-war who married locals and never left. Even today one is likely to be served the local chicken curry, *doro wat*, on a bed of *spirali* pasta. The defeat of the Axis powers, however, coupled with Haile Selassie's affection for England after having run his government-in-exile from Bath, gave Ethiopia an increasingly Anglophone flavour from the 1940s on; among the British settlers was Sylvia Pankhurst, of the Suffragette dynasty, a prominent wartime supporter of Haile Selassie whose son Richard would become the premier historian of the region. This Anglophilia meant, then, that Ethiopia, like the rest of East Africa, developed a surrogate public school to which the country's elite were sent; where Kenya had the Alliance School and Tanzania had Tabora Boys', Ethiopia had the General Wingate School. It was here that the precocious young Tsegaye Gabre-Medhin was sent in 1952 at the age of sixteen, and where shortly after his arrival he may have had his first formative encounter with Shakespeare, when the school's production of *Julius Caesar* was granted an Imperial audience. Welcome as the mark of favour must have been, however, it faced the school with a rather urgent dilemma – namely, whether they were to mangle Shakespeare's sacred text by cutting the scene in which Caesar is murdered, or to go through with a performance of regicide in a country where the very subject was taboo. In an elegant compromise, the eventual solution was for Caesar to be murdered behind a curtain.* It is impossible that a young man of a theatrical bent could fail to be struck by witnessing the Emperor as spectator to Shakespeare's staging of a tyrant's death, with only a literal veil obscuring the relationship between the royal observer and the murdered Caesar. Shakespeare himself seems to have revelled in the electric pleasure, somewhere between sacrilege and insurrection, of showing the all-powerful an image of their own death. His company, the Chamberlain's Men, agreed to perform *Richard II* on the eve of Essex's planned rebellion against the Queen, knowing perhaps that even Elizabeth saw herself in the isolated King; and Shakespeare also seems to have marked the beginning of James I's reign with *Macbeth*, a bloodbath which prominently features the gory deaths of two Scottish kings as well as James's ancestor Banquo. Indeed, one of the central merits of tragedy as understood by Shakespeare's contemporaries was that it 'showeth forth the ulcers' of human weakness and so makes 'kings fear to be tyrants and tyrants manifest their tyrannical humours'.[3] Perhaps most tellingly, Shakespeare's alter ego Hamlet – the inscrutable chameleon whose father is a Catholic ghost and whose name is almost that of the poet's recently deceased son, Hamnet – is writer-director-producer of a performance designed to show the death of one king to another.

---

* Though there are other reports of regicides being cut from Ethiopian Shakespeare performances, the Emperor evidently did not object to depictions of regicide per se, as he is recorded as enjoying the Marlon Brando/James Mason *Julius Caesar* aboard a US ship to New York in 1954.

During the years that Tsegaye was at school there were no fewer than four translations of *Julius Caesar* into Amharic being undertaken simultaneously, with the play's prominent regicide continually drawing both ire and interest. As one apocryphal story tells it, the censors were delighted to report after inspecting one script that only one small change need be made to what was evidently otherwise a masterpiece – that Brutus should be killed instead. It was perhaps because of saturation of *Caesar* plays that Tsegaye, after returning from studying at the Royal Court Theatre in London and the *Comédie Française* to be appointed Director of the National Theatre, chose to adapt *Othello* instead. It was, after all, a play that stood a better chance of being green-lighted for production by the Ministry. Yet for all that the play contained no overt representation of regicide, it was not true that Tsegaye's quiescence had been bought with the directorship. He later confessed that he had chosen the play, not out of some reverent attachment to Shakespeare nor a desire to meditate on jealousy, but rather because he felt its 'Byzantine intrigue' of 'cloak and dagger' were close to the bone of Haile Selassie's Ethiopia.

Artists often make use of a fortuitous resemblance between existing narratives and current circumstances to lend plausible deniability to public controversy, but there's a fine line to walk between deniability and making sure the audience doesn't miss the point. Shakespeare seems to have kept his nose studiously clean, but his fellow playwrights often landed themselves in Newgate prison for (say) giving buffoons Scottish accents too soon after James I's accession. Indeed, these instances of overstepping the mark are often our only way of discovering the subversive messages being offered to contemporary audiences. While Tsegaye openly gestured in the direction of the court by staging his play in modern Ethiopian dress, this in itself was too general to land him in hot water. But the striking resemblance between Iago (played as a *Fitawari* Ethiopian officer) and the Emperor's late half-brother, Dejazmatch Yilma, was too much for the censors at the Ministry of Information. Presumably they drew the unavoidable conclusion that if Iago was the Emperor's illegitimate elder brother, then Othello must be the Emperor who displaced him. Certainly Tsegaye's move had a ring of Shakespearean truth to it. While Iago's reckless loathing for Othello is never really adequately explained, Shakespeare found a more compelling reason for this bitter passion when he returned to it in *King Lear*, in the bastard Edmund's hatred for his younger brother Edgar. The Ministry, however, was evidently not impressed by the dramatic logic, and the production was discontinued.

There is, however, a strange and inexorable course followed by these things, and when reports of the production came to the Emperor's ears a year later, he expressed a desire to witness it himself. The revived production was duly staged in the National Theatre; Haile Selassie came with his train of attendants to see it not once but twice; and he was so struck that he ordered the state press, Berhana Sälam, to print 10,000 copies of Tsegaye's translation. Despite his titillating portrayal of a bloodbath at the Ethiopian court, the playwright had, at the tender age of twenty-eight, secured his place at the vanguard of Ethiopian cultural and literary life, and with the royal *imprimatur* to boot.

What the Emperor could not have known was that Tsegaye had at much the same time been witness to scenes that would make him a staunch opponent of his new Imperial patron. In an interview given late in his life, he recounted a trip he had taken to Asmara, through the northern Tigray province, in hopes of publishing a book somewhere outside of the strict censorship regime of the capital:

[W]e crossed this high plateau, across Alimata(?) mountain, and arrived in a small village, called Quaha(?). Again, it was toward evening. [long pause] And there was such a sound of humans screaming for food and help.

I was told to stay on the bus. Our bus was surrounded by police, to protect us from the people. They were surging forward, thronging toward the bus. [. . . The people on the bus] were handing out this bread with their hands, they were dropping bread and it was caught by so many hands trying to grab it, trying to get more. And some crumbs fell on the back of the head of a little woman who was carrying a lean, thin, hungry child. When the bread dropped, she tried to grasp it from the back of her neck, but the child had already grasped it and desperately stuffed it in his mouth. Then the police, who were carrying large sticks, struck this woman and she fell. Flat. The child was thrown off her back and onto the ground.

[. . . In the next town, Mekele] I sat up the whole night in a small cafeteria; they called it a hotel. The news was too much, something terrifying, something I had not heard of. And, of course, the police had surrounded the hotel; they were protecting us from the people.

But at dawn, the cafeteria service came in with a glass of tea and a piece of bread. I opened my window and I looked out toward where the noise was coming from, a sort of square. With my small piece of bread, I rushed toward where I saw a small human creature. The police had left it to die and were keeping the people away at the other end. This one was by itself.

I bent down and tried to lift it, to give it a piece of bread in its mouth. It bit it for a brief moment and its eyes opened and it fell in my hand. That's it. That's it. He died.[4]

While many Westerners today might reflexively associate Ethiopia with famine and drought, a legacy of the searing images circulated by television news and charitable campaigns in the 1970s and '80s, this is only half the story. The central highland province, in which Menelik II chose to found his royal capital of Addis Ababa ('New Flower') at the end of the nineteenth century, is overwhelmingly fertile and verdant, with rich and well-watered valleys running between hills wooded with eucalyptus groves. But there was virtually no communication between the capital and those provinces of the Empire to the north and south which were especially prone to crop failures. Not only were the routes between the north and the centre treacherous, beset by bandits and (in the words of Álvares) so steep-walled that it was 'as if it were the edge of a sword making this canyon and this valley', but the only newspapers were small-circulation, state-owned pet projects of the Emperor, and they reported only news of which the court could be proud.[5] Much as at European *ancien régime* courts, the provincial governors resided for the most part not in their regions but at court, for to be absent was to open oneself to slander and suspicion. Many of these governors knew enough about the famine to be profiteering off the crop failures by stockpiling what grain there was and jacking up prices, though they said nothing of this in the capital. But word increasingly began to filter through during the 1960s of experiences like Tsegaye's, a knowledge that would transform Addis from a blissful haven into the centre of unrest.

The disconnection between Ethiopia's ruling families and the lands over which they held sway, though, was something written deeply into the fabric of Ethiopian society. As one account of an Abyssinian royal residence had it,

Here the sons and daughters of Abyssinia lived only to know the soft vicissitudes of pleasure and repose, attended by all that were skilful to delight, and gratified with whatever the senses can enjoy. They wandered in gardens of fragrance, and slept in the fortresses of security. Every art was practised to make them pleased with their own condition. The sages who instructed them told them of nothing but the miseries of public life, and described all beyond the mountains as regions of calamity, where discord was always raging, and where man preyed upon man.

Fitting as the words above are as a description of the complacent oblivion in which Haile Selassie had secluded himself, they are in fact from the 1759 novella *Rasselas, Prince of Abyssinia*, by the Father of English dictionaries, Samuel Johnson. Johnson, who had as a young and penniless hack translated a Portuguese history of Abyssinia, wrote the philosophical tale in the evenings of a single week, in hopes of using his commission to visit his sick mother and pay her debts. (She died on the evening of the seventh day.) The story follows the life of Prince Rasselas, who with the rest of the royal children is confined to a Happy Valley in which their every desire is catered for, but who conceives a hunger to see the world beyond the valley in order that he might make his *choice of life* with all the options before him. It had long been assumed that Johnson chose Abyssinia more or less at random, as an arbitrary home for his whimsical romance; but recent scholarship has established that the details of his youthful translation stayed with him to a remarkable degree.[6]

There is, in any case, no doubt that Johnson's Happy Valley was a representation of the *real* mountain fortress in which all heirs and possible pretenders to the Abyssinian throne were sequestered to ensure that they did not present a challenge to the sitting Emperor. The mountain, which features prominently in Álvares's account (and which he sees as a model for European practice), evidently enthralled the Renaissance imagination. Giacomo Gastaldi's monumental 1564 map of Africa, the eastern portion of which was developed from Álvares's account, happily replaces the fantastical medieval landmarks of Prester John's kingdom – the

Fountain of Eternal Youth and Alexander's Gate – with this equally marvellous reality, and Gastaldi's example was followed until well into the nineteenth century. It was equally true, as in Johnson's *Rasselas*, that princes did escape from their heavily guarded prison into the outside world, a world where they were anathema and it was death even to speak to them; in one case during the 1520 expedition a fugitive disguised himself as a bush, only to be captured by nearby peasants and blinded. As Álvares makes clear, however, it was not the hunger for knowledge and the enervation of ceaseless pleasure that drove these captives to escape; instead, for all the Prester's protestations that they lived at ease and could want for nothing, it appears that these royal slaves regularly ran short of basic foodstuffs and lived in rags unsuited to the mountain climate.

After hearing of his mother's death, Johnson ended his novella abruptly by having Rasselas return to Abyssinia, having come to the conclusion that every possible *choice of life* has its own miseries and that the wilful ignorance of the Happy Valley was no worse than any other and better than most. Haile Selassie seems to have

Happy Valley on the 1564 Gastaldi map. The label reads 'Here is the mountain of Amara; the Lord Prester John keeps his children here under strict guard'.

come to much the same conclusion in his later life. The court from which he ruled increasingly became a bizarre world shaped to fit one man's fantasies. There was one attendant whose sole task was to wipe the Imperial lapdog's urine from the shoes of visiting dignitaries, and another who looked after the fifty-two pillows of various shapes and sizes designed to prevent the diminutive monarch's feet from dangling when he sat on his thrones.[7] Like his ancestor Lebna Dengel, he kept a menagerie that included chained lions, though he executed some of these lions for failing to fight against an abortive palace coup in 1960. The Emperor's decisions were communicated almost entirely via the Minister of the Pen, who could retrospectively be blamed for mishearing any policies that turned out to be unpopular; and, like his ancestor Solomon, the Emperor took pleasure in regularly dispensing verdicts in major and minor law cases from a platform in front of one of the palaces, draped in a floor-length black cape.

The world outside the palace was not spared this bizarre effrontery. The Ethiopian church, which was the major landholder in the realm, had always decreed fasting for nearly half the year, but this burden was increased to nearly 300 days, hoping to cover the deprivation with an air of sanctity. And it was into this world of delusion and tyranny that Tsegaye brought his translations of *Macbeth* and *Hamlet*. On the one hand these were attempts to make Ethiopia's mark on the world stage, and in late-life interviews Tsegaye spoke in one breath of his literary work and of the cultural precedence given to Ethiopia by another palaeontological discovery – Lucy, the specimen of *Australopithecus afarensis* uncovered in the Afar Triangle in the north of the country by the American Donald Johanson. But the Shakespeare translations were also deeply concerned with the internal politics of the country, and were undertaken with all the urgency of political acts during the period of Tsegaye's radicalization; they found, in the relationship

The cover of the 1972 edition of Tsegaye's *Makbez*.

ገቢር ሁለት

ት ፥ ፩

—ባንቆና ልጁ ፍሊያንስ ይገባሉ—

ማክቤዝ
ጌቶች ተኝተዋል አንተ ?

ፍሊያንስ
አዋ አባባ ተኝተዋል ።

ባንቆ
ምን መጠጥ ነው የጠጣሁት ? ክፉኛ አደብቶኛል ። . . . .
ማነህ አንተ ?

—ማክቤዝ ይገባል—

ማክቤዝ
ሰላማዊ ወዳጅ ።

ባንቆ
ገና አልተኛህም ጌታዬ ? . . . እሰይ ሳልረሳው መጥተሃል
እጅግ መደሰታቸውን ፤ ንገርልኝ ብለውኛል
በእልፍኝ አስከልካዩም በኩል ፤ ብዙ ስጦታ ልከዋል ። . . . .
ለእመቤት ሆይ ማክቤዝ ደሞ ፤ ይህቺን የዕንቁ በረከት
ቅድም ፈልገው አጡዋቸው ፤ ከምስጋና ጋር ለመስጠት ።

ማክቤዝ
ምን . . . . በበቂ ሳንዘጋጅ ፤ መጥታችሁብን በድንገት
ያልተሟላ ነገር ሆነ ፤ ግብገቶችን አልያዘም ሥርዓት ።

ባንቆ
ፈጽሞ ቅር እንዳትሰኝ ፤ እንዲህ አርጎም የለ በእውነት . . . .
እሬ የዚያ የሕልም ነገር ፤ ላንተ እንኳ አንድ ነገር ቢያጸድቅ
አልወጣ አለልኝ ከሃሳቤ ፤ እንዳባነነኝ ቀረ ይልቅ ።

፪

between human weakness and political power, something universal, something which spoke as powerfully while revolution stirred
in Ethiopia as it had during Shakespeare's lifetime. His *Makbez* was
completed in nine days in 1964, and *Hamlét*, widely considered his
masterpiece, over the course of two months while on a tour of
Israel. Both plays were published in 1972 by the Addis Ababa
branch of Oxford University Press, at which Tsegaye himself
worked as an editor, during a period when the capital was regularly
shut down by student protests and violent police reprisals. In the
National Library in Addis I inspected one of the few copies of
Makbez surviving in world libraries, and it is immediately obvious
that Tsegaye was pulling no punches: the cover shows a graphic
depiction, in black and red, of a crown, a skull and blood. It is no
surprise that he was not given permission by the Ministry of
Information to stage it, and that the few scenes included in a 1968
revue were censored after only three performances. The horrified
fascination with which Macbeth considers his impending act of
regicide in the 'dagger' scene, included in this selection, was
evidently too much for the censors; its hallucinogenic contemplation of a 'dagger of the mind' is perhaps too evident a metaphor for
a vision that incites the viewer to violence, as is the clarion-call
with which the speech ends: 'Whiles I threat, he lives. / Words to
the heat of deeds too cold breath gives' (II.i.60–61).

My main task in Addis is to unearth traces of these few performances, and those of the Ethiopian-dress *Hamlét* of 1967. The
world in which these plays were created has largely been washed
away by seventeen years of rule by the military-communist Derg
Council, bookended by civil wars, though local peculiarities have
of course survived that, to be found only slightly altered under the
new regime of Meles Zenawi. What first strikes the traveller
familiar with the rest of East Africa is the structure of the city: here
there are not so much well-to-do neighbourhoods and slums kept

entirely separate from each other, but rather a series of lavish islands – the palaces, the rail station, the university, the embassies and (today) the luxury hotels – set in an endless sea of humbler dwellings, from breeze-block buildings to lean-tos of cardboard and corrugated iron. Like many East African capitals, Addis was planned rather than growing up organically; but it was planned on a grand scale with little thought about what would inevitably fill the gaps. Whereas in Nairobi and Kampala one would never think to see slum dwellings from the presidential palace, there is a shanty town directly across from the gates of Zenawi's residence, as there was (I'm told) even when it served as Haile Selassie's Jubilee Palace right up to the moment of his overthrow and imprisonment. The British Embassy is reputedly the largest piece of sovereign territory outside of the British Isles, with its own golf course among other amenities; but it and the other embassies are placed at a great distance from the centre of town, positioned (as the story goes) over the river so that they would bear the costs of building and maintaining the bridge across it.

This mingling and dispersal have given rise to their own peculiar forms of social and political life. Current anti-government sentiments (surrounding both the undemocratic character of Zenawi's government and its response to an increasingly confident Islamic population) are given voice in so-called 'conversation taxis', crowded minibuses that provide the necessary anonymity for open political discussion. In the comfortable pre-revolutionary house where I am staying, and where the hostess, Yerusalem, proudly displays the dress uniform her grandfather wore at court, the local urchins have fashioned an opening in one of the fences to facilitate their entrance to the compound, where they play football and where Yerusalem sets out snacks for them.

As in much of eastern Africa, however, an increasingly confident and necessarily resourceful young population is leapfrogging traditional paths of industrial development to build a digital culture of its own, creating a curious hybrid of new technologies and non-existent infrastructure. Smartphones are in every hand, even those of many who do not have homes, and these together with mobile banking have fostered a networked economy among people who lack many of the basics which endless attempts to 'fix' Africa assumed must come first. When I arrive at the National Theatre building there is a line, snaking past Maurice Calka's glorious modernist sculpture of the Lion of Judah that Haile Selassie commissioned to sit outside his playhouse, which I later learn is made up of hopefuls for an Ethiopian equivalent of *Pop Idol*. It may be that the curious stares as I was ushered past the front of the queue – still something one can dishearteningly expect without question as a white person in East Africa – were drawn by the assumption that I had been dispatched by Simon Cowell as his surrogate. Inside there are the usual delays, requests for letters of introduction to see a rarely present director, the 'archives' in which unique documentary and photographic records are stacked and mouldering, the generous offers of help that are powerless to overcome decades of disorder, underfunding and neglect. I am reminded of Álvares's description of the endless waiting for an audience with Prester John: 'We all remained like the peacock when he spreads his tail and is gay, and when he looks at his feet becomes sad: so pleased were we with going, so sad at stopping behind.'[8] But eventually I am given access, and in the entrance hall and in the broken-doored cupboards of dust-shrouded rooms I find images of these productions that bring them richly to life: an Othello sporting a squared pharaonic beard, and his counterpart, Iago, in the military attire of the Emperor's dead brother; Horatio sporting a cape fixed at the shoulders in the aristocratic style.

There is also an image of the 1967 *Hamlét* with Täsfäye Gässäsä's prince in Abyssinian short-cloak stunned by the entrance of the

Ghost. Their shock may have been shared in some measure by the audience, as many observers saw in the Ghost a resemblance to Lej Iyasu, Menelik's appointed heir, who was deposed in favour of the Empress Zauditu and her successor, Ras Tafari Makonnen. Iyasu lived on for nearly twenty years as a prisoner in a mountain fortress, like Rasselas and the other captive princes, and it was widely believed that Ras Tafari had him murdered in 1935 to prevent the Italians from using his claim as a front for occupation.* To draw a comparison between the Ghost and Iyasu was as much as to remind the audience of the shady path by which the throne came to Haile Selassie, and to paint the Emperor as the blood-stained usurper Claudius. Tsegaye followed up *Hamlét* by beginning to translate *Lear*, starting with the third act's portrayal of the mad and abandoned king on the heath, and staging this in another revue in 1968 that was cancelled after three performances 'for technical reasons'.

Tsegaye's focus on scenes of tyrannical power, human weakness and violence bring him rather closer to a novel theory that was making the rounds at the time, a rather darker theory of what humans share and what sets them apart from other animals. Along with the Piltdown case for human intelligence, and Leakey's ideas about *Homo habilis* and his use of tools, the anthropologist Robert Ardrey had proposed in his book *African Genesis* that it was man's propensity for violence that set him apart from other species – a theory whose most popular image came in the film *2001: A Space Odyssey*, where the evolutionary leap comes by way of an ape who discovers that bones can be used as weapons.[9]

Earlier in the trip I had accepted the invitation of a lawyer friend

---

* In one of the endless mirrors that life held up to art in this story, Evelyn Waugh had constructed this precise plot in *Black Mischief* three years earlier, with the rightful heir, Achon, being dragged out of his mountaintop prison by the French to act as a stalking-horse for the Emperor Seth.

to sit in on the proceedings of the United Nations International Criminal Tribunal for Rwanda. The Tribunal, which occupies an office-block-fortress in the northern Tanzanian city of Arusha, is finally winding down its prosecutions of those implicated in the 1994 genocide of hundreds of thousands of ethnic Tutsis. The public gallery is a silent box with a one-way window into the courtroom, across which curtains can be drawn when the proceedings are closed; its proximity to a kind of morbid theatre is hard to ignore. Jonathan Swift once wrote that three 'engines' had the power to hold an audience in rapt attention – the pulpit, the stage and the scaffold – and the Tribunal is an uncanny mix of all three of these.[10] The details of the Rwanda Genocide are in some senses evidence of Ardrey's theories about the violence at the heart of man, and evidence that is hard to answer. The Tribunal, however, also reminds one of the singular capacity of humans to reflect communally on past acts of violence and to seek for justice and redress after the immediate crisis has passed, a capacity which is of course central to the narrative construction of Shakespearean drama. Audiences of Shakespeare's plays are, in some senses, juries in eternal preparation. The most striking thing about *actual* justice, however, is the deathly and untheatrical slowness of its proceeding. This is something I first learned working as a lawyer's clerk during odd hours at university, but which is infinitely more stark in this circumstance: there are very few scenes of revelation and triumph, and the challenge is to hold the solid fact of the crime in mind as days, weeks, years pass, time spent painstakingly reconstructing the trivial and often banal activities which filled the time around the criminal act. One of the fantasies that theatre often enacts is of a world evacuated of these trivia, a world in which doings stand bracingly clear of the tangle of circumstance, and judgement can be passed upon them with as much confidence as solving an equation.

For all that there was universal shock when the end did come for the Ethiopian Emperor in 1974, it was nevertheless the case that the country was awash with stories of unseated kings in the years before, even if these stories could be passed off as homage to Shakespeare. The symbolic power of staging these narratives at the National Theatre was amplified by cinema screenings which reached a much wider audience. The British Council showed films that attracted viewers in their thousands, with *Othello* and *Macbeth* among the most popular titles. My favourite story is of a screening of the Russian director Grigori Kozintsev's gorgeous and brooding 1964 *Hamlet* delighting crowds at Addis's Cinema Adwa despite the reels being shown the wrong way around. While the anecdote was probably originally told as evidence that the audience were amusingly uncomprehending, I think the prospect of a back-to-front *Hamlet* (with Claudius and Gertrude's deaths removed by officious censors) works rather well. In place of the well-known story of delayed revenge, we get the level-headed Hamlet of the last Acts dying in a duel at the mid-point, then living on through the first Acts as an increasingly frantic ghost at the Danish court, forever speaking to himself and unaware that he is one of the spectres he alone can see, haunting Ophelia to an early grave and finally expelled from the court on a ship bound for England. Hamlet's observations on 'The undiscovered country from whose bourn / No traveller returns' – which always had been confusing anyway, given that he has just been hearing from a ghost who *has* returned – take on a fresh and rich irony when the play is reconfigured in this way.

When the end did come, though, the efforts of the students and artists at the vanguard of protests against the Emperor did not win them any special recognition or protection. Instead, the Soviet-funded Derg military regime turned on the Ethiopian intelligentsia, branding them as bastions of bourgeois privilege and enemies of the Revolution. Many student activists were simply executed, including as many as a thousand during a single weekend after a protest on May Day 1977; the rest, those many of my father's classmates who did not have an escape route, were sent out to provincial villages to instruct the masses, provided with a narrowly defined syllabus for re-education in the foundations of socialism that doubtless did nothing to endear them to communities where they were regarded as aliens and as spies. A lucky few, like my hostess Yerusalem, found a new life in the United States and elsewhere, forming a diaspora that are only slowly renewing their links. The university was closed, as were the presses. A withdrawal of aid from the United States in reaction to reported human rights abuses drove the Derg council into the arms of the Soviet Union, whose warm welcome caused the immediate defection of Somalia to US protection. Statues of Pushkin and Lenin came to replace Shakespeare as representatives of European culture.

Tsegaye himself was briefly imprisoned, and there is a heartening story of his having saved a fellow inmate from the noose by means of a linguistic quibble. But like his counterpart Shakespeare, Tsegaye proved remarkably adept at weathering regime change. If he was proud of the fact that his work had been banned by three successive governments – Haile Selassie, Colonel Mengistu and the Derg, and Meles Zenawi – he was nevertheless also feted by all three as well. His *Otelo* was revived in 1980 and was reputedly seen by 100,000, earning the National Theatre a healthy $200,000 profit. The audience was ironically bulked up by crowds of civil servants seeking to avoid the compulsory weekly discussion meetings instituted by the regime to foster a sense of political solidarity. The praise for the production from the Minister of Information, however, shows how far Tsegaye's plays had lost their sting; the personal corruption of social elites could be lambasted, but this was mere preaching to the choir. In Shakespeare's London as in

Imperial Addis, the tragic intensity of these plays relied upon a contradiction, an intense fascination with the vulnerability of power, a fascination that is at once horrified and yet cannot look away, that recognizes the absurdity of power and its centrality to our imaginative and emotional lives. When productions today modernize Shakespearean tragedy they reach instinctively for mob bosses, military dictators and plutocrats, because these plays require that private life be exploded onto a public stage, giving rise to the public jubilation and catastrophe that we all (at some level) feel should follow our private affairs. The conspiracies and lusts of bureaucratic politicians are banal; they may expose petty hypocrisies, but they are far from catching the pulse between transcendence and annihilation that characterizes emotional experience.

Back in Yerusalem's compound, I am included in a family reunion, with stacks of spongey *injera*, hot and sour stews, and a spectrum of pickles. The drinks table teeters with mead-like *tej* and bottles of Johnnie Walker, which has never quite lost its Reagan-era status in the developing world as a symbol of access to the promise of the West. The gathering of around three dozen people, from elderly gentlemen in Italian camelhair overcoats and white cashmere scarves to young men with smartphones and baggy jeans, is blessed by a priest who swings an incense burner and stays for the whisky. Those of middling age are self-conscious yuppies, brandishing the marks of allegiance to a sacred domestic life with no interest in politics or transcendence. Their fantasy life is lodged securely elsewhere, as it was for Shakespeare, who went to Denmark, Venice and Scotland to explore the extremes of human experience. But interest in an increasingly reclusive leadership may soon lodge that otherworld closer to home once again. A game of football picks up in the dusty yard, and I obligingly accept the unquestioned authority held by someone who shares David Beckham's nationality (if precious little else).

PANAFRICA

Shakespeare in the Cold War

The language I have learned these forty years,
My native English, now I must forgo,
And now my tongue's use is to me no more
Than an unstringèd viol or a harp,
Or like a cunning instrument cased up,
Or, being open, put into his hands
That knows no touch to tune the harmony.
Within my mouth you have enjailed my tongue,
Doubly portcullised with my teeth and lips,
And dull, unfeeling, barren ignorance
Is made my gaoler to attend on me.
I am too old to fawn upon a nurse,
Too far in years to be a pupil now.
What is thy sentence then but speechless death
Which robs my tongue from breathing native breath?

Richard II (I.iii.154–68)

Like many people travelling to Nairobi for work – and, for that matter, many local professionals – I often arrange meetings at one of the new malls that have sprung up in the suburbs during the last decade and a half. These are arrestingly luxurious affairs, much more sophisticated than anything I've visited in England, featuring designer boutiques, fusion brasseries, antique shops worthy of Bond Street or Fifth Avenue, and frozen-yoghurt emporiums. They were just beginning to arrive when I was a child, though in much more modest form; I remember my first trips into their blank cool interiors of steel and glass, preserving like inverted aquariums a cube of high-spec design from the equatorial outside. I visited them as perhaps most children visit the zoo, ducking momentarily out of Africa into a world of gloss and industrial finish, and emerging with some souvenir of the impossibly distant world of Americana. They were self-consciously at odds with the gloriously non-standard Africa outside, where the logos of multinationals, Coca-Cola and Lucky Strike, were hand-painted onto the sides of buildings and buses in loose interpretations of the trademarks. Though I did not realize it then, however, these new places were not made for me: they were, rather, the first expressions of an increasingly confident Kenyan elite, not content for Africa to be an English playground in which a few well-heeled white settlers played out their fantasies of Darkest Africa, and generating demand for those comforts they had seen on the new satellite TV channels and on trips to Europe and America. The terrace of the Artcaffe, where I took many of my meetings, was packed with the children of that generation: glamorous interracial couples, ordering dishes in an accomplished international gastronomic argot, plying their smartphones and waiting while friends and clients newly arrived from abroad crawled towards them through the sclerotic Nairobi traffic.

Ten days after my last visit, the Westgate Mall which housed the Artcaffe was entered by a handful of gunmen from the Somalian al-Shabaab offshoot of al-Qaeda, scattering grenades and automatic gunfire. Shooting their way through the building, they secured a weapons cache that had previously been secreted in an empty shop and barricaded the entrances to the mall. The inverted aquarium became a scene of horror, and the world watched in real time as this happy little world imploded, first metaphorically and then literally. During the eighty-hour siege that followed, sixty-seven people were killed and a further 250 were injured. Although there are conflicting reports of the events at the Westgate, a number of the deaths have been blamed on Kenyan security services, including those resulting from the collapse of three floors of the mall after a botched use of munitions by the army. The army and police are also accused of having looted the shops after the siege had ended.

The Kenya in which the Westgate Mall had been built – and demolished – was one utterly foreign to that envisioned by the poets and independence leaders with whom the central part of this story has been concerned. It is, in a strange way, both more at ease with the former colonial masters and more isolated from the West than it has been for a century. If it is true that the al-Shabaab attacks in Kenya are just another front in a global war between Western capitalist nations and anti-Western forces, it is also true that they are more the product of a vacuum than a direct engagement, the hollow left by the momentous sequential withdrawals of British colonial power and American-led anti-Communist Cold War measures. It is within this eddying vortex that the final chapter of this strange story needs to be understood.

On the afternoon of 10 July 1988, President Daniel Arap Moi of Kenya spoke to a press gathering on the lawn of the State House in Nairobi after hosting a competition between thirty-five primary school choirs.[1] As well as congratulating the children on their singing, he exercised the trademark micromanagement of the autocrat by instructing the Ministry of Education to reorganize the festival so that the next year it would take place during the school holidays. Moi also used his speech to instruct the Ministry of Education to reinstate Shakespeare on the school syllabus. While Shakespeare's plays were still taught in Swahili translations by Nyerere and others, the English originals had been taken out of schools following a 1981 Kenya Institute of Education report which attacked Shakespeare as a 'colonial hangover' who had no place in an independent Kenya. Moi disagreed. He saw nothing wrong with Shakespeare's plays, which were written, as he said, by an 'international figure'. It is telling that neither of the wide-circulation Kenyan dailies, the *Nation* and the *Standard*, reported on this aspect of the speech, while the Robert Maxwell–owned former ruling party newspaper the *Kenya Times* made it front-page news that was picked up by the Associated Press and republished worldwide. The message that Kenya still wanted to be part of 'international' culture was clear, and was clearly directed more at an international audience than a home one.

For all that the intervention in the school syllabus by a President with supreme power who had never shown much cultural inclination seems odd, Moi's Shakespearean diktat was merely a last-resort, high-profile move in a conflict that had been in process for some time. In this conflict, Shakespeare always stood as the point of no return, the test-case in which dissent meant a final denial of anything in common with the culture of the former European colonizers, a denial of the possibility of a shared, universal set of cultural values. Banish Shakespeare, as fat Jack Falstaff would say, and banish all the world. As early as the late 1960s, even when translations by Nyerere and Tsegaye Gabre-Medhin were vaunting the power of African languages to take over Shakespeare and make it their own, academics in Kenyan universities were voicing increasingly strident condemnations of the lack of cultural independence that had been achieved with political independence. A 1974 conference on the teaching of literature in African schools pointed out that 'of 57 texts of drama studied at [secondary school] level in our schools between 1968 and 1972 only one was African'.[2] By the time these debates reached the Kenyan parliament in the mid-1970s, feelings were running so high that the initial calls to balance the syllabus had been replaced by demands to eradicate English literature altogether. Chelagat Mutai, the youngest MP in Kenya's history and one of the seven 'bearded sisters' who led opposition to the government, demanded that Shakespeare be banned from the curriculum in order to preserve national culture; a respondent warned, '*We should not Africanize for the sake of Africanizing*', a phrase which served as something of a talking point for Moi loyalists.[3] Mutai was jailed the next year for 'incitement'.

The opposing sides faced off in various public arenas: the National Theatre embarked on a conscious programme of Africanization, ending their heavy reliance on non-African drama; English-language drama, however, simply moved across the street to the Phoenix Theatre, which was founded by James Falkland in 1983, was largely supported by Western embassies, businesses and patrons, and had an annual Shakespeare performance in Elizabethan dress, largely staged by expat actors. Ngugi wa Thiong'o, the celebrated Kenyan novelist who had taken a lead part in discussions on the inclusion of English literature on African school syllabuses, swore off writing in English in favour of his mother tongue, Gikuyu, and was himself jailed after staging a play about women's and peasants' rights, a play whose cast of 2000 perhaps made it difficult to distinguish from an anti-government rising. Ngugi lists a volume of Shakespeare among the few books he was eventually allowed during his incarceration, but Shakespeare was increasingly isolated among a sea of anti-capitalist and anti-colonialist literature, and it was whilst in prison that Ngugi turned against even Shakespeare, denouncing the 'Shakespeare in Colonial Trousers' that he had been force-fed at the Alliance School.[4]

This was not, as one might be tempted to suspect, simply shrill indignation among intellectual elites over a matter of little consequence. The Cold War was after all a series of proxy battles, and though it was not often articulated, what was at stake was nothing less than the openness of Africa to Western influence, both cultural and (by extension) political and economic. The Cold War had flooded Africa with hundreds of billions of dollars of aid and development money, funds designed to prevent newly independent African nations from falling into the Soviet sphere of influence; the unintended (though perhaps inevitable) result was that dysfunctional kleptocracies were propped up with money for patronage that rarely came with strings attached, and the international community largely turned a blind eye to the brutal tactics employed to silence opposition.[5] But the CIA felt strongly that the war would not just be won with promises of political allegiance from artificially prolonged pro-capitalist governments; they also believed that planting the cultural resources of Europe and America in the hearts and minds of nations being wooed by the Soviets would act as a guarantee of free-market ideals. During the heady decades of the 1960s and '70s, the CIA channelled hundreds of millions of dollars into covert cultural operations through charitable foundations and other grant-giving bodies. In a curious way, the CIA shared Che Guevara and Julius Nyerere's belief that culture was less universal and more determined by economic systems; their idea, however, was to ensure the continuance of capitalism by placing Shakespeare, Jackson Pollock and Louis Armstrong on the front lines.[6]

Moi himself knew that demonstrative appreciation of Anglo-American culture was part of the dance. The Donovan Maule Theatre in Nairobi, which largely staged lighter theatrical fare for white settlers and expats, was repeatedly graced by visits from Moi and other government dignitaries when they staged Shakespeare; these productions, which were insufficiently profitable to pay for themselves, were regularly subsidized by the American oil company Caltex.[7] That was not to say that Moi was not equally capable of playing the pan-Africanist card when it suited him, though he did so in a manner less accessible to the international public; speaking in Swahili shortly after having urged the Ministry of Education to reinstate Shakespeare in English, Moi baited his audience by saying that

> African history dates back just to 1900. Does it go beyond? You, the learned people, tell me. Kenya's history starts at 1900. The rest, 'beyond 1900 is dim'. And if it stretches back further, it becomes darkness. Many of our children learn about Shakespeare and other matters, such as those of Sir Walter Raleigh. All this is other people's history. Where is your history?[8]

Whatever Moi said in the privacy of his own tongue, though, his public actions came in a language that the international community could understand. The Ministry of Education bent to his will, and Shakespeare was reinstated to the national curriculum; *Romeo and Juliet* was scheduled to be examined once again, appearing for the first time in the 1992 national tests.

In the end, of course, it did not matter. One afternoon in 1989, after 'Lillibulero' had called us to attention for the World Service bulletin, my mother learned that Lithuania had declared independence from the USSR, and she danced around the kitchen as I sat uncomprehending on the linoleum floor. I may not have understood, as the grown-ups did, that the great international game of dominos, which had been played between Washington and Moscow for half a century, had finally entered a terminal phase that would bring down Soviet Russia. But few I think had thought this endgame through; few were aware that the end to the Soviet Union also meant the end to the munificence of USAID, the IMF and the World Bank that had sustained the Anglo-American presence in the wider world, not only in the form of intelligencers and civil engineering firms but also the wide array of social, cultural and environmental organizations that served as a fifth column in the anti-Communist efforts. This thinly scattered tribe, for whom 'Lillibulero' was almost a national anthem, were in fact toasting the beginning of their own end.

The mass withdrawal of capital and personnel at the end of the Cold War, and the ensuing economic slump and crime wave, all but eradicated the theatrical culture in East African cities. The expat actors departed in droves and the diminished expat audiences were uninterested in performances by African actors.[9] Economic aid to Africa was cut in half during the 1990s, going from $30bn a year to $16bn, and money for cultural anti-Communist activity evaporated entirely.[10] I went away to boarding school and my parents left, first for Europe then other parts of Africa, as part of this general exodus. Attempts to fashion a new theatre-going public by staging performances in Swahili, including Nyerere's *Julius Caezar*, faltered; there were too few actors who could speak Nyerere's classical Swahili verses, and they proved too obscure to draw a new generation of theatregoers. If Moi's government dropped all attempts to censor theatrical activity, this was in part because it had ceased to matter.[11]

The abrupt withdrawal of Shakespeare from the front lines of East African life gives a strong indication of the extent to which his place there was sustained by power struggles rather than by disinterested love of his works. This, like so many other aspects of the story I have been pursuing, makes clear how difficult it is even to ask questions about Shakespeare's universal appeal. The Victorians' idolization of Shakespeare meant that he would have a place at the foundations of language learning in their colonies, and would serve as a totemic standard of beauty for the peoples over whom they ruled. In this respect there was a certain inevitability to the central place that he would have in East African history – first as something kept from the natives, then a test through which they could prove their allegiance to their colonial masters, then as something they could take over and make their own, and finally as something to be cast off, as the final and most internalized form of colonial power. It is possible that *something* would have served this role even had it not been Shakespeare's works.

These rather bleak conclusions are, in a sense, the ones reached in Shakespeare's most poignant description of the way culture moves between peoples. Faced with the threat of being taken, as a captive, to Rome by Octavius Caesar, Cleopatra evokes a nightmarish vision of the cultural conquest which will follow on from the military one:

> . . . Saucy lictors
> Will catch at us like strumpets, and scald rhymers
> Ballad us out o'tune. The quick comedians
> Extemporally will stage us, and present
> Our Alexandrian revels. Antony
> Shall be brought drunken forth, and I shall see
> Some squeaking Cleopatra boy my greatness
> I' th' posture of a whore.

> *Antony and Cleopatra* (V.ii.213–19)

In the hands of the conquering nation, the culture of the conquered is reduced to the lowest possible level, a target for mockery and prurient, exotic sexual fantasies, a way to rewrite history and give the victor's account of the past and the foreign. Here it is clear that the Egyptians and the Romans do *not* see beauty in the same things, and that the playwrights and poets, 'quick comedians' and 'scald rhymers', are using drama and verse as means of cultural domination.

In true Shakespearean style, however, these words are being spoken by one of the most complex and engaging figures ever to grace the English stage, at the end of a play that has by no means flattened the exotic world of Egypt in order to let European values triumph over it. Cleopatra has not been 'balladed out of tune', and if Cleopatra *would* have been played by a boy on Shakespeare's stage, there is no sense in which we think of her and Antony in the reductive way she expects. Cleopatra's bleak vision of cultures failing to see eye to eye is in stark contrast to the masterpiece of empathy in which the lines are spoken. In a similar sense, while it is inescapably true that the story of Shakespeare in East Africa is one caught up in colonial history and its failings, it is still hard to be entirely satisfied with these gestures to broad historical forces as the explanation for this astonishing series of events. The many accounts of reading, translating and performing Shakespeare here are not exhausted by a fuller understanding of the contexts in which they took place; too often this can explain how Shakespeare got into these hands or those, but it doesn't explain what happened when he got there.

What, then, might be the nature of this universalism, this peculiar quality that repeatedly drew readers to his works? Part of this, of course, has to do with the breadth of Shakespeare's canon and the relentlessly unmoralizing tone that can be found across his works, meaning that everyone can, to an extent, find their own Shakespeare. Stanley, Steere, Blixen, Farah, Nyerere and Tsegaye all turned to different plays, or read the same plays in markedly different ways, in pursuit of a particular Shakespearean voice that spoke to them. This might be said to constitute a very weak form of universalism – a universalism born not of a shared and distinct experience but of mutual contemplation of something so vast and varied as to accommodate every point of view. In a sense, however, this variety of interpretation comes close to demonstrating what the great critic Erich Auerbach suggested was the key component of Shakespeare's literary power. Auerbach's *Mimesis*, a magisterial history of European literature that is still introductory reading for literary students, was written with limited access to research materials during the Jewish scholar's exile to Istanbul after he was expelled from his university post by the Nazis in 1936. Without unlimited possible avenues of research to distract him, and writing in fear that the culture he was studying might be destroyed by the Second World War, Auerbach produced a sweeping account of the Western literary tradition which few have managed to equal. For Auerbach, Shakespeare represents a pivotal moment in the history of the 'mixed style', which adamantly refuses to separate the comic from the tragic, the everyday things of life from the sublime events by which we define our existence. It is the very fact that Cleopatra finds herself contemplating the common theatre in the grand historical moment of her suicide that marks Shakespeare out from the rest. And it is only in the light of this aspect of Shakespeare's realism, which Auerbach calls 'godlike in its non-partisan objectivity', that the variety of interpretation found in this East African history can be achieved. Shakespeare seems a semi-divine 'creator of man', as Pushkin and Haile Selassie suggested, because his writings never turn aside from the messy mixture of life; and in seeming like life itself, his works open themselves to as varied a reaction as life does. The critic Edward Said has pointed out that the kind of broad perspective that Auerbach achieved, drawing out the essential components of a culture stretching over 3000 years, was only possible when writing from outside that culture, from a vantage point that allowed him to rise above the noise of detail and gain a broad overview. In some sense, then, it is fitting to think that the proof of Auerbach's conjecture could only be found by once again taking Shakespeare outside of the culture in which he was created, as happened during the stories I have been telling here.

I'm still, however, a little dissatisfied.

During the rainy seasons in Kenya, when the wet smell on the wind warned us indoors from our usual routines, I sometimes sought out the key to the storage room under our verandah. This place could not have been better designed for childish intrigue. The latch-key needed to be singled out from a bunch united by their forgotten uses, and the door, half obscured by bougainvillea, was made of wooden slats and lined inside with wire mesh, allowing the scent of dust and mould to seep out and bring the passerby into its zone. The room was a puzzle of drawers and boxes, from out of and under which peeped the materials of make-believe. The skins of zebras and the skulls of larger beasts; crested brass buttons long separated from their uniforms; tribal shields and masks; light switches and bell pulls now lying in a heap and wrapped up in the pages of outmoded magazines. These were co-opted into a fantasy life that was already a mishmash of other people's pasts played out in the African surroundings: to my habitual uniform of oversized T-shirt, made a tunic by the addition of a belt and short-sword, I took from this storeroom the decorations to be awarded for my acts of valour, and the totems for my private cults. Much later I learned that these things were the belongings of a settler couple who had once lived in the house and died on a steamer holiday to India; no one remained to claim their belongings, though it didn't seem right to throw away the collected remnants of their lives. I didn't need to know their story, however: anyone would have intuited the wonder and the sadness of the place, how it held symbols that were beautiful and significant to someone else but were quickly receding from the realm of the understood.

I think of that room now because this strange sequence of episodes is itself receding from the realm of the understood, and also because Shakespeare is the poet *par excellence* of this feeling, that beauty lies in the constantly frustrated search for meaning. For all that Shakespeare often cleanly captures the mixture of the comic and tragic, of the mundane and the sublime, there is nothing more ever-present in his plays than the border of meaning, the cliff's-edge beyond which lies the incomprehensible realm in which answers are thought to reside. This feeling is often represented by a character in the plays who knows more than we do but who is ultimately unknowable by us – the Ghost in *Hamlet* or the witches in *Macbeth* or the fools in *Lear* and *Twelfth Night*; maybe even Caliban in *The Tempest*, who knows the island in a way that Prospero never can. They make present to us our own lack of understanding, a lack which we constantly attempt to drive away, like Hamlet or Lear or Macbeth trying to clear their minds of doubt. As Shakespeare got older, however, the number of these characters proliferates, and in the later plays the world is nothing but a collection of people who find each other utterly baffling. Antony cannot understand Cleopatra, and both are a mystery to Caesar, who in turn makes no sense to them. Leontes is driven mad by his inability to grasp Hermione, and his own mind-frame is a mystery to everyone else. Prospero, Caliban, Ariel, Miranda, Sebastian and Stefano each reside in a world that is all but incomprehensible to each of the others. Shakespeare perhaps most precisely captured this borderland between the most significant things and insignificance in Sonnet 64:

When I have seen by Time's fell hand defaced
The rich proud cost of outworn buried age,

When sometime lofty towers I see down razed,
And brass eternal slave to mortal rage;
When I have seen the hungry ocean gain
Advantage on the kingdom of the shore
And the firm soil win of the wat'ry main,
Increasing store with loss and loss with store;
When I have seen such interchange of state,
Or state itself confounded to decay,
Ruin has taught me thus to ruminate
That Time will come and take my love away.
    This thought is as a death, which cannot choose
    But weep to have that which it fears to lose.

This seemingly simple elegy, about how general decay in the world reminds us of the losses that lie in store for us, has a sting in its tail. The final description of anguished love – that 'weep[s] to have that which it fears to lose' – is really a description of all experiences of beauty which force upon the present an awareness that it is the future's past. It is thought 'as a death', confronted with its usually submerged sense of mortality by a premonition of that great slipping-from-the-grasp that awaits us all. But it is also this awareness of a future loss that causes us to gather to ourselves what we can; a suggestion that – along with the ideas of man as *sapiens* (knowing), *habilis* (handy) and aggressive, we should also add what the philosopher George Steiner calls *homo quaerens*, 'questioning man', the man who is never sated with seeking.[12] In a sense, the experience of reading Shakespeare is rather like a form of exploration or an encounter with another culture: its essence, like the kingdom of Prester John, is always beyond the next horizon, like the right word is always just beyond the translator's reach, and the meaning of history is always an instant away from our grasp.

. . .

Shakespeare, the old survivor, would live to fight another day. His new form, however, would be virtually unrecognizable to those who fought the culture wars of the 1970s and 1980s. The Shakespeare that began to creep back on stage in Nairobi, after the Phoenix Theatre was taken over by its current director, George Mungai, at the millennium, was neither a totem of European culture nor a radical attempt to make Shakespeare African, but rather a kind of theatre with which Shakespeare himself would have been more familiar – a kind that needed to make money in order to make sense. Touring the theatre out of hours – an experience that always has a touch of disenchantment – George tells me the thinking behind his recent Shakespeare productions. The plays have been performed in English but with African intonations, in African locations but ones not cleansed of the intrusion of the outside. A production of *The Merchant of Venice* with Gikuyu businessmen as suitors; a *Macbeth* with Zanzibari witches and Kamban assassins; a *Romeo and Juliet* set on the streets of Nairobi, where the lovers speak by text message. These productions don't always make sense to outsiders. A production team recruiting African actors for a major Hollywood film set in Kenya were shocked to see a production of *Othello*, set in Maasailand, in which Iago won greater sympathy than the *chothara* (half Indian, half Maasai) Moor of Venice. They failed, perhaps, to see how the dynamics of the play might change if the outsider who takes both the prestige and the girl comes from a more privileged ethnic group.[13] I don't suppose it matters, though. Like the shock of Indian Shakespeare to English reviewers in turn-of-the-century Mombasa, their incomprehension seems like a sign of health, a sign that the performers are brashly making the material their own, just as Shakespeare himself would have done.

It was from this reviving scene that an East African production of *The Merry Wives of Windsor* was sent to the London Cultural Olympiad in 2012, an uproariously funny take on bourgeois sexual antics in new-age Kenya. But given that Shakespeare has survived in East Africa in this hybrid, modern, African, English-speaking form, it was all the more notable that the Globe policy during the Cultural Olympiad was that all performances had to be in the language of the performing country, and that no English was to be spoken during the plays.[14] This was a rule that, apparently, they were repeatedly called upon to enforce, as troupe after troupe played for laughs by including words that the whole audience understood. Their idea, I suppose, was to underline Shakespeare's universal appeal by demonstrating how his works could be performed in so many different languages. But behind the neatly arrayed spread of Shakespeare from different cultures a much more complex story could be seen: many of the actors spoke fluent English (some better than the language of performance) and did their main acting in English; others even lived in London already; still others had developed their productions outside the country they supposedly represented, and many of the troupes did so with the assistance of professional theatre producers from the English-speaking world.

However good-natured this attempt to show the global appeal of Shakespeare while at the same time promoting English awareness of foreign theatrical traditions, it may have averted its gaze from the true nature of this latest phase in Shakespeare's universalism. The Globe's attempt to preserve cultural difference was nostalgic and artificial, and could only be sustained by the use of arbitrarily imposed and strictly enforced rules. In truth, of course, the most recent incarnation of Shakespeare's universalism exists not despite cultural differences but because of an increasing lack of them. In the age of the internet, even attempting to ask the question of whether Shakespeare is universal is fraught with difficulty, because it means finding a society sufficiently isolated from English and American culture that its understanding of the works can be seen as a crossing of supposedly unbridgeable divides. In place of the constantly elusive proof that something in Shakespeare's works transcends cultural differences and speaks directly to a common humanity, we have the somewhat thornier *de facto* universalism of Shakespeare's works: available everywhere for free online and increasingly accessible to a world eager to participate in American economic success through its language and cultural history.

JUBA

Shakespeare, Civil War and Reconstruction

GUIDERIUS:

Fear no more the heat o'th' sun,
Nor the furious winter's rages.
Thou thy worldly task hast done,
Home art gone, and ta'en thy wages:
Golden lads and girls all must,
As chimney-sweepers, come to dust.

ARVIRAGUS:

Fear no more the frown o'th' great;
Thou art past the tyrant's stroke.
Care no more to clothe and eat,
To thee the reed is as the oak.
The scepter, learning, physic must
All follow this and come to dust.

Cymbeline (IV.ii.257–68)

I was preparing to draw a line under this story at the end of the Cold War when I came across a BBC World Service piece about South Sudanese independence.[1] In explaining the decision to make English the official language of the world's newest country after it split from the Arabic-speaking northern part of Sudan, the regional correspondent noted the remarkable part played by Shakespeare in this decision: the man charged with making English the working language of the Sudan People's Liberation Army (SPLA), which formed the backbone of the fledgling state, had himself fallen in love with English and with Shakespeare while fighting the guerrilla independence war in the bush. Shortly after this, I also became aware that South Sudan's first international outing as a country would not be a diplomatic or sporting event, but rather an adaptation of Shakespeare's *Cymbeline* in Juba Arabic produced for the 2012 Cultural Olympiad. This evidently was an opportunity not to be missed, an opportunity to come face to face with this strange mixture of Shakespeare and African state formation that I had so far been studying as a fascinating but very much historical phenomenon.

It was not, however, without some trepidation that I arranged my travel to the new capital of South Sudan, Juba. This was, after all, an area that had only recently emerged from a thirty-year civil war of extraordinary brutality, and it was evidently not yet open to the casual visitor. The process for obtaining a visa at the London embassy – on the third floor of a nondescript office building in St John's Wood – was rudimentary and evidently designed with diplomats, corporations and aid workers in mind. This impression is confirmed on arrival at Juba Airport, where I must be one of the few travellers without a local 'handler' to smooth my passage through customs. These handlers, mostly young men from the exceptionally tall Dinka people, form a striking welcoming party, combining a taste for sharp Western suits in extravagant cloths –

silver or bright yellow – with the ritual facial scarring that distinguishes one clan from another, for those who can read the signs.

The man who drives me to the 'camp' where I am staying, one of the few institutions that outsiders can book to fulfil their visa requirements, is not Sudanese but rather Gikuyu, a member of Kenyatta and Leakey's sharp-eyed tribe who are proverbial in their ability to spot the main chance. While this one-storey town in the middle of a vast scrubland might not seem the obvious place for a goldrush, any fool in Africa knows that the birth of a country is a time when fortunes are made. Independence from the Arabic Sudan run from Khartoum gives the Juba government access to potentially massive oil resources – though some of these are still under dispute in the border regions – and the West has a vested interest in a functioning state friendlier to them than the Chinese-leaning government in Khartoum. Enormous grants are distributed by USAID, the World Bank and the IMF, and infrastructure contracts or mining concessions are secured by international companies well versed in this kind of feeding frenzy. Doubtless money is creamed off by the government as it passes between the international funds and the international companies they pay – widely accepted as the price of doing business in Africa – but all too often one gets the feel of money being brought in the front door and swiftly moved out the back by much the same people. But even if this is a closed-circuit economy, where only major international institutions and government officials get a share of the official spoils, the corporate and diplomatic agents have generous *per diems* that mean small-time operators can also get a look-in. The five-minute taxi ride from the airport costs $20; the air-conditioned shipping containers which serve as accommodation in the heavily guarded 'camp' start at $150 a night, though I doubt if that raises many eyebrows among the management consultancies and US congressional delegations who have taken over large parts of the compound. Later, visiting one of the supermarkets where you need a passport and dollars to shop after winding through the streets of lean-tos on the one paved road, I witness the largest selection of Champagne magnums I've ever seen outside of Harrods. As there is virtually no internal transport network in South Sudan, all this has to be flown in at great expense, primarily (I understand) from Nairobi and Lebanon. All of this has sprung up overnight; when my father visited five years back to survey what wildlife had been left intact by the war, he lived for several days off a sack of roast groundnuts, all that was to be had from the local stores. The edict from the Ministry of Broadcasting that prohibits photography *anywhere* in South Sudan without a special permit reinforces the impression that, as so often before in Africa, this fledgling nation is being carved up in a way no one is supposed to see.

This is, of course, only the latest in a series of political experiments in this region, stretching back to where this story began – with an attempt, by the same British governments which sent expeditions and built railroads to discover and secure the headwaters of the Nile, to defend its lower stretches and the passage to India by taking over this Ottoman-held territory and administering it in a joint 'condominium' with Egypt. Britain was eventually prompted to take over as sole administrator, in part because of public outcry at home over the fate of General Gordon of Khartoum and his troops, who were massacred in 1885 by Mahdist Islamic forces. But because British interests were largely focused on the Arab north, instead of the Nubian (and eventually Christian) south, their withdrawal in 1955 at the end of Empire left a country of two separate peoples, a separation that was reinforced by a 'Closed District Ordinance' that prevented immigration and intermarrying between the north and south. This disparity was only made worse by the overwhelming dominance of the Arabic north. The unsurprising result was civil war, though perhaps no one could have foreseen the extraordinary brutality of the Sudan conflict in the second half of the twentieth century, which mingled an anarchy of cattle raids and attempts to impose Sharia Law from the north with inter-tribal conflicts in the south and the kind of wholesale slaughter seen at other times in the Congo and Rwanda. Elements of this caught the attention of the outside world, such as the extraordinary scale of suffering among refugees in Darfur province, but at many times the conflict was so intractable, complex and grotesque that the collective mind of the West simply turned away in horror.

Shortly after I arrive at the camp a ferocious rainstorm forces me away from the Nile-side table, where I have been making notes for my meetings, to take shelter under the thatch roof of the camp bar. Huddled away from the misting downpour and shouting over the resonantly African sound of heavy rain on corrugated iron, I strike up a conversation with an aid worker. She tells me she works in conflict resolution – something, she adds dryly, with a certain amount of job security in these parts. She tells me that the locals have 700 different words for cattle and that many place names are simply words for shades and types of cow; also that arguments over place names, which figure highly in local notions of sovereignty, are one of the main sources of conflict between local tribes. Islands of sedge float by on the swollen Nile, and the hunched egrets stand still in hope that theirs isn't the next to be swept away. I think of the shanty huts that fill the low-lying places outside the camp.

After the rain subsides I manage to track down Brigadier General Awur Malual, who is not in Juba but engaged in army manoeuvres in the west of the country. I do, however, manage to speak to him by satellite phone, and he is (as I had been led to believe) very loquacious and even eloquent. He tells me that, for all that Arabic had been the *lingua franca* of the south since the time of Ottoman rule, English had been widely used among Sudanese liberation fighters from the time when his father had taken up arms following independence from Britain in 1955, a symbol of resistance to the Arabic north. His own education was in Arabic in the 1970s, but he had begun using English when he joined the SPLA in 1983 at the age of eighteen, after the Khartoum government's refusal to abide by the 1972 Addis Ababa agreement establishing a South Sudanese autonomous region led to a fresh round of fighting. Brigadier, as he is cordially known despite not standing on ceremony, had fought almost continuously between then and when the ceasefire was signed in 2005.

We speak for some time about his experience as a fighter; he is reticent and modest in his descriptions, and I do not press for more. I have read some accounts of the war, including the many appalling stories of the 'lost boys', those children and adolescents orphaned by the fighting who grew up variously recruited into the SPLA ranks and criss-crossing the barren, savage and gunship-raked conflict zone to reach one of the refugee camps in bordering regions. There are episodes in these accounts beyond the capacity of most to listen to without shutting down, and so I am grateful not to be exposed. Like many of the SPLA soldiers, Brigadier seems to have moved fluidly as a young man between periods in the camps, where rest and recuperation could be had, and the areas of Sudan where the resistance was concentrated. It was, he tells me, on the way to one of these safe havens at Kurmuk on the Ethiopian border in 1991 that he lost the first volumes of Shakespeare he had carried with him during his time as a soldier. 'When we started trekking to go to Ethiopia, we were actually carrying some cartons of books, but because the area is always swampy and drowning so some of the books were eaten by rain or got lost while trekking to Ethiopia.' His unidiomatic but highly resonant description cannot fail to recall Prospero's drowned books, the source of all his magic. When

Brigadier reached the border the volumes were replaced by an English missionary and he rejoined the fighting.

What strikes me in Brigadier's account is its similarity to the stories with which this book began, stories by the likes of Henry Morton Stanley in which Shakespeare was being read in unthinkably harsh conditions, and being read as a kind of protest against the hardships being encountered, as well as a talisman to keep them from total dissolution by the horrors around them. Stories like these characteristically focus on the destruction of these beloved volumes – as Stanley had in his tale of the burnt Shakespeare – in part because this is reading defined not so much by the intimate encounter with each page as by the defiant act of reading at all, a drama intensified (in truth and in the telling) by reading the words most dense with significance at the edge of a wordless and unsignifying abyss. This is, of course, at the heart of many sacred textual traditions: the Pentateuch was revealed to Moses while Israel wandered in the Sinai desert, and the Koran to Muhammad in the Cave of Hira, and Jerome, compiler of the Vulgate Bible, is conventionally pictured in a desert with his book. Dante receives his vision of Hell, Purgatory and Heaven when in a *selva oscura*, and the Welsh Bards were said to be given their poetic powers after spending a night alone on windswept Snowdonia. Shakespeare is often pictured as a poet in a garret, recording the plays revealed to him by his genius, because the idea of him mingling with the crowd seems wrong. Nor should we assume that the information age is beyond this ritual belief that the most intense significance has some profound connection with the void. When the Voyager spacecraft was sent out in 1977 with its recordings of Bach and Chuck Berry, the chance that it would ever be heard or understood by extraterrestrials was less than slender; what was guaranteed was that a crucible of human culture would venture once more into the dark, all the more defiantly set off by being the something in an infinite nothing. If the English-speaking nation of South Sudan needed a foundation myth, Brigadier's swamp-eaten Shakespeare certainly hits many of the right notes.

We must, however, be careful not to will these stories into existence. I had expected Joseph Abuk, the translator of *Cymbeline* for the South Sudan Theatre Company's London production, to add to my fund of Shakespeare-in-the-bush stories – indeed, the press surrounding the Globe production repeatedly mentions him reading Shakespeare under the stars in the wilderness. But when I press him on this he quickly admits that it was the invention of a Western reporter with a story they had wanted to pursue. Abuk, who despite being the national poet and having served briefly as the Minister of Culture has to wait at the gates of the camp until I come to vouch for him, seems painfully resigned to having his story written by others. 'Whatever you want to write will be okay', he says. I am reminded of Caliban's damning final judgement on Prospero in Aimé Césaire's *Une tempête*:

> And you have lied so much to me
> (lied about the world, lied about me)
> that you have ended by imposing on me
> an image of myself.[2]

He has the milky eyes and faraway look that cataracts give to many East African elders, and he speaks slowly, enjoying the small amount of food he accepts from the lavish buffet, while the story of the South Sudan *Cymbeline* unfolds. The simple story of a new nation telling its history to the world through Shakespeare quickly becomes more complicated. There is, to begin with, the language question: though Abuk, who spent most of his life as part of the cultural scene in Khartoum and first read Shakespeare in the Arabic translations of the Egyptian *al-Nahda* cultural renaissance, says Juba Arabic was the obvious choice as the language for the play, he admits that this wasn't popular with the SPLA government, for whom Arabic was a reminder of the northern oppressor. Some concession seems to have been made in that Abuk wrote the play in Roman characters, but many of the actors had to have this re-transcribed into Arabic in order for them to read it. Though it remains unspoken, the reason that the play could not have been put on in the new nation's official language – English – is obvious: this would simply not have been exotic enough to figure in the Globe's demonstration of Shakespeare's universalism. The Anglophone audience demands that Shakespeare's universalism be heralded in strange tongues, even if for those cultures *English* in some sense provides a communal identity and a release from oppression. It is also obvious that the choice of *Cymbeline*, one of Shakespeare's least known plays in part because it is almost impossible to stage successfully, was driven by circumstance as much as by choice: not every nation represented at the Globe could have *Hamlet*, so some nations needed to be nudged towards the backwaters of the canon.

For all these limiting factors, Abuk is clearly a natural dramaturge, and he speaks compellingly of the connection between *Cymbeline* and South Sudan. Shakespeare's late tragicomedy is, after all, a story of plucky young Britain's defiance of the Roman Empire, and so offered easy parallels for a young nation trying to escape from the dominance of colonial overlords, both from Khartoum and beyond that from London; the Romans were dressed in the khaki uniforms of the British Imperial police. On a more detailed level, Cymbeline's villainous queen, who acts as spokesperson for the rebellion but has her own interests at heart, was quickly seen as a parallel for the widely disliked wife of John Garang, the resistance leader who died shortly before independence and whose status as father of the nation is celebrated in the vast and closed-off John Garang memorial square. Yet though *Cymbeline* may have been offered to the South Sudanese as a parable of an underdog nation's triumph – and this was, indeed, how it was played in London during many times of patriotic fervour in the eighteenth and nineteenth centuries – neither Shakespeare's play nor the South Sudanese take on it was that simple. *Cymbeline* was written at a moment when England was having to set aside the anti-Catholic fervour by which it defined itself under Elizabeth I in favour of the more conciliatory approach taken by James I, and it ends with the triumphant British army voluntarily resubmitting itself to Roman rule. It is a play which shows itself to be deeply unsure about British identity and its reliance on foreign imports; those who resist any outside influence are revealed to be traitors, and those who survive are much more open to what Rome can offer. It was rather fitting, then, that the South Sudan production, which resulted from an invitation from the former colonial master to perform Shakespeare in the motherland, didn't adopt any simple ideas of Sudanese national identity. For those who knew how to spot it, the actors in the play were distinguished by the beads of the Nilotic Dinka and Nuer peoples, or the barkcloth skirt of the Bari, or a Lotuka helmet made of spent bullet cartridges.

For all that the South Sudan *Cymbeline* was not the spontaneous and simple overflow of patriotic feeling that it might have been, it has nevertheless been a source of great pride to the new nation. The government, Abuk tells me, is warming to the idea of Juba Arabic – which was not even included on the list of the twenty-five languages of South Sudan at a recent UNESCO conference – after the warm reception it brought the country on the world stage. We discuss a plan to publish the Juba *Cymbeline* as a monument to the newly founded nation. There are also plans, I hear, to build a national cultural centre for the performing arts, using traditional materials and local craftsmen, but based on the design of

Shakespeare's Globe theatre on the South Bank in London. The London-based firm of architects who have developed the idea is called Metaphor.

Once again I am struck, as I have so often been during this journey, by the infinite resourcefulness and variety that readers have brought to their readings of Shakespeare, and the majestic consistency with which the works have risen to the task. In a century and a half during which eastern Africa had witnessed the most rapid and radical transformation of any human settlement in history, Shakespeare had provided an amulet against the dark recesses of an unknown continent and the human heart, a primer for children's reading in a foreign tongue, a prompt for fantasies in the wilderness and urban revelry, a tool for testing what we share with others and a weapon used by colonizer and colonized, a cover for resistance to foreign and domestic tyranny, and a way for people without power to take for themselves something from the world of power. Even if Shakespeare cannot be said to be *universal* in any simple sense – in that his global celebrity can never be fully extricated from the political history that produced it – there is surely a hint of the miraculous in the fact that I share something with a man like Joseph Abuk, whose life could hardly have been more different from my own. The achievement, of course, is all on the side of Abuk and his ilk, all those many readers whom I've met (or got to know) during my research: I came by this inheritance easily, and their fluency in it makes cheap any claims that might be made for my own Shakespearean knowledge. It has also seemed wondrous that, through all these various changes of use, Shakespeare's works have never once felt out of place. The surprise that initially came with finding Shakespeare in these places and forms was quickly replaced by an awareness that Shakespeare now *meant* the poet of Mughal railroads or the Ethiopian court, of Swahili and Maasailand. Like language itself, which changes in the speaking and makes all previous versions obsolete, the Shakespeare made in Africa has come to replace the one that was taken there. It is a strange and beautiful renewal: he is much the better for it, and I am grateful to have seen this latest bloom.

Abuk sits with the riverbank behind him and I can see beyond to where the massive stern of a half-sunk ferry sticks out of the water. I cannot help but think of Shakespeare's lines about his strange and isolated nation from *Cymbeline*:

> . . . I'th' world's volume
> Our Britain seems as of it, but not in't:
> In a great pool a swan's nest.

(III.iv.137–9)

While the sunken ferry often has a fishing boat moored to it, it becomes clear over the ensuing days that at least one fisherman has taken up residence in the wreck.

APPENDIX

A Partial List of Theatrical Performances Licensed in the *Official Gazette of the East Africa Protectorate*, 1915–16*

An Act of 16 October 1912 required all stage plays and cinematograph exhibitions to be licensed by the colonial authorities. This is a list of licences published in the official organ of the East Africa Protectorate between February 1915 and June 1916; it is not intended to be exhaustive, but merely suggestive of the scope and range of Indian theatre being performed at this time. Although some of the Shakespeare plays are given their English titles, it is clear from their inclusion in long lists of Indian-language plays that almost all of these must have been Indian translations as well. I have tried as far as possible to identify those other plays which come from Shakespearean sources, though it is almost certain that I have missed a large number of these; the corpus of Indian Shakespeare translations is enormous and even if the poorly transliterated titles in the *Gazette* could be correctly identified, there is no authoritative guide.

---

* The relevant pages of the *Official Gazette of the East Africa Protectorate* are 14 April 1915 (p. 281), 7 July 1915 (p. 564), 13 October 1915 (p. 831), 12 January 1916 (p. 16), 12 April 1916 (p. 277) and 26 July 1916 (p. 651).

Licence	Location	Title of Play	Author	Source
5.2.1915	Mombasa	*Bhul Bhuliya*	[Mehadi Hasan]	*Twelfth Night*
6.2.1915	Mombasa	*The Merchant of Venice*		*The Merchant of Venice*
12.2.1915	Mombasa	*Narsi Meta*	Trambaklal Dev-Shanker Raval	
13.2.1915	Mombasa	*Richard III*		
27.2.1915	Mombasa	*Silver King*	Agha Mohammed Shah [i.e., Agha Hashr Kashmiri]	
5.3.1915	Mombasa	*Hamlet*		*Hamlet*
13.3.1915	Mombasa	*Quatal-i-nazeer*	Narain Purshad Betab	
18.3.1915	Mombasa	*Sanbhagya Sundri*		*Othello*
9.4.1915	Mombasa	*Haris Chandra**		
29.5.1915	Nairobi	*Padmani*		
13.6.1915	Nairobi	*Saidi Hawas*	Agha Hassar [i.e., Agha Hashr Kashmiri]	*King John* and *Richard III*
25.7.1915	Nairobi	*Sufed Khun*	Agha Hashr	*King Lear*
1.8.1915	Nairobi	*Dage Hasrat*		
6.8.1915	Nairobi	*Alibaba Chalis Chore*	Munshi Murad Ali	
20.8.1915	Nairobi	*Vina Vele*	Dahyabhai Dhalshah	
26.8.1915	Nairobi	*Insafe Mahamoodshah Gaznavi*	Mohammad Abdulla	
5.9.1915	Nairobi	*Kwabe Hasti*	Agha Hashr Kashmiri	*Macbeth*
15.9.1915	Nairobi	*Khubsurat Bala*	Agha Hashr Kashmiri	*Macbeth*†

* A slightly confusing entry, which might either be the name of the play – and Harish-Chandra is the name of various figures in Indian mythology and history – or the name of the playwright Bharatendu Harishchandra, a prolific translator of Shakespeare.

† These appear to be distinct versions of *Macbeth* by Agha Hashr Kashmiri.

Licence	Location	Title of Play	Author	Source
1.10.1915	Nairobi	*Chandravali*	'Ashon' [i.e., Durgeswar Sarma?]	*As You Like It*
17.10.1915	Nairobi	*Intekam*	M. S. Jouhar	
27.12.1915	Kisumu	*Julius Caesar* (abridged)		*Julius Caesar*
16.1.1916	Nairobi	*Malanki Beti*	M. S. Jouhar	
12.2.1916	Mombasa	*Zenebracho Soro*		
12.2.1916	Nairobi	*Fateh Jang*	M. S. Jouhar	
3.3.1916	Nairobi	*Udaybhan*	Jiwesi Chandu Lal	
3.3.1916	Nairobi	*Ranakdevi Rakhengar*		
11.3.1916	Nairobi	*Indar Sabha*		
18.3.1916	Nairobi	[*Ramavarma ?*] *Lilawati*	[A. Anandrao?]	*Romeo and Juliet?*
25.3.1916	Nairobi	*Naval Kusum*	Vijay Shanker	
29.3.1916	Nairobi	*Khudadost*	Jamnadaass Bhagwandass	
8.4.1916	Nairobi	*Bharathuhari*	Vaghi Assaram	
15.4.1916	Nairobi	*Sarda Vijay*		
29.4.1916	Nairobi	*Gopichand*	Qualam Jan	
7.5.1916	Nairobi	*Triyaraj*		
13.5.1916	Nairobi	*Zehri Samp*	Betab	
20.5.1916	Nairobi	*Madhav Kamkundala*	Rajkan Nathuram Sundarji Shukla	
28.5.1916	Nairobi	*Chapraj Hado & Sourani*	Vaghi Assaram Ojha	
10.6.1916	Nairobi	*Khudprast*	M. S. Jouhar	
28.6.1916	Nairobi	Scene from *The Merchant of Venice*		*The Merchant of Venice*

A Note on Sources and Further Reading

While the sources for specific facts and quotations can be found in the endnotes, where I have also pointed towards some of the major scholarship and criticism relevant to individual events and texts, it seemed useful here to provide a general overview of the sources used in writing this history, as well as some guidance for those who would like to read further about the subject of each particular chapter.

The only attempt prior to this to deal with Shakespeare in East Africa at any length was an important article by Alamin M. Mazrui entitled 'Shakespeare in Africa: Between English and Swahili Literature', in *Research in African Literatures*, vol. 27, no. 1 (1996), 64–79. Mazrui sketches out some of the basic lineaments of the stories of Steere, Nyerere and Moi, but without the context of the use of Shakespeare by the explorers, the Indian and European settlers, or within the independence and post-independence pan-Africanist movement. The history of Shakespeare in Ethiopia is treated authoritatively by Richard Pankhurst in an article in the same journal ('Shakespeare in Ethiopia', *Research in African*

Literatures, vol. 17, no. 2 (1986), 169–86), though no connection is made there with the uses of Shakespeare in the rest of Africa. Ngugi wa Thiong'o's *Decolonising the Mind* (Heinemann, 1986) provides an important overview of the use of literature (and more particularly drama) in colonial education.

Over the past three decades a considerable literature has grown up treating Shakespeare and his relation to colonization – both the prehistories of English colonization which can be found in his works and the parts played by his work in colonial and post-colonial history. While this book is a highly personal account of Shakespeare's impact on one specific location (and a location that has, I believe, certain historical peculiarities), it is of course related to wider debates on the role played by culture (and Shakespeare more specifically) in the geopolitics of the colonial and post-colonial periods; for obvious reasons, a book for the general reader could not be expressed in the highly recondite theoretical termi-nology developed in this scholarship, though it is perhaps appro-priate here to say briefly what the relation of this book is to that scholarship. Many of the stories told here fall into that category of cultural 'hybridity' which is seen by some to be characteristic of the colonial and post-colonial condition, and indeed some of these episodes (as well as the narrative arc as a whole) suggest the capac-ity of this hybridity to supplement and interrupt discourses of power. The best place to start for those interested in reading more about this is Ania Loomba and Martin Orkin's volume *Post-Colonial Shakespeares* (Routledge, 2003), which also provides a useful introduction to other literature on the subject; Peter Hulme and William H. Sherman's *'The Tempest' and Its Travels* (Reaktion, 2000) is also useful in demonstrating the immense complexities that can be drawn out of both the contexts and afterlives of a single play. Those wishing to read further into theories of cultural exchange and hybridity should start with Homi K. Bhabha's *The*

Location of Culture: Critical Theory and the Postcolonial Perspective (Routledge, 1991) and Kwame Anthony Appiah's *In My Father's House* (Oxford University Press, 1992).

There are several good and accessible general histories of East Africa in this period which helped to give a backdrop to this history and which will serve anyone wishing to know the history more generally: Thomas Pakenham's *The Scramble for Africa* (Weidenfeld and Nicolson, 1991) covers the nineteenth-century exploration and exploitation, Charles Miller's *The Lunatic Express: An Entertainment in Imperialism* (Macdonald and Co., 1972) provides a good introduction to the early social history of eastern Africa in service of telling the story of the Uganda railroad, and Martin Meredith's *The State of Africa: Fifty Years of a Continent in Crisis* (Free Press, 2005) gives a pithy distillation of African political and economic history since independence. For those interested in the literary history of East Africa, Simon Gikandi's *Columbia Guide to East African Literature in English Since 1945* (Columbia University Press, 2007) is a good place to start.

Tim Jeal's excellent biographies *Livingstone* (Heinemann, 1973) and *Stanley: The Impossible Life of Africa's Greatest Explorer* (Faber and Faber, 2007), as well as his group biography *Explorers of the Nile: The Triumph and Tragedy of a Great Victorian Adventure* (Faber and Faber, 2010), give an excellent introduction both to these complex characters and to the literature of exploration more generally; the latter is more thorough than Alan Moorehead's *The White Nile* (Hamish Hamilton, 1960; rev. edn 1972), though Moorehead's book remains a classic of the genre. Edward Rice's biography *Captain Sir Richard Francis Burton: The Secret Agent Who Made the Pilgrimage to Mecca, Discovered the Kama Sutra, and Brought the Arabian Nights to the West* (Scribner's, 1990) is also highly readable.

There is no modern biography of Edward Steere beyond the short life in the *Oxford Dictionary of National Biography*; the nineteenth-century *A Memoir of Edward Steere, D.D., LL.D.: Third Missionary Bishop in Central Africa* (George Bell, 1888) by R. M. Heanley is rather dated, but is nevertheless readable and available for free online. For those interested in in-depth research on the Universities' Mission to Central Africa, the papers lodged in Rhodes House became available in digital facsimile during the final stages of this project, and can be accessed through the British Online Archives. Derek Peterson's *Creative Writing: Translation, Bookkeeping, and the Work of the Imagination in Colonial Kenya* (Heinemann, 2004) provides a much more detailed and scholarly consideration of the relationship between literacy and colonialism in an East African context than was possible here. D. S. Higgins's *Rider Haggard: The Great Storyteller* (Cassell, 1980) is the best biography available, and Wendy Katz's *Rider Haggard and the Fiction of Empire* (Cambridge University Press, 1987) is also useful. There are no modern accounts of the other adventurers treated in Chapter 3, beyond the brief vignettes provided in Miller's *The Lunatic Express*.

The history of Indian settlement in eastern Africa is woefully undertreated, though there are good foundations laid in several works by the late Cynthia Salvadori (*We Came in Dhows* [3 vols; Paperchase Kenya Ltd, 1996] and *Through Open Doors: A View of Asian Cultures in Kenya* [Kenway, 1989]); Neera Kapur-Dromson's *From Jhelum to Tana* (Penguin Books, 2007) provides an enjoyable personal account of one family's immigration to East Africa, as well as a sense of general atmosphere. There is welcome new work on the Indian theatre in the period dealt with in this chapter, among which Kathryn Hansen's *Stages of Life: Indian Theatre Autobiographies* (Anthem Press, 2011) stands out.

While Blixen is her own best biographer, the key work on the political and historical contexts of this period is Bruce Berman and John Lonsdale's two-volume *Unhappy Valley: Conflict in Kenya and Africa* (Heinemann Kenya, 1991). There are also interesting studies looking at life on Blixen's farm from the perspective of her servants, including Peter Beard's *Longing for Darkness* (Harcourt, Brace, Jovanovich, 1975) and Tove Hussein's *Africa's Song of Karen Blixen* (T. Hussein, 1998).

There are no good widely available sources on the history of Makerere University and on East African education more generally, though a general sense of the atmosphere is easily gained from the novels of Ngugi wa Thiong'o, M. J. Vassanji (especially *The In-Between Life of Vikram Lall* [Doubleday, 2003]), and the writings of Paul Theroux. David Johnson's *Shakespeare and South Africa* (Clarendon Press, 1996) is more limited in scope than the title suggests, but provides a broadly analogous account of the use of Shakespeare in the colonial education system. David Schalkwyk's *Hamlet's Dreams: The Robben Island Shakespeare* (Bloomsbury, 2013), on Mandela's 'Robben Island Shakespeare', is an excellent introduction to the complexities of that particular episode and to South African prison literature more generally, and might be used as a way to approach East African prison writings by Ngugi, Jack Mpanje and others.

The excellent coverage of Nyerere's pre-political life in Thomas Molony's *Nyerere: The Early Years* (James Currey, 2014) is much harder to come by in accounts of his later life, and it is to be hoped that Molony will continue his account in a companion volume. Readers are otherwise reliant on picking through various European eyewitness accounts of this period in Tanzanian history (such as Judith Listowel's *The Making of Tanganyika* [Chatto and Windus, 1965] and Charles Meek's *Brief Authority: A Memoir of Colonial Administration in Tanganyika* [Radcliffe Press, 2011]) and hagiographical biographies, both of which have severe shortcomings.

Richard Pankhurst's *The Ethiopians: A History* (Blackwell, 1998) and Ryszard Kapuściński's *The Emperor: Downfall of an Autocrat* (Quartet, 1983) provide excellent and highly readable accounts of

Haile Selassie's last years and of Ethiopian history more generally. There is no good general account of the early Portuguese explorations in Abyssinia, but Francisco Álvares's account is available in a mid-twentieth-century edition (1961) by the Hakluyt Society (*The Prester John of the Indies*) and is generally enjoyable.

David Eggers's *What Is the What* (Hamish Hamilton, 2007), a ghost-written account of the life of Valentino Achak Deng – one of the Sudanese 'Lost Boys' who made their way to America – provides an excellent (if often harrowing) introduction to recent Sudanese history.

Unless otherwise specified, all quotations from Shakespeare's works are taken from Stephen Greenblatt et al. (eds), *The Norton Shakespeare* (3rd edn; W. W. Norton and Company, 2015).

Acknowledgements

This book has benefited from the expertise, advice, encouragement and couches of an almost interminable list of individuals, and I can only hope that those who have somehow slipped from this list will attribute my remissness, as the essayist Montaigne says, to an uncooperative memory rather than to the duties of friendship which I hold in such high regard.

My first debts of thanks go, of course, to my parents, who gave me my experiences of Africa (and much else) without much regard for the comfort of their old age; and the British Academy, who (with the help of the Sir Ernest Cassel Educational Trust) funded much of my research for this book. I am also grateful to the Master and Fellows of Sidney Sussex College, Cambridge, who have provided me with research funding and leave (not to mention gainful employment and a roof) during the writing of this book.

This book has been shepherded into its final order by an extraordinary group of people from the publishing world, from my wonderful agent Isobel Dixon and her colleagues at Blake Friedmann, to Arabella Pike, Kate Tolley and the team at HarperCollins, to

Mitzi Angel, Ileene Smith and John Knight at Farrar, Straus and Giroux. They have relentlessly supported this book and made invaluable suggestions for improving it.

I am grateful for the help and advice, during my African travels, of Jan Janmohammed, Daniel Sambai and John Baptist da Silva (in Zanzibar); Neera Kapur-Dromson, Allaudin Qureshi, Tove Hussein, George Mungai, John Sibi-Okumu and Mary Epsom (in Nairobi); Derek Pomeroy, Austin Bukenya, Timothy Wangusa and Abasi Kiyimba (in Kampala), where Susan Kiguli was not only a gracious host but also provided aid in photo researching; Tony Calderbank, Philip Winter, Joseph Abuk and the South Sudan Theatre Company (in Juba); Tom Miscioscia, Meron Solomon, and Richard and Rita Pankhurst (in Addis). Shaila Mauladad-Fisher and Jaswant Vohora proved a formidable team in organizing my life in Kenya, and I am also grateful to the Vohoras for stays in Nairobi and Arusha. I am further grateful for the advice of Shernaz Cama and others linked to the Parzor Foundation for information about Parsi theatre and culture.

Back in Cambridge, I have been endlessly supported and encouraged by my colleagues in Sidney English (Chris Page, Claire Preston and Clive Wilmer). I also benefited from readings of early chapters by fellow young scholars (Jo Craigwood, Ruth Ahnert, Sarah Howe and Joe Moshenska) and by my good friend René Weis; Joe Moshenska and Clive Wilmer also later read a complete draft and provided invaluable feedback. I also benefited from help and advice, at key stages, from Emma Hunter, John Lonsdale and Pauline Essah at the Centre for African Studies. Sanne Rishoj-Christensen helped me with Karen Blixen's Danish. I am also grateful for having had the opportunity to read early versions of these chapters to audiences at the British Academy, at the Shakespeare Institute in Stratford (at the invitation of Michael Dobson), and at the Aga Khan University in London (at the invitation of Philip Wood), and for the feedback given by audiences on those occasions.

The following libraries and archives have provided indispensable materials, as well as guidance and information during the course of my research: the Commonwealth and Rare Books Rooms at Cambridge University Library; the Rhodes House Library in Oxford; the Zanzibar National Archives; the Tanzania National Archives; the Kenya National Archives; the Uganda National Archives; the Makerere University Archives; the Nova Scotia Archives; the Archive of the National Maritime Museum; the Archive of the Royal College of Surgeons in Ireland; the Karen Blixen Museet; the Huntington Library; the British Library, including the technicians at the Sound Archive; the SOAS library; the Library of Congress; the library of the University of Michigan.

Finally, there are two debts which should be acknowledged last. The first of these is to Ambrogio Caiani, who encouraged me to write this up as a book in the first place, and who has been a great supporter since. The last is to my wife, Kelcey, whose idea this really was, and who, as well as reading innumerable drafts, saved me from my constant instincts to ruin it.

Notes

Prelude: Beauty Out of Place

1. They did, it should be said, count Castilian, Mexican and Argentinian Spanish as three different languages, as well as making 'Hip Hop' its own tongue, in order to make the advertising slogan work.
2. W. H. Auden, *The Complete Works*, vol. 3: *Prose, 1949–55*, ed. Edward Mendelson (Faber and Faber, 2008), p. 159.
3. The term is used by Alamin M. Mazrui in 'Shakespeare in Africa: Between English and Swahili Literature', *Research in African Literatures*, vol. 27, no. 1 (1996), p. 68, and has seemed a convenient shorthand for the geographical area covered by this book; the term is not, of course, without its problems, defining as it does a broad region in the terms of a local culture which owes its significance within wider eastern Africa to colonial history – though the cultural, political and social coherence of this region are themselves to a large extent a product of the same history.

1. The Lake Regions: Shakespeare and the Explorers

1. Pliny the Elder, *Natural History: A Selection*, trans. John F. Healey (Penguin Classics, 1991), p. 35.

2. Adam Phillips, 'Freud's Idols', *London Review of Books*, vol. 12, no. 18 (27 September 1990), pp. 24–6; Albert Hourani, *A History of the Arab Peoples* (Faber and Faber, 1992), ch. 16, pp. 265–8. See Tim Jeal, *Explorers of the Nile: The Triumph and Tragedy of a Great Victorian Adventure* (Faber and Faber, 2010), pp. 13–19, for Livingstone's response to the resistance of the Nile to discovery. For Murchison's presidential address, see Ian Cameron, *To the Farthest Ends of the Earth: The History of the Royal Geographical Society, 1830–1980* (Macdonald, 1980), pp. 76–9.

3. For the British ambivalence on the benefits of the colonies, see Adam Smith, *An Inquiry into the Nature and Causes of the Wealth of Nations* (1776), bk IV, ch. vii, 'Of Colonies'; Gladstone's 'Midlothian Speeches' (for instance, the opening speech of the Midlothian Campaign in *Gladstone's Speeches*, ed. Arthur Tilney Bassett (Methuen and Co., 1916), pp. 570–72; Mira Matikkala, *Empire and Imperial Ambition: Liberty, Englishness, and Anti-Imperialism in Late Victorian Britain* (I. B. Tauris, 2011), pt I, ch. 1. On the age of tycoon-philanthropists who sponsored these expeditions, see (for instance) John S. Galbraith, *Mackinnon and East Africa, 1878–1895: A Study in the New Imperialism* (Cambridge University Press, 1972), and Charles Miller, *The Lunatic Express: An Entertainment in Imperialism* (Macdonald and Co., 1972), pp. 172–6.

4. Richard Francis Burton, *Personal Narrative of a Pilgrimage to Al-Madinah and Mecca* (Longman, 1857), pp. 7–8. See also Burton's defence of travelling in disguise in the Preface to the third edition (1879), reproduced in the Memorial Edition (Tylson and Edwards, 1893), vol. I, pp. xix–xxvi.

5. Richard Burton, *Zanzibar: City, Island, and Coast* (1872), 2 vols, vol. II, pp. 388–9. For further examples of Burton's Shakespeare quotations in his accounts of his East African expeditions, see, for example, *The Lake Regions of Central Africa: A Picture of Exploration* (Longman, Green, Longman, Roberts, 1860), vol. I, pp. 65, 163, 338; vol. II, pp. 89, 204, etc. Burton does not include Shakespeare among the list of 'miscellaneous works' in the *Lake Regions of Central Africa* (vol. I, p. 155) – these are all linguistic, navigational and ethnographic treatises – but he makes it clear in his later accounts that Shakespeare was one of the few non-functional texts that accompanied them on the trip.

6. See Alan H. Jutzi, 'Burton and His Library', in *In Search of Richard Burton: Papers from a Huntington Library Symposium*, ed. Alan H. Jutzi (Huntington Library, 1993), pp. 85–106. Burton's copy of the *Sonnets* is now held as part of the Burton Library Collection at the Huntington Library in San Marino, California. I am very grateful to Alan Jutzi of the Rare Books Department for his guidance on the Collection and for sending me copies of relevant pages of Burton's *Sonnets*.

7. *Lake Regions of Central Africa*, vol. I, p. 338.

8. Ibid., vol. II, p. 204.

9. Theodore Roosevelt, *African Game Trails: An Account of the African Wanderings of an American Hunter-Naturalist* (John Murray, 1910), pp. 24–5.

10. Karen Blixen, *Out of Africa* (1937; Penguin Classics, 2001), p. 195.

11. 'The Pigskin Library', *Outlook*, 30 April 1910, pp. 967–70. C. W. Eliot's opposing selection of the greatest books, originally known as 'Dr Eliot's Five Foot Shelf of Books', soon afterwards became the Harvard Classics series; see his 'Editor's Introduction' to *The Harvard Classics* (P. F. Collier and Son, 1909). The Harvard Classics are now available to download for free online.

12. Roosevelt, *African Game Trails*, Appendix F, pp. 569–75, at p. 570.

13. Walter Montague Kerr, *The Far Interior: A Narrative of Travel and Adventure from the Cape of Good Hope across the Zambesi to the Lake Regions of Central Africa* (2 vols, 1886), vol. I, p. 121. For other examples of travellers who took Shakespeare with them on East African travels, see (for instance) George Francis Scott Elliot, *A Naturalist in Mid-Africa: Being an Account of a Journey to the Mountains of the Moon and Tanganyika* (A. D. Innes, 1896), pp. 65 and 369; *The Life and Letters of Arthur Fraser Sim, Priest in the Universities' Mission to Central Africa* (1896), p. 109.

14. Thomas Heazle Parke, *My Personal Experiences in Equatorial Africa, as Medical Officer of the Emin Pasha Relief Expedition* (Sampson, Low, Marston & Co., 1891), p. 384.

15. Lawrence F. Abbott, ed., *The Letters of Archie Butt, Personal Aide to President Roosevelt* (William Heinemann, 1924), p. 86, quoted in Patricia O'Toole, *When Trumpets Call: Theodore Roosevelt after the White House* (Simon & Schuster, 2005), p. 58.

16. Marjorie Hessell Tiltman, interviewing Gertrude Benham in *Women in Modern Adventure* (Harrap & Co., 1935), p. 90.

17. Parke, *My Personal Experiences*, p. 8; I have added the italics.

18. Joseph Conrad, *Heart of Darkness* (1899; Penguin Classics, 2007), p. 60.

19. William G. Stairs, expedition diary, microfilm 11028, Nova Scotia Archives; also printed in *African Exploits: The Diaries of William Stairs, 1887–92*, ed. Roy McLaren (Liverpool University Press, 1998), p. 218. I am very grateful to the staff of the Nova Scotia Archives for sending me copies of the relevant pages of Captain Stairs's diary.

20. Arthur H. Neumann, *Elephant Hunting in East Equatorial Africa* (Rowland Ward, 1898), p. 115.

21. Except where otherwise indicated, my account here is indebted to Tim Jeal's authoritative biography, *Stanley: The Impossible Life of Africa's Greatest Explorer* (Faber and Faber, 2007).

22. See Jeal, *Stanley*, p. 254, and *H. M. Stanley: Unpublished Letters*, ed. Maurice Albert (W. & R. Chambers, 1957), pp. 87–8.

23. See Jeal, *Stanley*, p. 198, and Norman R. Bennett (ed.), *Stanley's Despatches to the New York Herald, 1871–77*, p. 387, as well as the account in Henry Morton Stanley, *Through the Dark Continent* (S. J. Low, 1880), vol. II, pp. 385–6.

24. Stanley, *Through the Dark Continent*, vol. II, pp. 385–6. Both of these accounts strangely insist on the reader knowing that he took the Chandos edition with him, something that I have not yet been able to explain. Answers on a postcard, please.

25. Richard Stanley and Alan Neame (eds), *The Exploration Diaries of H. M. Stanley: Now First Published from the Original Manuscripts* (William Kimber, 1961), pp. 192–3.

26. See the discussion of cannibalism in early modern New World reports in Montaigne's essay 'On the Cannibals', and in David Abulafia, *The Discovery of Mankind: Atlantic Encounters in the Age of Columbus* (Yale University Press, 2009), pp. 3–9, 187–92, *et passim*; Anthony Pagden, *European Encounters with the New World* (Yale University Press, 1993), 'Introduction' and ch. 1; Stephen Greenblatt, *Marvellous Possessions: The Wonder of the New World* (Oxford University Press, 1991), ch. 3 *et passim*.

27. Rabelais proposes laughter as a defining human quality in the prologue to *Gargantua* (Caliban is 'merry' and 'jocund' at III.ii.111–12), and the

love of wine appears as a version of enlightenment throughout his books and related writings (indeed, the parallel between Caliban's worship of the bottle and the cult of the Divine Bottle in *Le Cinquiesme Livre* is interesting and – to my knowledge – unnoted). On the appreciation of music as a sign of higher intelligence, see Elizabeth Eva Leach, *Sung Birds: Music, Nature, and Poetry in the Later Middle Ages* (Cornell University Press, 2007), pp. 1–11.

2. Zanzibar: Shakespeare and the Slaveboy Printworks

1. There is some ambiguity in the archival evidence about when the *Hadithi* was first printed and even who was given the main credit for the translation (as well as whether the original edition was entitled *Hadithi Kiingereza* or *Hadithi za Kiingereza*; I have chosen to standardize it here as the latter, following Marcel van Spaandonk's *Practical and Systematical Swahili Bibliography* (E. J. Brill, 1965), §700, p. 47). While all of the printed historiographies of Swahili literature are consistent in attributing the translation to Steere (see, for instance, Rollins's *History of Swahili Prose*, p. 62), and the fact of Steere's translation has become common knowledge among those few who are interested in this area, a few documents in the Archive of the Universities' Mission to Central Africa attribute the translation instead to A. C. Madan, who was resident at the Zanzibar mission from the late 1870s and who revised a number of Steere's works for publication; see UMCA D(8)3/75 (confusingly, this box is also labelled 'c', and there is confusion in the catalogue, where it is listed as '3' in the index, but the page appears to be missing from the detailed catalogue) and the *List of Swahili Books Published by the Universities' Mission with the Names of the Translators* (Zanzibar: Universities' Mission Printing Office, 1905), p. 8; it is unclear whether the mention here of 'Hadithi Ingereza 4' is a reference to the fact that there are four tales or to this being the fourth edition. It should be noted that it is only the 1900 edition of the *Hadithi* that is attributed to Madan, and that by the time that the attribution is made Steere was long deceased and Madan had been away from Zanzibar for nearly a decade. Both Steere and Madan are frustratingly vague when referring to their translations and publications in their letters (see, for instance, UMCA A(VI)A, f. 860v), each referring

NOTES TO PAGES 30–38

repeatedly to 'my translations' without specifying which one(s) they mean and, in the case of Madan, often referring to 'his' publications when these are actually revisions or expansions of works by Steere. In the absence of strong evidence for overturning the attribution of the works to Steere and assigning the initial publication date to 1867, I stick with the established chronology here.

2. See R. M. Heanley, *A Memoir of Edward Steere, D.D., LL.D.: Third Missionary Bishop in Central Africa* (George Bell, 1888), p. 163.

3. Karen Blixen, *Out of Africa* (1937; Penguin Classics, 2001), p. 50.

4. Some details can be provided about these translations after it was transferred to the Sheldon Press imprint of the Society for Promotion of Christian Knowledge, though the archives of the SPCK are uncatalogued and so information is rather patchy. The records of the SPCK Foreign Translation Committee (Cambridge University Library) record the following editions: a new 1938 edition of *The Merchant of Venice* in Swahili (*Biashara was Venisi*), 5000 copies, p. 336; a 1940 edition (61 pp., illustrated, 6d) of *Tales from Shakespeare* (number of copies unspecified, though 5000 was the usual number for this kind of book), p. 378. SPCK MS A16/8. The same volume (for instance, p. 240) shows that Swahili was by far the biggest market for the SPCK, selling well over 100,000 volumes a year in the 1930s and '40s. In addition to the 1940 edition, the SPCK archive in the Cambridge University Library holds (as yet uncatalogued) editions from 1951, 1961, 1963, 1964, 1966, 1967 and 1972. I am very grateful to Claire Welford-Elkin of the Rare Books Room for unearthing these for me.

5. *Hadithi za Kiingereza* (Sheldon Press, 1940), p. 22.

6. *Anjili kwa Yohana* (Cambridge University Press for the British and Foreign Bible Society, 1875), p. [3].

7. Edward Steere, *Some Account of the Town of Zanzibar* (1869), p. 6.

8. Tim Jeal, *Livingstone* (Heinemann, 1973), ch. 7.

9. Heanley, *Memoir of Edward Steere*, p. 62.

10. The Ware Collection and various newspaper cuttings, British Online Archives img. 781. www.britishonlinearchives.co.uk/browse.php?did=72542cE1 (accessed 18 February 2015).

11. Timothy Holmes, *Journey to Livingstone: Exploration of an Imperial Myth* (Canongate, 1993), p. 273.

12. Steere, *Some Account of the Town of Zanzibar*, p. 13.
13. Heanley, *Memoir of Edward Steere*, pp. 79–80.
14. An inventory of April 1863 suggests that Tozer and Steere brought the printing press with them on their voyage from England, and left it in Cape Town to be sent on to them at a later date (UMCA Archive, Rhodes House Library, A1(I)A 2, fol. 270); the press was certainly up and running by April 1865, when he requests a box of printing ink and says that the one he has is nearly finished (UMCA A1(I)A/2 fol. 275). Steere mentions Owen Makanyassa as the head of the print operation in a letter of October 1879 (Heanley, *Memoir of Edward Steere*, p. 248), but Samuel Speere suggests that he was in charge of the press as early as 1872 (*Suffolk Boy in East Africa*, 86). An account of the conditions of the printing house from slightly later can be found in G. W. Mallendar's 'Missionary Life in Central Africa' (UMCA Archive), available at www.britishonlinearchives.co.uk/browse.php?did=72542cE3 (accessed 14 September 2015), pp. 28–9.
15. *Central Africa: A Monthly Record of the Work of the Universities' Mission*, 1 January 1886, p. 7.
16. Heanley, *Memoir of Edward Steere*, p. 49.
17. Ibid., p. 101.
18. Abdulrazak Gurnah, *By the Sea* (Bloomsbury, 2002), pp. 77–8. A similar quasi-autobiographical memory is repeated and reflected upon in his novel *Desertion* (Bloomsbury, 2006), pp. 145–7 and 215.
19. Zanzibar National Archives MS CB1/5, p. 32.
20. *Central Africa*, 1934, p. 166.
21. The other interesting conclusion that can be drawn from this is that the *Hadithi* was still in circulation in 1934, despite not yet having been taken up and printed in the large Sheldon Press editions (which began in 1940); either further, as yet undocumented editions were printed in Zanzibar (or elsewhere), or the people of Mbweni were still cherishing flimsy pamphlets that were now a half-century old.
22. Heanley, *Memoir of Edward Steere*, p. 80.
23. For a discussion of the experience of print, see Marshall McLuhan, *The Gutenberg Galaxy: The Making of Typographic Man* (University of Toronto Press, 1962), and Jonathan Sawday, *Engines of the Imagination: Renaissance Culture and the Rise of the Machine* (Routledge, 2007), ch. 3.

24. Letter to John Festing, July 1872, UMCA Archive, Rhodes House; digital image www.britishonlinearchives.co.uk/browse.php?did=72542cB01 (Letters and Images Relating to Dr Steere Part 1, img. 145).
25. UMCA D(8)/2/7, fol. 7. See also fol. 17v for 'All the world's a stage'.
26. Heanley, *Memoir of Edward Steere*, p. 146.

3. Interlude—The Swahili Coast: Player-Kings of Eastern Africa

1. There is an extensive literature on African appropriations of *The Tempest*, including Rob Nixon's 'Caribbean and African Appropriations of *The Tempest*', *Critical Inquiry*, vol. 13, pp. 557–78, and Thomas Cartelli's 'Prospero in Africa: *The Tempest* as Colonial Text and Pretext', in J. Howard and M. O'Connor (eds), *Shakespeare Reproduced: The Text in History and Ideology* (Methuen, 1987), pp. 99–115. See also, however, Jerry Brotton's critique of the anachronistic mapping of colonialist discourses onto the early modern text in '"This Tunis, sir, was Carthage": Contesting Colonialism in *The Tempest*', in A. Loomba and M. Orkin (eds), *Post-Colonial Shakespeares* (Routledge, 2003), pp. 23–42.
2. The figures about the MV *Spice Islander* disaster used here are from a report by the Tanzanian firm IPP Media (www.ippmedia.com/frontend/index.php?l=34437); figures from the Zanzibar prosecutors' case put the figure slightly lower at 2740 in March 2013.
3. 'Ambrose Gunthio', 'A Running Commentary on the Hamlet of 1603', in *The European Magazine, and London Review*, vol. I, no. 4 (December 1825), pp. 339–47, at p. 347.
4. Samuel Purchas, *Purchas his pilgrimes in five books* (1625), vol. III, no. 6, §2–3, pp. 191–3.
5. The fullest recent account of this controversy can be found in Bernice W. Kilman's article 'At Sea about *Hamlet* at Sea: A Detective Story', printed in *Shakespeare Quarterly*, vol. 62, no. 2 (2011), pp. 180–204. Kilman's article, while compelling in many respects in its quest to prove the entries to be forged and to be forged by Collier, does not entirely convince that Collier would have undertaken such an audacious forgery only to then let it wallow in obscurity for forty or fifty years before gaining general traction among Shakespeare scholars. While Collier's most recent and authoritative biographers, Arthur Freeman

and Janet Ing Freeman, do note several instances of Collier forgery which *do* seem to have been undertaken with no view to having the evidence widely known and generally accepted, they nevertheless do not see Collier's hand in the publication of the 1825–6 Gunthio article which gives the suspect Keeling entries for the first time. Further complexity is added to the story by the fact that the entries were published again, in a slightly variant form, in Thomas Rundall's *Narratives of Voyages towards the North-West, in Search of a Passage to Cathay and India, 1496 to 1631* (1849) for the Hakluyt Society, and it is not clear how Rundall came by the entries or why they exist in a variant form in his version.

6. Zanzibar National Archive, MS CB 1/5, p. 5.

7. Evelyn Waugh, *Remote People* (1931; Penguin Classics, 2002), p. 115.

8. The details of Rider Haggard's life here are drawn largely from D. S. Higgins's *Rider Haggard: The Great Storyteller* (Cassell, 1981), though with additional details from Peter Beresford Ellis's *H. Rider Haggard: A Voice from the Infinite* (Routledge and Kegan Paul, 1978) and Tom Pocock's *Rider Haggard and the Lost Empire* (Weidenfeld and Nicolson, 1993).

9. Higgins, *Rider Haggard*, p. 83.

10. H. Rider Haggard, *Allan Quatermain* (Longmans, 1887), p. 94.

11. See John Ruskin, *Lectures on Art, Delivered before the University of Oxford in Hilary Term of 1870* (Clarendon Press, 1870), esp. pp. 27–31, where he calls upon England to 'found colonies as fast and as far as she is able, formed of her most energetic men:– seizing every piece of fruitful waste ground she can set her foot on, and there teaching these her colonists that their chief virtue is to be fidelity to their country, and that their first aim is to be to advance the power of England by land and sea' (p. 29).

12. Rider Haggard, *Allan Quatermain*, pp. 120, 149, 174. Rider Haggard's description of Milosis is actually reminiscent of England as it *should* be, as laid out in Ruskin's *The Two Paths* (1859), where thirteenth-century Pisa, with its 'dome and bell-tower, burning with white alabaster and gold', is held up as an example of what England has lost.

13. The story of this phenomenon in 'high' literature is outlined by Edward W. Said in *Orientalism* (Vintage, 1979), esp. pt II. ch. IV, 'Pilgrims and Pilgrimages, British and French'.

14. Charles Miller, *The Lunatic Express: An Entertainment in Imperialism* (Macdonald and Co., 1972), pp. 79–82.

15. This footnote first appears in the cheap edition of *King Solomon's Mines* (Cassell, 1898), p. 35, and appears to be a tongue-in-cheek admission that Rider Haggard himself had misremembered the source of this quote and allowed it to stand misattributed in many editions of the novel over thirteen years.

16. Higgins, *Rider Haggard*, p. 74.

17. Ibid., pp. 75–6; Ellis, *Rider Haggard*, pp. 204–5.

18. The fullest account of this venture is given in an article by R. W. Beachey, '"Freeland": A Socialist Experiment in East Africa – 1894', in the *Makerere Journal*, vol. 2 (1959), pp. 56–68. Beachey's account, which is based on Foreign Office correspondence, makes clear that A. S. Rogers, thought by Miller in *The Lunatic Express* to be the leader of the Freeland Expedition, was actually the Sub-Commissioner of the newly formed province of Tanaland. See also Miller, *Lunatic Express*, ch. 11.

19. Information for the table is taken from Beachey, '"Freeland"', pp. 60–61.

20. For details of the IBEA Company, see John S. Galbraith, *Mackinnon and East Africa, 1878–1895: A Study in the New Imperialism* (Cambridge University Press, 1972), ch. 6.

21. Rejection of the European spelling of the tribal name ('Kikuyu') in favour of a spelling that more accurately reflected correct pronunciation ('Gikuyu') took on a political edge at an early stage (see Jomo Kenyatta, *Facing Mount Kenya: The Tribal Life of the Gikuyu*, Preface). I use 'Gikuyu' here except when directly quoting from a source that uses the European spelling, but (to keep things simple) use 'Gikuyu' in place of all the various premodified versions required by that tongue ('Mu-Gikuyu' – a Gikuyu person; 'A-Gikuyu' – Gikuyu people, etc.).

22. Sonia Cole, *Leakey's Luck: The Life of Louis Seymour Bazett Leakey* (Collins, 1975), p. 55.

23. John Boyes, *John Boyes: King of the Wa-Kikuyu* (Methuen, 1911), p. 29.

24. Ibid., p. 32.

25. *The Journal*, Grahamstown, South Africa, 23 December 1898, p. 3; *Bulawayo Chronicle*, Bulawayo, Rhodesia, 28 January 1898, p. 6.

26. *Natal Mercury Weekly Edition*, 10 September 1897, p. 11.
27. See Denis Schauffer, 'Shakespeare Performance in Pietermaritzburg before 1914', *Shakespeare in Southern Africa*, vol. 19 (2007), pp. 17–18, and the notices page of the Grahamstown *Journal* between 24 and 31 December 1898, for the repertoire of the Haviland–Lawrence company; they also had *The Taming of the Shrew* in their repertoire, but don't appear to have played it in Durban in 1898; the *Natal Mercury Weekly Edition* for 27 May 1898 (p. 11) adds *Hamlet* to this list. The Haviland–Coleridge company is alternately referred to as the 'Haviland–Lawrence' company.
28. See the *Natal Mercury Weekly Edition*, 2 September 1898, pp. 26–7. Schauffer appears to have mistakenly attributed the same repertoire to the Wheeler company in May–June, but the Wheeler company, primarily a comic ensemble, do not seem to have visited Durban that year. See Schauffer, 'Shakespeare Performance', p. 17.
29. William Shakespeare [and Colley Cibber], *The Tragical History of King Richard III as it is Acted at the Theatre Royal* (London: For B. Lintott . . . and A. Bettesworth, 1700), p. 50.
30. Ruskin, *Lectures on Art*, p. 29.

4. Mombasa: Shakespeare, Bard of the Railroad

1. Charles Miller, *The Lunatic Express: An Entertainment in Imperialism* (Macdonald and Co., 1972), p. 15.
2. Luís de Camões, *Os Lusiadas (The Lusiads)*, trans. Richard Francis Burton, ed. Isabel Burton (Bernhard Quaritch, 1880), pp. 37–9.
3. A translation of the poem is given in Lieut.-Col. John Henry Patterson, *The Man Eaters of Tsavo and Other East African Adventures* (Macmillan, 1907), Appendix II, pp. 332–8; see also Miller's account in *Lunatic Express*, pp. 318–47. I have continued to employ the term 'Hindustani' here as it is used in contemporary sources, as it is unclear there when Urdu and when Hindi variants are being used. Agha Hashr Kashmiri translated Shakespeare into Urdu, but in other instances the standards used are not clear.
4. Sisir Kumar Das, 'Shakespeare in Indian Languages', in *India's Shakespeare*, eds Poonam Trivedi and Dennis Bartholomeusz (Delaware University Press, 2005), p. 55.

5. See, for instance, Karen Blixen's chapter on 'Pooran Singh' in *Out of Africa* (1937; Penguin Classics, 2001), Evelyn Waugh in *Remote People* (1931; Penguin Classics, 2002), William Boyd's *An Ice-Cream War* (Hamish Hamilton, 1982), etc.

6. Appendix I gives a list of the plays licensed in 1915–16, with a note of the author or translator (where known) and location of performance.

7. Once again it is the colonial administration's impulse to control that provides us with evidence of much of the theatrical activity; the Societies Ordinance of 1952 required that all associations be registered with the authorities – in order to prevent undesirable political associations – a requirement from which the Mombasa Shakespeare Group is exempted in the *Kenya Gazette* of 21 March 1961. I am grateful to Allaudin Qureshi and Neera Kapur for information on the other theatrical troupes; see Neera Kapur Dromson's *From Jhelum to Tana* (Penguin Books, 2007), pp. 242–3, 329.

8. Kathryn Hansen, *Stages of Life: Indian Theatre Autobiographies* (Anthem Press, 2011), p. 172.

9. For summaries of Indian versions of Shakespeare, see P. K. Yajnik, *The Indian Theatre* (George Allen & Unwin, 1933), pp. 125–82, and Poonam Trivedi and Dennis Bartholomeusz, *India's Shakespeare: Translation, Interpretation and Performance* (University of Delaware Press), esp. Sisir Kumar Das's chapter, 'Shakespeare in Indian Languages'.

10. Yajnik, *Indian Theatre*, pp. 156–8.

11. 'Shakespeare in Mombasa', *East African Standard*, 22 August 1908, p. 12. Yajnik, *Indian Theatre*, p. 134.

12. 'Hindu Theatricals at Mombasa', *East African Standard*, 6 June 1914, p. 4.

13. The identification of the play as *Khubsurat Bala* is made by Gaurav Desai in his article 'Asian African Literatures: Genealogies in the Making', *Research in African Literatures*, vol. 42, no. 3 (2011), pp. vi–xxx (ix–x).

14. The likely reference to Shakespeare as an 'upstart Crow, beautified with our feathers' occurs in Robert Greene's *Greenes groats-worth of witte* (London: for William Wright, 1592), sig. F1v; see discussion of this in, among others, Arthur Schoenbaum, *Shakespeare: A Documentary Life*, ch. 10, and Katherine Duncan-Jones, *Shakespeare: An Ungentle Life* (Methuen, 2010), ch. 2. The reference to Shakespeare's 'small *Latine*, and lesse *Greeke*' comes from Ben Jonson's prefatory poem in the First Folio, 'To the memory of my beloved, The Author', and is of course

affectionate, if still characteristically barbed affection from the dedicated classicist Jonson.

15. See the British Universities' Film and Video Council Record: Shakespeare, 'Khoon Ka Khoon', http://bufvc.ac.uk/shakespeare/index .php/title/av37438 (accessed 20 April 2015). See also Neera Kapur-Dromson, 'Asian Drama Productions Light Up Nairobi', *Old Africa Magazine*, February–March 2012, pp. 15–19.

16. F. W. Gaisberg, *Music on Record* (Robert Hale, 1948), p. 54.

17. The recordings are listed in Michael Kinnear's *The Gramophone Company's First Indian Recordings, 1899–1908* (Bombay: Popular Prakashan). For *Bhul Bhuliyan*, see p. 263. The British Library copy of the recording is held under 1CU0002108 S1 HIS MASTER'S VOICE, which may suggest that this recording is from a trip made subsequent to the Gramophone Company's adoption of the HMV title in 1909.

18. I am grateful to Rohit De and Suren Sista for help with translation from Indian languages.

19. *Bhul Bhoolaian, or Twelfth Night or What You Will. With some changes as performed by Parsee Original Theatrical Company* [synopsis] (Parsee Orphanage Captain Printing Works, 1905).

20. The manuscript is translated, and the circumstances of its acquisition described, in Alice Werner, 'Some Notes on East African Folklore (Continued)', in *Folklore* 26.1 (1915), 60–78, pp. 63–67. Werner writes further about the manuscript in 'Shakespeare in Africa', in *The Crisis* 12.3 (1916), p. 144. I am grateful to Brian Willan for drawing my attention to this.

5. Nairobi: Expats, Emigrés and Exile

1. Evelyn Waugh, *Remote People* (1931; Penguin Classics, 2002), pp. 135–6.

2. This particular rendering of Longinus's word comes from *Longinus. On the Sublime*, trans. A. O. Prickard (Clarendon Press, 1906), p. 13.

3. Elspeth Huxley, *White Man's Country: Lord Delamere and the Making of Kenya* (Chatto and Windus, 1968); Charles Miller, *The Lunatic Express: An Entertainment in Imperialism* (Macdonald and Co., 1972), pp. 415–26.

4. Details of this festival can be found in the *East African Annual* for 1954–5, pp. 137–45.

5. All details of Blixen's Shakespeare volumes are from Pia Bondesson, *Karen Blixens bogsamling på Rungstedlund* (Karen Blixens selskabet,

1982), §396–407. I am grateful to Anne-Marie Teideman Dal for sending me the relevant pages, and to Sanne Rishoj-Christensen for help with Danish translation.

6. Isak Dinesen (ed. Frans Lasson), *Letters from Africa* (Weidenfeld and Nicolson, 1981), p. 410.

7. Edward Grigg, *The Faith of an Englishman* (Macmillan, 1936), p. viii.

8. Karen Blixen, *Out of Africa* (1937; Penguin Classics, 2001), p. 321.

9. Ibid., pp. 221–3.

10. Laura Bohannan, 'Shakespeare in the Bush', *Natural History*, August–September 1966.

11. For further stories of Shakespearean narrative being misunderstood, see David Schalkwyk, *Hamlet's Dreams: The Robben Island Shakespeare* (Bloomsbury, 2013), pp. 34–5.

12. For an interesting reversal of this, which insists on universal mental structures in a language derived from Freud's reading of Shakespeare, see Andreas Bertoldi's essay on 'Shakespeare, Psychoanalysis, and the Colonial Encounter: The Case of Wulf Sach's *Black Hamlet*', in A. Loomba and M. Orkin (eds), *Post-Colonial Shakespeares* (Routledge, 2003), pp. 235–58.

13. *The Indian Voice of British East Africa*, 29 January 1913, p. 6.

14. Harry Thuku with Kenneth King, *Harry Thuku: An Autobiography* (Oxford University Press, 1970), p. 11. Thuku describes the forgery incident on p. 13; the file on the court case had already disappeared by the time of his 1922 trial (see Kenya National Archives, S/288/45/122 – AP 1/3/7), so we are unable to add further details to this incident; but it was clearly not so serious as to have prevented him being employed by the Treasury shortly afterwards.

15. Bruce J. Berman and John M. Lonsdale, 'The Labors of *Muigwithania*: Jomo Kenyatta as Author, 1928–45', *Research in African Literatures*, vol. 29, no. 1 (Spring 1998), p. 22.

16. J. Bailey and G. Bundeh, *Kenya: The National Epic. From the Pages of Drum Magazine* (Kenway, 1993), p. 35.

17. Jean de Brunhoff, *The Story of Babar*, trans. Merle S. Haas (Random House, 1933), p. 38.

18. Quoted in the *Daily Telegraph*, 'Mystery of Kenyatta Marriage', 1 March 2005.

6. Kampala: Shakespeare at School, at War and in Prison

1. For reviews of these productions, see *Makerere: A Literary Magazine, Published in East Africa at Makerere College*: 'Julius Ceasar', by 'R.A.S', September 1948 (vol. 2, no. 6), pp. 114–15; '*Richard II*', by Alastair Macpherson, Sept.–Nov. 1949 (vol. 3, no. 3), pp. 6–8; and 'Shakespeare at Makerere', Jan.–March 1953 (vol. 4, no. 1), pp. 10–12 (for the 1950 *A Midsummer Night's Dream*, the 1951 *Coriolanus*, and the 1952 *Henry IV, Part 1*).

2. Margaret MacPherson, 'Makerere: Place of the Early Sunrise', in Eckhard Breitinger, *Uganda: The Cultural Landscape* (E. Breitinger, 1999), pp. 27–8.

3. Yasmin Alibhai-Brown, *The Settler's Cookbook: A Memoir of Love, Migration and Food* (Portobello Books, 2008), pp. 205–10.

4. See also Ngugi wa Thiong'o, *Decolonising the Mind* (Heinemann, 1986), p. 38.

5. *Makerere*, September 1948, pp. 114–15.

6. MacPherson, 'Makerere', pp. 27–8.

7. Ngugi wa Thiong'o, *Dreams in a Time of War: A Childhood Memoir* (Harvill Secker, 2010), p. 166.

8. For another case study of this kind, see David William Cohen and E. S. Atieno Odhiambo's *Burying S.M.: The Politics of Knowledge and the Sociology of Power* (Heinemann, 1992).

9. Colony and Protectorate of Kenya, *Legislative Council Debates. Official Report* (1955), 5 October 1955, vol. LXVI, col. 21–22.

10. There is an extensive literature on the Mau Mau and the Emergency of the 1950s, which is developing as newly declassified documents are being released, and which can only be gestured to here. I am reliant for my account here largely on the two volumes of John Lonsdale and Bruce Berman's *Unhappy Valley: Conflict in Kenya and Africa* (Heinemann Kenya, 1991), E. S. Atieno and John Lonsdale's *Mau Mau and Nationhood: Arms, Authority and Narration* (James Currey, 2003) and Caroline Elkins's *Britain's Gulag: The Brutal End of Empire in Kenya* (Jonathan Cape, 2005).

11. My account here is heavily indebted to David Schalkwyk's excellent recent book on the Robben Island Bible and Apartheid Shakespeare, *Hamlet's Dreams: The Robben Island Shakespeare* (Bloomsbury, 2013).

12. See Sonia Cole, *Leakey's Luck: The Life of Louis Seymour Bazett Leakey* (Collins, 1975), p. 196, but also Peterson, *Creative Writing, Translation, Bookkeeping, and the Work of Imagination in Colonial Kenya* (Heinemann, 2004), which provides an interesting revisionist account of the relationships between the languages of Protestantism and Kenyan nationalism.

13. Gakaara wa Wanjaū, *Mau Mau Author in Detention*, trans. Paul Ngigĩ Njoroge (Heinemann Kenya, 1988), p. 190.

14. This episode is recounted in ibid., pp. 190–92.

15. A useful short account of the forgery is provided in Stephen Jay Gould's essay 'Piltdown Revisited' in *The Panda's Thumb: More Reflections in Natural History* (Norton, 1980).

16. Cole, *Leakey's Luck*, p. 297.

7. Dar es Salaam: Shakespeare in Power

1. My account of Nyerere's early life is largely based on Thomas Molony's groundbreaking biography *Nyerere: The Early Years* (James Currey, 2014). As Molony points out, no adequate biography exists of Nyerere's life as a whole, given the extreme hagiographical flavour of most existing accounts; Molony's account, which takes us up to the time of his entry into politics in 1954, begins to repair this gap. Nyerere mentions himself that the day of his birth was a rainy day in David Ganzuki and Ad' Obe Obe's *Rencontres avec Julius K. Nyerere* (Descartes, 1995), p. 19.

2. Cited in Molony, *Nyerere*, p. 54.

3. As Molony points out (p. 85), joining the Catholic St Mary's instead of Tabora Boys' meant that Nyerere was not a civil servant and therefore would have expected less government oversight of his views.

4. Molony, *Nyerere*, p. 85.

5. Julius K. Nyerere, *Freedom and Unity/Uhuru na Umoja: A Selection from Writings and Speeches, 1952–1965* (Oxford University Press, 1966), pp. 40–41.

6. *Nyerere on Education/Nyerere kuhusu elimu: Selected essays and speeches, 1954–1998*, eds Elieshi Lema, Marjorie Mbilinyi and Rakesh Rajani (HakiElimu, 2004). On *Barriers to Democracy*, where Nyerere also quotes *Julius Caesar*, IV.iii.218ff. ('There is a tide in the affairs of men'), see Alamin A. Mazrui, 'Shakespeare in African Political

Thought', in *The Anglo-African Commonwealth: Political Fiction and Cultural Fusion* (Pergamon Press, 1967), p. 113.

7. Charles Meek, *Brief Authority: A Memoir of Colonial Administration in Tanganyika* (Radcliffe Press, 2011), p. 166.

8. Ibid.

9. Ibid., pp. 170–71.

10. For a discussion of Nyerere's ambitions for Swahili, as well as the objections to this project, see Alamin A. Mazrui, 'Shakespeare in Africa: Between English and Swahili Literature', *Research in African Literatures*, vol. 27, no. 1 (1996), as well as Judith Listowel, *The Making of Tanganyika* (Chatto and Windus, 1965), pp. 417–18, which also contains the mention of the Shakespeare anniversary of 1964.

11. See Lyndon Harries, 'Translating Classical Literature into Swahili', *Swahili: Journal of the Institute of Swahili Research*, vol. 40, no. 1 (1970), pp. 28–31; *Sunday News* (Dar es Salaam), 8 September 1963; John Allen, 'A Note on Dr. Nyerere's Translation of Julius Caesar: Preliminary Thoughts on the Value and Importance of the Translation', *Makerere Journal* (March 1964), pp. 41–53; and Ali Mazrui, 'The African Symbolism of Julius Caesar', in *The Anglo-African Commonwealth*, pp. 121–33.

12. See the review of Nyerere's translation of *Julius Caesar*, *Sunday News* (Dar es Salaam), 8 September 1963; and Mazrui, 'The African Symbolism of Julius Caesar', in *The Anglo-African Commonwealth*, pp. 121–33.

13. See Ali A. Mazrui and Lindah L. Mhando, 'On Poets and Politicians: Obote's Milton and Nyerere's Shakespeare', in *Julius Nyerere: Africa's Titan on a Global Stage* (Carolina Academic Press, 2013), p. 212 (in an essay first published in 1971), where Mazrui focuses on Nyerere's link to his namesake 'Julius' and confines his discussion to the first part of the play, where the dangers of a personality cult forming around a leader are discussed.

14. 'Sitaki Kutishwa Kwa Migomo', *Ngurumo*, 20 November 1961, p. 1, quoted in Molony, *Nyerere*, p. 39.

15. The literature on Renaissance friendship is vast; those interested in reading further might start with Cicero's *De Amicitia* and Montaigne's essay 'De l'amitié' (translated as 'On Affectionate Relationships' in M. A. Screech's edition of the *Essays* [rev. edn; Penguin Classics, 2013]), and consult Jacques Derrida's *Politics of Friendship* (Verso, 2005) and

Edward Said's essay on 'Secular Criticism' in *The World, the Text, and the Critic* (Harvard University Press, 1983); and (on specifically English literary takes on friendship), Lorna Hutson's *The Usurer's Daughter: Male Friendship and Fictions of Women in Sixteenth-Century England* (Routledge, 1994) and Thomas MacFaul's *Male Friendship in Shakespeare and his Contemporaries* (Cambridge University Press, 2007). There is also an interesting discussion of friendship in an African context in the final chapter of David Schalkwyk's *Hamlet's Dreams*.

16. See Meek, *Brief Authority*, p. 171, and Nyerere's speech to the Legislative council on 18 October 1961, printed as 'The Principles of Citizenship' in Nyerere, *Freedom and Unity/Uhuru na Umoja*, pp. 126–9.

17. See 'Democracy and the Party System', in Nyerere, *Freedom and Unity/ Uhuru na Umoja*, pp. 195–203.

18. Molony, *Nyerere*, pp. 70–71.

19. See '*Ujamaa* – The Basis of African Socialism', in *Freedom and Unity/ Uhuru na Umoja*, pp. 162–71. For background on Marxist attitudes to the family, see Friedrich Engels, *The Origin of the Family, Private Property, and the State* (compiled after Marx's death from his notes).

20. The information for this passage comes from Che Guevara's own diaries (available in an English edition as *The African Dream: The Diaries of the Revolutionary War in the Congo* [Harvill Press, 2000]), as well as Paco Taibo's *Senza perdere la tenerezza: vita e morte di Ernesto Che Guevara* (Il Saggiatore, 2009), Jon Lee Anderson's *Che Guevara: A Revolutionary Life* (Bantam Press, 1997) and Aleida March's *Remembering Che: My Life with Che Guevara* (Ocean Press, 2012).

21. March, *Remembering Che*, p. 125.

22. Ibid., p. 126.

23. Taibo, *Senza perdere la tenerezza* (my translation). Aleida's mention of their programme of reading together is mentioned in Anderson, *Che Guevara*, pp. 674–5; and Coleman Ferrer also mentions Che's reading habits in an interview in Jorge G. Castañeda, *Compañero: The Life and Death of Che Guevara* (Bloomsbury, 1997), pp. 326–8.

24. March, *Remembering Che*, p. 121.

25. Interestingly, in an article written in 1974 the Cuban writer Roberto Fernández Retamar suggested that Caliban was the most apt symbol for Cuba's hybrid identity. See Retamar, 'Caliban: Notes Towards a

Discussion of Culture in Our America', *Massachussets Review*, vol. 15 (1974), pp. 7–72.

26. See Mazrui and Mhando, 'On Poets and Politicians', p. 212. Faisal Devji argues that this associates Shylock specifically with the Indian shopkeepers who were seen to be at the root of East African capitalist evils; this argument does, however, turn on Nyerere having misunderstood (or ignored) the fact that the 'Merchant' is Antonio, not Shylock. See 'Subject to Translation: Shakespeare, Swahili, Socialism', *Postcolonial Studies*, vol. 3, no. 2, p. 182. Interestingly, a fictional version of this history *does* take place in V. S. Naipaul's *A Bend in the River* (André Deutsch, 1979), where one of the characters joins a theatre troupe in London after studying in Oxford and spots the similarity between the position of the East African Indians and Shakespeare's Jews: 'Another time there was the idea of rewriting *The Merchant of Venice* as *The Malindi Baker*, so that I could play Shylock. But it became too complicated' (p. 177).

27. For an excellent recent discussion of this, see Emma Smith, 'Was Shylock Jewish?', *Shakespeare Quarterly*, vol. 64, no. 2 (Summer 2013), pp. 188–219.

28. Montaigne, 'On Affectionate Relationships', pp. 211–12.

8. Addis Ababa: Shakespeare and the Lion of Judah

1. Richard Pankhurst, 'Shakespeare in Ethiopia', *Research in African Literatures*, vol. 17, no. 2 (1986), pp. 169–86, at p. 175. Pankhurst's excellent article is the only source for most material on the Shakespeare translations and performances of the 1960s and 1970s, and though I have confirmed many of the findings and been able to add details and context here and there, my account here relies heavily on his work.

2. The translations here are taken from the Hakluyt Society edition, *The Prester John of the Indies: The translation of Lord Stanley of Alderley, 1881, rev. and edited with additional material by G. F. Beckingham and G. W. B. Huntingford* (2 vols, Cambridge University Press, 1961). The quotations in this paragraph are from vol. 1, pp. 157, 69, 97, 132 and 70.

3. Philip Sidney, *The Defence of Poesy*, in *Sidney's Defence of Poesy and Selected Renaissance Literary Criticism*, ed. Gavin Alexander (Penguin Classics, 2004), p. 27.

4. Wendy Belcher, 'Interview: Ethiopia's Poet Laureate Tsegaye Gabre-Medhin', *Ethiopian Review*, September 1998. There is some confusion over the ostensible date of this episode; Tsegaye affirms both that it happened in 1959 and that it happened when he was twenty-nine years old (i.e., in 1965). It is possible that Tsegaye was using the Ethiopian calendar, in which case this episode would have taken place in 1966.

5. *Prester John of the Indies*, vol. 1, p. 258.

6. See Wendy Belcher's *Abyssinia's Samuel Johnson: Ethiopian Thought in the Making of an English Author* (Oxford University Press, 2012), which notes the many parallels between Johnson's writings and the histories of Abyssinia with which he was familiar, which included not only the history by Jerónimo Lobo that he translated (via Legrand's French), but also the sections of Álvares and Pedro Páez that had been excerpted in the great travel compilation *Purchas' Pilgrims*. Belcher makes the further claim that Johnson had a fuller and deeper trans-historical affinity with the Habesha people of northern Abyssinia and its culture and customs, which she argues offered Johnson an alternative ancient Christian heritage beyond the European Protestant–Catholic divide.

7. We are reliant for many of the details of life in Haile Selassie's late court on Ryszard Kapuściński's extraordinary book *The Emperor: Downfall of an Autocrat* (Quartet, 1983), which purports to transcribe interviews with courtiers conducted just after the Emperor had been dethroned by the Derg in 1974. While it is immediately apparent that Kapuściński's uniformly eloquent informants, with their strange blend of naïveté and knowing irony, are at least to some extent an imaginative recasting, the book remains our only source of information on many aspects of court life.

8. *Prester John of the Indies*, vol. 1, p. 281.

9. Robert Ardrey, *African Genesis: A Personal Investigation into the Animal Origins and Nature of Man* (Athenaeum, 1961).

10. Jonathan Swift, 'A Tale of a Tub', in *Major Works* (Oxford World's Classics, 2003), pp. 87–8.

9. Panafrica: Shakespeare in the Cold War

1. Ali Mazrui ('Shakespeare in Africa: Between English and Swahili Literature', *Research in African Literatures*, vol. 27, no. 1 [1996], p. 64)

mistakenly suggests that this speech is reported in the 26 July 1989 edition of the *Daily Nation*, but no such report appears there; the speech, in fact, took place on 10 July 1988 and was only reported in the *Kenya Times*, on 11 July 1988. I am grateful to Megan Halsband at the Library of Congress for sending me the relevant pages of the *Kenya Times*.

2. Ngugi wa Thiong'o, *Decolonising the Mind* (Heinemann, 1986), p. 100.

3. *Kenya Gazette*, 12 June–25 July 1975, cols 1178, 1331.

4. Ngugi wa Thiong'o, *Detained: A Writer's Prison Diary* (Heinemann, 1981), p. 132.

5. See, for instance, Michela Wrong, *In the Footsteps of Mr Kurtz: Living on the Brink of Disaster in the Congo* (Fourth Estate, 2001); Ngugi, *Detained*.

6. See Frances Stonor Saunders, *Who Paid the Piper?* (Granta, 1999).

7. See Annabel Maule, *Theatre near the Equator*, pp. 105 and 134, where she records performances of *The Merchant of Venice* (1964) and *The Taming of the Shrew* (1971) subsidized by Caltex, the first attended by J. M. Otiendo as Minister for Education and the second by Vice-President Moi.

8. Foreign Broadcast Information Service Daily Reports, 20 July 1989, translated from a speech in Swahili at Kiharu on 14 July.

9. See, for instance, 'Kenyan expats kiss the good life goodbye', *DailyTelegraph*, 16 July 2001, which suggests that 'The number of white settlers in Kenya, as opposed to foreigners on two-year contracts, is widely believed to have shrunk from about 50,000 in 1963 to fewer than 8,000 today.' For obvious reasons, the number of departing expats is rather difficult to record precisely from published migration data, as many kept British citizenship and so were not recorded as migrants on returning to Britain.

10. See the OECD report on *African Economic Outlook* for 2005/6, especially Figure 6 (p. 22) and Table 11 (pp. 566–7). The fall in aid flows from around $30bn in 1990 to around $16.7bn in 1999 was also exacerbated by the changing value of the dollar; by some indexes (such as the economic power of the dollar during the period), the fall in aid would actually be closer to a reduction by two thirds.

11. George Mungai suggests that the end to government censorship of the theatre came about in 1992 through the challenge of a lawyer on the

Board of Governors of the Phoenix, who pointed out that there was no constitutional basis for the use of these powers nor for the habit of Special Branch in regularly shutting down theatrical performances.

12. George Steiner, *Grammars of Creation* (Faber, 2001), p. 16. As the philosopher Giorgio Agamben points out, the epithet *Sapiens*, added to the tenth edition of Linnaeus's *Systema Naturae*, appears 'not [to] represent a description, but [. . .] rather an imperative', simplifying the adage *nosce te ipsum* ('know thyself' or, as Hobbes suggests, 'read thyself') which had appeared in the margin next to *Homo* in previous editions. In other words, this was not Man the Wise, but rather an injunction upon man *to become wise*. Giorgio Agamben, *The Open: Man and Animal* (Stanford University Press, 2004), p. 25.

13. See Ania Loomba's analysis of Janet Suzman's Johannesburg production of *Othello* (A. Loomba and M. Orkin (eds), *Post-Colonial Shakespeares* (Routledge, 2003), p. 148), where she points out that *Othello* is 'not just a play about race in general but a play about a black man isolated from other black people', something which both explains the significance of the adaptations in the Phoenix production and may account for the fact that *Othello* does not figure as prominently as one might expect in the history of East African Shakespeare.

14. See Susan Bennett and Christie Carson (eds), *Shakespeare Beyond English: A Global Experiment* (Cambridge University Press), Introduction, p. 7.

10. *Juba: Shakespeare, Civil War and Reconstruction*

1. Rosie Goldsmith, 'South Sudan Adopts the Language of Shakespeare', 8 October 2011, www.bbc.co.uk/news/magazine-15216524 (accessed 8 October 2015).

2. Translation by Clayton Eshleman and Annette Smith.

List of Illustrations

Plate Section

P. 1: [top] Richard Burton reading (*Photo by Rischgitz/Getty Images*); [bottom] Henry Morton Stanley with his servant Kalulu (*Smithsonian Institution Archives. Image SIL28-277-01*)

P. 2: [top] Roosevelt on Safari (*Smithsonian Institution Archives. Image SIA2009-1371*); [bottom] anonymous lithograph of Edward Steere from Heanley's *A Memoir of Edward Steere* (*George Bell, 1888*)

P. 3: [top] Procession announcing a performance of *Khoon ka Khoon*; [bottom] Hiralal Kapur in costume for this production (*reproduced with kind permission of Neera Kapur-Dromson*)

P. 4 [top]: Karen Blixen and her servants (*The Royal Library, Copenhagen, The Rungstedlund Collection*); [bottom] Milton Obote in the 1948 *Julius Caesar* at Makerere (*Makerere University Library Archive*)

P. 5: [top] Images from the Makerere production of *Coriolanus* (*Makerere University Library Archive*); [bottom] Julius Nyerere in 1960 (© *Hulton-Deutsch Collection/CORBIS*)

P. 6: [top] Ernesto 'Che' Guevara (*Photo by AFP/Stringer/Getty Images*); [bottom] Haile Selassie (*author's collection*)

P. 7: Images from Tsegaye's *Hamlét* and *Otello* (*National Theatre of Ethiopia*)

P. 8: *Cymbeline* in Juba Arabic (*Shakespeare's Globe*)

Illustrations in Text

P. 5: [top] The Gastaldi map (*from the American Geographical Society Library, University of Wisconsin-Milwaukee Libraries*); [bottom] Stanley consulting a map (© *Corbis*)

P. 13: Roosevelt in the jungle (*Library of Congress LC-DIG-ppmsca-36551*)

P. 24: Stanley with the members of the Emin Pasha Relief Expedition (*Photo by De Agostini Picture Library/Getty Images*)

P. 33: *Hadithi za Kiingereza* (*Reproduced by kind permission of the Syndics of Cambridge University Library*)

P. 37: The European quarter of Zanzibar (*Reproduced by kind permission of the Syndics of Cambridge University Library*)

P. 42: Christ Church, Zanzibar (*Reproduced by kind permission of the Syndics of Cambridge University Library*)

P. 67: Illustration from 1888 edition of *King Solomon's Mines* (*Reproduced by kind permission of the Syndics of Cambridge University Library*)

P. 91: Indian railway employees (*Nairobi Railway Museum*)

P. 103: Indian nautch girl (*Images of Asia*)

P. 119: Shylock from *Mabepari wa Venisi* (*Oxford University Press, Dar es Salaam, 1969*)

P. 158: [top] Richard Leakey (© *Marion Kaplan/Alamy Stock Photo*); [bottom] Laurence Olivier in *Hamlet* (© *Underwood & Underwood/Corbis*)

PP. 203–204: Cover and page from the Amharic *Macbeth* (*Oxford University Press, Addis Ababa, 1964 [i.e., 1972]*)

Index

8/16

MYS
MOOSE

Moose, Ruth.

Doing it at the Dixie
Dew.

$24.99   WITHDRAWN

DATE			